Racism
IN CANADIAN SCHOOLS

Racism
IN CANADIAN SCHOOLS

Ibrahim Alladin
CAMBRIAN COLLEGE

HARCOURT BRACE CANADA

Harcourt Brace & Company, Canada

TORONTO MONTREAL FORT WORTH NEW YORK ORLANDO
PHILADELPHIA SAN DIEGO LONDON SYDNEY TOKYO

Canadian Cataloguing in Publication Data

Alladin, Ibrahim M., 1956–
Racism in Canadian schools

ISBN 0-7747-3492-2

1. Discrimination in education — Canada.
2. Minorities — Education — Canada. 3. Racism — Canada. I. Title.

LC212.3.C2A55 1995 370.19'342 C95-930612-9

Publisher: Heather McWhinney
Editor and Marketing Manager: Joanna Cotton
Projects Manager: Liz Radojkovic
Projects Co-ordinator: May Ku
Director of Publishing Services: Jean Davies
Editorial Manager: Marcel Chiera
Production Editor: Louisa Schulz
Production Manager: Sue-Ann Becker
Production Co-ordinator: Carol Tong
Copy Editor: Robert Templeton, First Folio Resource Group, Inc.
Cover Design: Opus House
Interior Design: Dave Peters
Typesetting and Assembly: Tom Dart, First Folio Resource Group, Inc.
Printing and Binding: Best Book Manufacturers, Inc.

Cover photo: Courtesy of Shaw Cable, Alex Taylor Community School, and Dr. Steve Ramsankar

This book was printed in Canada on acid-free paper.

1 2 3 4 5 00 99 98 97 96

Dedicated to two very special children,
Tariq and Kemal,
who have just started their schooling.

FOREWORD

Many of our leaders consider Canada to be a truly multicultural country; a nation where people are free to practise the customs and language of their native cultures without fear of reprisal. As Canadians, we take a great deal of pride in this adoptive attitude. We rejoice in our cultural mosaic with an annual Heritage Days celebration. The federal government has a ministry to promote and maintain the ideology of multiculturalism. The Charter of Rights and Freedoms guarantees equality without discrimination based on race, national or ethnic origin, colour, or religion.

Perhaps the Charter should be revised to include equality within the education system. According to Ibrahim Alladin, racism in Canadian schools is pronounced and evident at all levels of education. In *Racism in Canadian Schools*, Alladin presents a compilation of research that illustrates that multiculturalism in Canada is more illusion than reality. Multiculturalism is aimed at tolerance; but tolerance is not enough. It is not proactive. What is required is antiracist action which is directed at transforming power relations. This type of action is necessary, and an appropriate place to begin is in the classroom. Our education system maintains the inequalities that exist in society through biased curriculum and teaching materials, methodology, and teacher attitudes and beliefs.

Let this be the first text to examine racism in Canadian schools. It is theoretical, objective, and provides a critical analysis of institutional racism, and race and curriculum. It provides a clear distinction between prejudice, racism, discrimination, and racial harassment. It is a valuable resource for anybody in the field of education. After reading *Racism in Canadian Schools*, you will begin to reflect on your own beliefs, values, assumptions, and knowledge. In creating your own personal awareness, you will begin to challenge long-held beliefs.

One theme of this book is strategies for overcoming racism. This book is an important reference tool that you will consult repeatedly. It illustrates how textbooks are neither neutral nor value free, and lists ways to analyze children's books for suitability. It also provides a model for antiracist experiential learning. Whether you are an elementary school teacher, a university professor, a researcher, or an administrator, you will find this an important resource. Racism has a detrimental effect on society. The school can be an agent of change; in implementing antiracist action we can indeed challenge racist behaviour and beliefs.

Harvey Zingle, Dean
Faculty of Education
University of Alberta.

PREFACE

Racism, like sexism, is an ideology. Racist ideologies, as rationalizations for various forms of social, political, and economic control, have contributed to the maintenance of minority groups in social positions of inferiority. Racism in schools is not something that has surfaced recently. It is a problem that has existed for a long time, but has not been dealt with effectively. It is often ignored and racial incidents in schools are either dismissed or downplayed. The victims of racism continue to suffer psychologically and socially.

This book has several unique features. The authors, who represent several institutions in Canada, are experienced teachers and researchers. All the chapters are original essays written for this volume. The chapters take a multidisciplinary approach and they bring to the attention of teachers how racism persists in schools. Each chapter offers a provocative discussion of contemporary issues and problems, allowing students and teachers to take part in the controversies from an informed perspective.

Specifically, *Racism in Canadian Schools* fulfills three objectives. First, the contributors to this volume present a multidisciplinary appraisal of the conceptualization of the race category. Attention is paid to clarify the meaning and misconceptions on race and ethnicity. Second, the volume addresses how racism persists and how minorities are represented in education. It questions the social power relations and the specific arrangement of social relations in schools. Issues of identity and representation raise the question about who has power to define whom, when, and how. Third, the volume offers a forum for dialogue on race relations in schooling and society.

As we approach the twenty-first century, we in North America are witnessing a radical intensification of neo-conservative offensives within the major social and cultural institutions of American and Canadian society. The school is among the institutions that are contested for their attempts to deal with groups outside the "mainstream." The recent assault on multiculturalism and equality of educational opportunity, has given rise to a social movement that is highly motivated to challenge the politics of the new-conservatives. The developments in Canadian universities and schools are painful: minority levels of achievement and rates of graduation are declining at the same time as these institutions are championing the cause of minorities. The racial antagonism and minority underachievement intensify in schools, and contemporary educators and researchers seem to be overtaken by what is happening.

Racism in Canadian Schools offers both a theoretical and an objective, yet critical, analysis, of the thorny issues of racial inequality and minority underachievement now facing educators across the country. After presenting a critical overview of mainstream and radical accounts of racial inequality and schooling, the volume examines race relations and the persistence of racism in schools. Taking a multidisciplinary approach, racial inequality in education is understood from a number of perspectives. Attention is directed to the complex nature of race relations in the institutional life of social organizations such as schools. Rather than dwelling on single causes of racial inequality, the importance of social context and nuance in understanding race relations is stressed.

Racism in Canadian Schools draws from recent research in Canada. It presents a Canadian perspective on race relations. It was written for students and teachers. In researching the book, we tried to keep in mind contemporary issues and changes. The case studies reflect what is being attempted; the stories and the examples make the text easier to understand. The entire book deals with racism in Canadian schools, giving a Canadian perspective on this serious issue. We have included statistics, excerpts from documents, and reports, and cases reported in the newspapers. Most of the references and additional readings are drawn from Canadian sources. The questions raised in this book could be further researched and the discussion questions at the end of each chapter could become part of a written assignment or a classroom project.

This book has ten chapters, each one analyzing a different aspect of racism in schools. The chapters are organized around a number of central questions or issues. Each chapter begins with an introduction that raises key questions. The questions and issues are explored in detail, with real examples that seek to link theory with practice. Each chapter raises fundamental concerns and offers an opportunity for further research and reflection.

Racism in Canadian Schools has three parts: Part I looks at institutional racism, Part II focuses on race, identity, and curriculum, and Part III explores strategies for overcoming racism.

This book helps the reader understand how racism persists in school. It gives practical examples and draws from case studies to present alternative views on how to deal effectively with racism.

The exercises at the end of each chapter focus on the issues raised in the chapters. They have been selected to stimulate classroom discussion and for use as course assignments. Other issues can be explored independently. The additional readings afford the reader the opportunity for further investigation. We encourage the reader to seek other points of view and to engage in dialogue with others.

Acknowledgements

Racism in Canadian Schools would not have been possible without the efforts of the contributors. The willingness to prepare and revise their chapters on several occasions shows their great dedication to this project. Thanks to all of them and to those who assisted with the preparation of the manuscript.

We are thankful to the Department of Canadian Heritage for supporting the project, in particular, Speros Vlassopoulos for his advice and suggestions. A special thanks to the staff and Board of the Edmonton Immigrant Services Association, in particular Molly Koo and Bill Warwaryick, for their assistance in the preparation of the manuscript. We are grateful to Donna von Hauff for editing the text. Thanks also to our colleagues at the University of Alberta, especially to Allen Pearson, Chair of the Department of Educational Policy Studies, for his support and encouragement.

Special thanks to Heather McWhinney, Joanna Cotton, and Tony Luengo, at

Harcourt Brace for all their advice and seeing the book to completion. We would also like to thank the reviewers, whose suggestions helped to develop the book. They are: June Benin of Simon Fraser University, Fred Drew of the University of Manitoba, Richard Hirabayashi of the University of Calgary, Norrel London of the University of Western Ontario; and Don Santos of the University of Western Ontario.

Thanks to all the authors and publishers for their kind permission to reprint materials. While every attempt has been made to secure the necessary copyright, we apologize for any omission.

A Note From the Publisher

Thank you for selecting *Racism in Canadian Schools* by Ibrahim Alladin. The author and publisher have devoted considerable time and care to the development of this book. We appreciate your recognition of this effort and accomplishment.

We want to hear what you think about *Racism in Canadian Schools.* Please take a few minutes to fill in the stamped reply card at the back of the book. Your comments and suggestions will be valuable to us as we prepare new editions and other books.

TABLE OF CONTENTS

PART I INSTITUTIONAL RACISM

PART III STRATEGIES FOR OVERCOMING RACISM

PART I

Institutional Racism

INTRODUCTION

This section begins with a theoretical analysis of racial inequality and education. The discussion draws from the historical development of Canada, which has led to the marginalization of the aboriginal people. In spite of various efforts, the school has not been a positive factor to eliminate the discrimination of natives. Recently, other minority groups have fallen victims. Racism in Canadian society is increasing according to the Decima Report (1993), and racial discrimination in education and employment are denying minority groups opportunities for social mobility. From this view, the policy on multiculturalism does not seem to have addressed problems of racial inequality. The four chapters in this section provide an analysis of how racism persists in Canadian society and how institutional racism tends to marginalize certain groups.

Chapter One, by Ibrahim Alladin, seeks to clarify the concept of race. It examines some of the misconceptions involved and offers a theoretical explanation of race and ethnicity. Immigration has changed the demographic composition of Canadian society and it is argued that some groups are deliberately subjected to various forms of discrimination. The school has not been effective in reducing racial discrimination. On the contrary, it is argued that certain school practices discriminate. It is suggested that school should institute antiracist education programs and empower teachers and students to talk about racism more openly.

Chapter Two, by Syd Pauls, examines racism and Native education from an historical perspective. Pauls begins by clarifying terms such as racism, genocide, and indigenous peoples. By drawing from the Indian Act, he establishes the status of a Native and the rights of aboriginal people. He argues that education for Natives was based on racist principles and as a result, Natives have suffered tremendous injustice. The intention of the residential schools for example, was to "civilize" the Natives, who were regarded as inferior. The residential school system tried to destroy Native culture and Native values, which were sacred to the Native people. Pauls gives a detailed analysis on the state of Native education and considers its future.

In Chapter Three, George Dei examines racism from the point of view of Black/African-Canadian students. Based on a recent study he conducted in Ontario, he looks at the practice of exclusion. He is concerned with both individual and institutional racism, and the marginalizing effects on some students. Dei argues that all educators should take racism in schools seriously and, if we are to address the fundamental issues of educational equity, then we should pursue an antiracist education policy.

Previously, there has been little attempt to examine campus racism. In Chapter Four, Augie Fleras, provides a lucid analysis of racism in academe. Racism is a pervasive feature of Canadian institutions, argues Fleras, and the magnitude and scope of this racism are expressed in different ways. Fleras uses both primary and secondary data to explore the politics of ivory-tower racism from the perspective of problem and solution.

The chapters in this section are:

1

RACISM IN SCHOOLS: RACE, ETHNICITY, AND SCHOOLING IN CANADA

Ibrahim Alladin

If racists as a category all wore horns, the battle against them would be a great deal easier. But this is not the case...The type that chilled me the most, in fact, was not the hard-nosed bully who wanted to kick somebody's teeth in, but rather the highly educated man, wealthy and sophisticated, who sat sipping his cognac while elaborating on the nobility of the white race and the necessity of excising the "mud people" from our midst.[1]

Stanley R. Barrett
Is God a Racist? The Right Wing in Canada.

Introduction

The racial and ethnic composition of Canadian society has been transformed. Our schools have also changed and the classrooms are truly international. The multi-ethnic nature of our society has been recognized. Educators, teachers, and parents are trying to come to terms with the diverse nature of our schools. There is an increasing awareness that Canadian society is multicultural and that the education system should prepare our citizens to cope with the national and global realities. Unfortunately, the present educational system is unable to deal with the complexities of a changing modern society. Institutional barriers to occupational and social mobility have created a deeply stratified society, in which power relations are defined in terms of class, race, and gender (see, for example, Li 1988). In a society where there is institutionalized racism, prospects for social and economic advancement for minority groups remain daunting. This chapter explores racial inequality in Canadian society. It begins with a theoretical discussion on race and ethnicity. The concept of race and ethnicity is explored from different perspectives, and some of the misconceptions are clarified here. It is argued that racism is systemic in Canadian society and that it is manifested in different ways. The political space that education occupies today continues to de-emphasize a pedagogy that emancipates; it generally serves to reproduce the dominant ideologies. The school therefore has become an instrument whose function is primarily to sustain and legitimize the status quo (McCarthy 1993). The minority groups who occupy subordinate positions within the society are both economically and socially disadvantaged. Racism is an attempt to further keep some minority groups marginalized. This chapter raises a number of questions on educational equity and explores an inclusive education that empowers both teachers and students.

Race and Ethnicity: Meanings and Misconceptions

Race is not a stable category. Its meaning changes over time. What it means, how it is used, by whom, and how it is conceptualized by policy makers and educational practitioners, is contingent and historical. The complex issues surrounding race have to be understood from different perspectives and the approach is multidisciplinary. As Apple (in McCarthy 1993) notes, it needs to draw from studies of popular culture, literature, the role of the state in struggles over race, class, and gender relations, national and international economic structures, and the cultural policies of imperialism and post-colonialism. In taking this position, we can recognize race theoretically as a social and cultural production.

There are several perspectives within sociology and the social sciences that may assist us in understanding social forces in Canadian society. The study of race and ethnicity has been approached from different viewpoints. Each perspective highlights certain features of society and intergroup dynamics. Together, these perspectives demonstrate how ethnicity and ethnic relations in Canadian society are shaped and how consensus is reached.

The term ethnicity, as employed in sociology and social anthropology, is not easy to define, as it is used in a number of social contexts. As a theoretical concept, ethnicity remains quite vague. Sociologists, for example, have taken different positions with respect to what is race and ethnicity. These positions represent theoretical orientations that focus on different aspects of intergroup relations. The way race and ethnicity are defined have a bearing on the explanations and analysis. Furthermore, the theoretical status accorded to ethnicity has influenced the political focus in the development of the public policy on multiculturalism.

Race Is Not only a Black and White Issue

> What is at issue here is the recognition of the extraordinary diversity of subjective positions, social experiences and cultural identities which compose the category "black," that is the recognition that "black" is essentially a politically and culturally constructed category, which cannot be grounded in a set of fixed transcultural or transcendental racial categories and which therefore has no guarantees in Nature.[2]

Sociologists have generally focussed on the question of subjective identity as a basis for their definition of ethnicity and race. Ethnicity, is therefore, ascribed or given at birth. An important aspect of an ethnic group is that its members share a sense of peoplehood or identity that is based in part on descent, language, religion, tradition, and other common experiences (Weber 1968, 385-398). According to this view, ethnic identity provides a basis for members of an ethnic group to develop closures or boundaries, within which ethnic institutions, neighbourhoods, beliefs, and cultures are developed and maintained.

Studies on ethnicity indicate that the most frequently mentioned attributes of ethnicity are ancestry, culture, religion, race, and language (Li 1988, Isajiw 1974). Driedger (1978) identified six factors of ethnic identification that form the components of an ethnic community. These factors are: identification with an ecological territory, an ethnic culture, ethnic institutions, historical symbols, an ideology, and charismatic leadership. Rosen (1965) has gone further in arguing that an individual may identify himself or herself with others on three levels. First, one may identify with an important person in one's life, for example, a parent or friend (that is, a significant other person). Second, one may identify with a group from which one draws one's values, for example, family or co-workers (that is, a reference group). Third, one may identify with a broad category of persons, for example, an ethnic group or occupational group (that is, a social category). It is on the third level that ethnic identification occurs.

Race and ethnicity can also be examined as a consequence of unequal relationships, produced and maintained by differential power between dominant and subordinate groups (Li 1989). From this view, racial and ethnic groups are constructed on the basis of social relationships and are not based on genetic differences or primordial features. The focus is on the institutional framework within which groups are defined as racial or ethnic, and how social interactions are organized accordingly (Bolaria and Li 1985). Physical and cultural traits are the basis of defining social groups only in so far as they are socially recognized as important. The dominant group has the power, and therefore capacity, to use physical and social features to define socially a subordinate group.

Race and Ethnicity: A Theoretical Analysis

What emerges from the literature on race and ethnicity is a confrontation between two powerful theoretical perspectives for the analysis of ethnic group relations. The theory of assimilation has dominated policies on multiculturalism since the Second World War. Only recently has it been challenged by theories of social pluralism.

The theory of assimilation or the "melting pot," is basically social Darwinism, and essentially claims that the dominant group is socially superior. Milton Gordon's *Assimilation in American Life* (1964), was a pioneer work in the theory of assimilation. Gordon posits four distinct types of assimilation: cultural assimilation (adoption of dominant group culture, values, and life-style), structural assimilation (entrance into group institutions, clubs, and cliques), amalgamation (defined and measured by intermarriage rates), and "identificationable" assimilation (in which minority group members think of themselves as American, Canadian, Mexican, and so on). In addition to these four types of assimilation, he argues that assimilation may be measured by the absence of three phenomena: prejudice, discrimination, and power or value conflicts between groups (Newman 1978, 43).

Assimilation Theory

The assimilationist and melting-pot integrationist policies that emerged in North America were consistent with the liberal ideals identified by Smith (1981, 2). Smith argues that liberal theorists had generally taken the view that "as mankind moved from a primitive, tribal stage of social organization toward large-scale industrial societies, the various primordial ties of religion, language, ethnicity and race which divided it would gradually but inexorably lose their hold and disappear." With mass migration and with the expansion of industrial capitalism, it was expected that there would emerge a time when it would be necessary to organize production and trade on a global scale. The rational use of labour would mean that old cultural differences and political divisions would become increasingly irrelevant. The growth of mass tourism, the expansion in communication systems, and the standardization of mass culture would inevitably lead, according to the liberals, to a global cosmopolitan culture (Rizvi 1986, 5). According to Smith, however, this dissolution of ethnicity has not occurred. Indeed, he maintains that modern history, if anything, has demonstrated that economic and industrial trends have tended to reinforce ethnic and cultural divisions.

Van den Berghe (1981, 2-3) develops his analysis of race and ethnicity on the basis of his rejection of both the assimilationist ideology and what he refers to as the liberal tradition in race and ethnic relations. According to van den Berghe, this liberal tradition in ethnic and race relations is constituted by the following propositions:

- All humans are members of a single species, and there are no biologically meaningful subspecies within it. Races are social constructs corresponding to no biological reality.
- Differences between human populations are smaller than within them, and such differences as exist (for example, in IQ test performance) are largely, if not entirely, the product of the social environment.
- Racism and ethnocentrism are irrational, dysfunctional attitudes, if not downright aberrations, to which certain rigid, authoritarian types of personality are especially prone. Such attitudes must be combated through a social therapy promoting equal status contact between groups.

Van den Berghe contends that assimilationist and melting-pot ideologies are fundamentally misguided because they are based on the assumption that cultural diversity can be eradicated through the forces of urbanization, industrialization, and modernization. For van den Berghe, cultural diversity is a necessary condition of human evolution and adaptation. On the basis of this view, ethnicity, according to van den Berghe, has something to do with kinship, a deeply rooted biological affiliation, which is often referred to in social-science literature as primordialist. It is this kinship and biological affiliation that brings people together to acquire common cultural attributes, like language, religion, rituals, and other customs, and that these constitute ethnicity (van den Berghe 1981).

In a powerful criticism of the primordial conception of ethnicity, Barth rejects the views that ethnic groups have a primordial quality, that is, the characteristic of being biologically self-perpetuating, and that they share fundamental cultural values, realized in overt unity in various cultural forms (Rizvi 1986). In Barth's view, what is missing from the primordial view of ethnicity is any account of how individuals come together to see each other as sharing a common culture, and others as having a distinctively different culture. Barth accepts the view that the classification of persons and local groups as members of an ethnic group depends on their exhibiting the traits of a particular culture. But he denies the assumption that this is something that can only be "judged objectively by the ethnographic observer, in the culture-area tradition, regardless of the categories and prejudices of actors" (Barth 1969, 12). For Barth, it is the subjective, interpretive, dimension of ethnic classification that is of crucial importance. So, in contrast to van den Berghe's analysis, Barth is concerned with the social processes by which groups identify themselves and maintain their difference from other groups. Barth explains these processes by reference to his concept of boundary maintenance (Rizvi 1986).

Cultural Pluralism

Another version of assimilation theory, pluralism, stresses both the demise and persistence of ethnic cultures. In a culturally pluralistic society, ethnic groups are believed to share aspects of a common culture and participate collectively in its economic and political life, while retaining their unique ethnic culture in their networks, residential enclaves, churches, and languages. The notion of cultural pluralism has led to the development of policies of multiculturalism, which seeks to encourage cultural diversity, and promote racial and cultural harmony, with the aim of reducing racial/ethnic discrimination. Cultural pluralism assumes that every individual and group desires to maintain a distinctive ethnic identity and heritage, and multiculturalism as a policy recognizes the fact that some individuals will find greater human affinity outside their ethnic group than within it. Furthermore, the voluntary nature of maintenance of ethnic ties, loyalties, and identities under the multicultural policy protects the individual rights of members to freely dissent or dissociate themselves from the collective values of their ethnic origin.

Critics of pluralism argue that it downplays the problem of ethnic and racial inequality, and that the view of a pluralistic society often assumes a basic equality for all groups (Li 1988, 8). This same criticism can be applied to multicultural policies, which often fail to combat racism and discriminatory practices, but succeed in managing race and ethnic relations within a state apparatus (Bolaria and Li 1985).

The accounts of race and ethnicity indicate that there is an assumption that cultural traditions are static phenomena, divorced from the broader social context in which they acquire meaning. In the analysis given above, ethnicity remains a key concept, but the questions of the dynamics of cultural change are either pushed aside as being irrelevant or simply ignored. In short, culture is reified (Rizvi 1986). Reification occurs whenever culture is treated as a thing unto itself, independent of other spheres of life. The reification of ethnic values has made a mystique of ethnicity, creating phenomena that do not lend themselves to rational explanation. This is particularly the case when ethnic groups are assumed to be endowed with a given set of cultural values that are taken to be unrelated to the material and political context in which they arise and acquire significance (Rizvi 1986, 17).

Racism and Discrimination in Canada

Racial inequality in Canada dates back to the original contact between the European colonizers and the Natives and the Inuit. The Europeans quickly established their political and economic dominance over the indigenous population and the Natives soon came under the direct control of the European colonial powers, namely Britain and France. The British and the French emerged as the dominant national groups, while the natives were pushed onto the reserves and subjected to discrimination. They were denied access to economic and political power (see Elliott and Fleras 1992).

By controlling immigration policies, both the English and French consolidated their cultural and institutional dominance. They determined which groups would be allowed entry, where they would settle, what jobs should be allocated, and which languages should be spoken. English Canadians offered preferred status to immigrants from Britain and Northern and Western Europe, who were culturally and socially similar, while the less preferred ethnic groups, mainly from Southern Europe, Asia, and Central America, took low occupational and social roles (Porter 1965, 63).

Until 1962, the Canadian Immigration Act openly discriminated against nonwhite immigrants. Changes in immigration laws in 1967 altered Canada's racial composition, resulting in a multiracial society, but the stratification system has not significantly changed. Reitz (1989, 153) notes that, despite a reduction in ethnic inequality, immigrants from Southern Europe continue to exhibit lower socioeconomic status, unlike immigrants from Northern Europe. English and French Canadians continue to dominate public and political life, while the Natives exist as a marginalized group.

The demographic characteristics of Canada are undergoing a dramatic change and will continue to do so according to immigration forecasts. As Figure 1.1 indicates, the main source of immigrants to Canada is no longer the United Kingdom and Western Europe, but Eastern Asia, South East Asia, and Southern Asia. Figure 1.2 summarizes the gradual increase in the number of immigrants in the past decade. The number of "visible" immigrants has increased. There is a public concern that too many immigrants from Asia are allowed into Canada. Some Canadians perceive immigrants from Asia as a threat. They are often accused of taking jobs away from Canadians, although that is not the case. Studies by Hawkins (1972) and Li (1988) show that immigrants create more employment and contribute positively to the economy. But at a time of high unemployment, immigrants tend to become the target for racial discrimination Some groups, for example Blacks and Chinese, remain victimized (Curtis and Tepperman 1988, 603).

Canada has a reputation of being a tolerant and compassionate country. But its poor treatment of racial and ethnic minorities cannot be ignored. Elliott and Fleras (1992) list some shameful episodes: public attitudes and political responses to Chinese and East-Indian immigrants around the turn of this century, the evacuation and relocation of Japanese Canadians during the Second World War, and the anti-Semitism of the 1920s and 1930s that prevented the entry of Jewish emigrants from Germany. Prejudice and discrimination cannot be dismissed. In urban centres, visible minorities have experienced widespread discrimination in housing, employment, and education (see, for example, Curtis and Tepperman 1990, Li 1988).

FIGURE 1.1

Places of Birth of Canada's Immigrant and First-Generation Canadian Population, 1991 Census

	CANADA
TOTAL	4 343 000
United States of America	249 000
Central America	69 000
South America	151 000
Caribbean and Bermuda	233 000
United Kingdom	718 000
Other Northern Europe (31)	83 000
Western Europe	432 000
Eastern Europe	420 000
Southern Europe	712 000
Africa	166 000
Western Asia and Middle East	147 000
Eastern Asia	377 000
South East Asia	312 000
Southern Asia	229 000
Oceania and Other (31)	46 000
TOTAL POPULATION	**26 994 000**

Source: Compiled from *1991 Census of Canada* and reports from Immigration and Citizenship Canada.

A recent study by the Canadian Council of Christians and Jews found that racism in Canada is increasing. One in four Canadians (25 percent) believe that there is a "great deal of racism" in Canada, 61 percent say there is "some" racism, 12 percent say there is "not very much" racism, while 3 percent believe that there is "no racism at all." Thirty-one percent of younger Canadians feel that a "great deal of racism exists in Canada, while only 17 percent of older Canadians are so inclined. (Decima Report 1993, 19-20). The report also found that those most likely to be discriminated against are Canadians of African origin, Native Canadians, Canadians of South-Asian/East-Indian descent, Asians, and Jews (p. 25). It seems that immigrants of a non-European background are more likely to be victims of racism.

We're People, Just Different by Colour and Look

> Prejudice towards natives happens because people have no understanding of the history of Canada's first peoples, says Val Kaufman, community relations coordinator for the Canadian Native Friendship Centre in Edmonton. "When people see the high rates of unemploy-

ment and welfare dependency on Indian reserves today, they assume it's a result of inherent laziness" says Val. All Canadians must "take into account forced relocations, and the destruction of traditional aboriginal economies leaving aboriginal people dependent on welfare and alcohol."[3]

Racism, like sexism, is an ideology, the belief that one racial or ethnic group is inferior to another and that unequal treatment is therefore justified. The characteristic feature of racist ideologies is that they try to make social and economic inequalities among

FIGURE 1.2

Immigration to Alberta and Other Provinces, 1980-1990

Year	BC	AB	SK	MB	ON	PQ	Atl.	YK/ NWT	Not Specified	Total
1980	24 437	18 839	3 603	7 683	62 257	22 538	3 554	189	17	143 117
	(17.1)	(13.2)	(2.5)	(5.4)	(43.5)	(15.7)	(2.5)	(0.1)	(0.0)	
1981	22 007	19 294	2 401	5 359	54 890	21 118	2 997	201	351	128 618
	(17.1)	(15.0)	(1.9)	(4.2)	(42.7)	(16.4)	(2.3)	(0.2)	(0.3)	
1982	18 996	17 948	2 125	4 931	53 031	21 331	2 576	180	29	121 147
	(15.7)	(14.8)	(1.8)	(4.1)	(43.8)	(17.6)	(2.1)	(0.1)	(0.0)	
1983	14 447	10 688	1 735	3 978	40 036	16 374	1 767	132	0	89 157
	(16.2)	(12.0)	(1.9)	(4.5)	(44.9)	(18.4)	(2.0)	(0.1)	(0.0)	
1984	13 190	10 670	2 150	3 903	41 527	14 641	2 042	116	0	88 239
	(14.9)	(12.1)	(2.4)	(4.4)	(47.1)	(16.6)	(2.3)	(0.1)	(0.0)	
1985	12 239	9 001	1 905	3 415	40 730	14 884	2 021	107	0	84 302
	(14.5)	(10.7)	(2.3)	(4.1)	(48.3)	(17.7)	(2.4)	(0.1)	(0.0)	
1986	12 552	9 673	1 860	3 749	49 630	19 459	2 180	116	0	99 219
	(12.7)	(9.7)	(1.9)	(3.8)	(50.0)	(19.6)	(2.2)	(0.1)	(0.0)	
1987	18 913	11 975	2 119	4 799	84 807	26 822	2 486	152	25	152 098
	(12.4)	(7.9)	(1.4)	(3.2)	(55.8)	(17.6)	(1.6)	(0.1)	(0.0)	
1988	23 204	14.025	2 223	5 009	88 996	25 789	2 539	144	0	161 929
	(14.3)	(8.7)	(1.4)	(3.1)	(55.0)	(15.9)	(1.6)	(0.1)	(0.0)	
1989	25 335	16 211	2 142	6 138	104 799	34 171	3 005	200	0	192 001
	(13.2)	(8.4)	(1.1)	(3.2)	(54.6)	(17.8)	(1.6)	(0.1)	(0.0)	
1990	28 617	18 908	2 358	6 629	113 173	40 680	3 124	158	0	213 647
	(13.4)	(8.9)	(1.1)	(3.1)	(53.0)	(19.0)	(1.5)	(0.1)	(0.0)	
Total	**213 937**	**157 232**	**24 621**	**55 593**	**733 876**	**257 807**	**28 291**	**1 695**	**422**	**1 473 474**
	(14.5)	**(10.7)**	**(1.7)**	**(3.8)**	**(49.8)**	**(17.5)**	**(1.9)**	**(0.1)**	**(0.0)**	

Source: *Immigration to Alberta. Decade in Review.* Alberta Career Development and Employment. Immigration and Settlement, January, 1992, p. 60. Reprinted with permission of Public Works and Government Services.

racial and ethnic groups seem natural or right (Robertson 1987, 291). Discrimination is the unequal treatment of people on the grounds of their group membership. Racial discrimination results from the negative attitudes and actions of majority groups who define and enforce patterns of exclusion toward ethnic or minority groups. In Canada, minorities have been subjected to three forms of discrimination: individual discrimination, institutional discrimination, and cultural discrimination (Ramcharan 1989, 119).

Individual Racism

Individual racism is the belief that one's race is superior to another (racial prejudice) and behaviour that suppresses members of the so-called inferior race (racial discrimination). Racism is based on the erroneous assumptions that physical attributes of a racial group determine the social behaviour of its members, as well as their psychological and intellectual characteristics (Robertson 1987). For example, we have heard about the stingy Scots, and the antisocial and strange Jews. A racist, therefore, is an individual who believes that members of another race are inferior. The racist further believes (often unconsciously) that the inferior person's behaviour, morality, and intellectual qualities are determined by a few visible physical traits. Sometimes these racist beliefs remain submerged as hidden racial prejudice, but usually the racist believes this inferiority is a legitimate basis for inferior social treatment.

Institutional Racism

Racial discrimination also involves institutions. Institutional racism consists of those established laws, customs, and practices that systematically reflect and produce racial inequalities, regardless of whether the individuals maintaining those practices have racist intentions. For example, the criminal justice system in Canada is more likely to incarcerate Natives than white Canadians (see, for example, Mercredi 1994). Individual lawyers and judges may not be racists, but they function within a system that deals with Natives differently. Similarly, in schools, Christian values and moral codes are more widely taught because the society is built predominantly upon Christian values. While we are not consciously discriminating against other faiths, we take it for granted that there are children who are non-Christians. In the same way, schools have hot-dog days, but we seldom hear of a chow-mein day. We assume that every child eats hot-dogs and celebrates Christmas. Other examples of institutional racism include formal and informal real-estate practices that prohibit some races from buying or renting in particular sections of town, and practices that deny certain races access to clubs and organizations such as fraternities. Textbooks and educational materials that present erroneous information about certain racial groups or omit their contributions are other examples of institutional racism. Books tend to give an ethnocentric and Eurocentric view of the world, denying other cultures of what they are capable of. Minority groups are portrayed in a negative way. The Natives in Canada for example, are often presented as uncivilized and barbaric. No nation, no race, can face the future unless it knows what it is capable of (see Bolaria and Li 1985, Elliott and Fleras 1992).

Cultural Racism

Cultural racism is the belief in the inferiority of the implements, handicrafts, agriculture, economics, art, music, language, tradition, and story of non-Anglo-European peoples, and the belief that these people have no distinctive culture apart from that of mainstream white Anglo-Europeans. For example, during colonial times it was a deliberate policy to rewrite the history of colonized peoples and replace it with European history (see Rodney 1972). In Europe, racist scholars obliterated the influence of African and Asian civilizations. The colonial curriculum taught the history of Europe and the Gospels. Christianity was the only accepted religion. Either one was a Christian or a barbarian. European colonizers, France in particular, saw colonization as a way of civilizing the world. Colonization took on a civilizing mission (see Carnoy 1974, Fanon 1968).

Although it is possible to discriminate in favour of a group, discrimination usually implies negative actions. In particular, discrimination involves the refusal to give members of one group the opportunities that would be granted to similarly qualified members of another group. Discrimination occurs, for example, if an employer refuses to hire or promote someone solely because of that person's racial or ethnic background.

Racial Inequality in Schooling

Rick's story...Being target of prejudice and racism hurts a lot

> I had not even heard of the words prejudice and racism. My first exposure was in Grade 5. While watching several television commercials about prejudice and racism, I started to wonder what the words really meant. Hating other people for their race? I thought it was not all that true until I became more knowledgeable about the topic. Gradually I was shocked by all the things I had seen and heard. What kind of country had I come to?...When I think about it, prejudice and racism hurt not only the victim, but the person who is creating the problem. Do they not have anything better to do than to make fun of other people about their race? Whenever I see a person getting hurt for their race, I cry inside. As I got insulted, how much I wish that I was white instead. I thought if I was the same race he was, I would not get teased by him.[4]

For racial or ethnic antagonisms and inequalities to develop, some basic conditions must be met. First, there must be two or more social groups, identifiable by their visible physical characteristics or cultural practices. Unless people are aware of differences, conflict between them cannot develop. Second, there must be competition for resources, such as power, jobs, land, and housing. In this case, one group will seek to deny access to these resources to another group. Third, there is an unequal distribution of power between the groups. One group eventually makes claim over scarce resources at the expense of other groups. At this stage inequalities become structured into the society.

The structured inequalities in the society are reinforced by our institutions. Schools, are perhaps, a prime example. Since formal education is free and compulsory in Canada, one would expect that a random member of any given social class or racial group would have the same probability of entering college that a random member of any other group would have. Factors such as sex, race, or class would not affect educational achievement. Yet, there are varying differences and treatment. For example, the residential segregation of Native students in Canada has created separate local school systems.

Since the Second World War, most advanced capitalist societies have spent a major proportion of their gross national income on expanding the capacity of the educational system. One of the reasons for the expansion of the educational system was to equalize opportunities, especially for the socially and economically disadvantaged. Notably, in Canada the increased educational expenditures from 1950 to 1970, the peak period, saw the school participation rates for Indians, Inuit, and other minorities increase at a faster rate than the national averages (Li 1988, 74).

The Accommodation of Immigrants and Languages

> Canada has for a long time been substantially a nation of immigrants. Part of the reason for developing public schools in central Canada in the mid-nineteenth century had to do with a desire to ensure that the large numbers of German, Scottish, and Irish immigrants were socialized into the dominant values of the Canada of that day. There was no thought to accommodating or supporting the maintenance of immigrants' own cultures and languages. The same was true of the great waves of immigration around the turn of the last century, when hundreds of thousands of Ukrainians, Mennonites, Jews, Icelanders, Poles, and others came to Canada. The schools saw their task as being one of teaching these people "Canadian" ways, that is, teaching them to adjust to Canada as it existed when they arrived.
>
> An inspector of schools in Saskatchewan wrote in 1918: "The people of foreign countries who come to Canada after having reached maturity...will never become 'true Canadians'...but there is an important duty to perform in seeing that the children of these newcomers are given every opportunity to receive proper training for intelligent citizenship...(the) public school...is the great melting-pot into which must be placed these diverse racial groups, and from which will eventually emerge the pure gold of Canadian citizenship."
>
> More recently, there has been an increasing, though by no means universal, tendency to allow greater diversity in the schools; to be more accepting of different ways of living that Canadians of different origins may have. Schools have begun to offer programs in the languages of immigrant communities. But this general statement disguises the controversies that persist. Heritage Language programs are

> primarily offered outside of regular hours. The Peel Board of Education in Ontario lost a court battle to prevent a Sikh student from wearing a *kirpan* (a ceremonial dagger) to school. There has been heated debate in many Canadian communities about the creation of French immersion schools, which has sometimes meant busing English language students to schools outside their local area. Disputes about what, if any, religious exercises should be held in schools have been quite bitter in some provinces.[5]

Immigrant Children Drop Out of School

In spite of the attempts to equalize educational opportunity for all groups, research on immigrant children's successful integration into the education system shows that there is a high drop-out rate among these students. In a recent study, Watt and Roessingh (1994) show that school jurisdictions across Canada are moving towards an educational model of inclusion in response to the growing cultural, ethnic, and linguistic diversity of their student populations. However, equitable inclusion involves access to the curriculum, participation, and benefit. Failure to meet these criteria results in the marginalization of English-as-a-Second-Language (ESL) students. In Alberta, for example, Watt and Roessingh's findings indicate that the ESL drop-out rate is 74 percent. At the beginner level they found 95.5 percent of students dropped out before attaining a high-school diploma. Students drop out for several reasons: lack of confidence with spoken English, ridicule by English-speaking classmates, lack of support from teachers, and teachers underestimating their potential.

For immigrant children to succeed in school, access to instruction in English is the key. This access is a right, not a privilege. The Alberta School Act defines this right as being for: "those whose first language is not English and whose knowledge of English is insufficient to permit them to succeed in school and society" (Alberta Education Policy Document No. 02-03-03). The ESL drop-out is a sign that immigrant children are marginalized and their academic chances of success are greatly reduced. From a policy point of view, access to ESL and its delivery must be examined to include ESL students into the mainstream.

Despite the widely shared ideology of equality, social inequality remains well entrenched in Canadian society. Policies on equity, which advocate equality of opportunity for all groups, are full of rhetoric. These policies have sparked false hopes. Rather than equalizing unequal opportunities, the school system reproduces class and ethnic inequality by preparing those from privileged backgrounds for higher education, and sorting out and channelling others from deprived upbringings to lower-class positions (Li 1988, 131).

Native Students Victims of Racism

> Native students on Winnipeg's campuses say they face acts of racism as brutal as any found in the poverty-stricken city. Aboriginal students are constantly bombarded with racist acts, from death threats spray-painted on the elevator walls to insensitivity from professors.

> In class people won't sit beside native students. As the economy worsens, so do incidents of racism. Native students at the University of Winnipeg have to endure racism more from professor than their peers. A third year student from the Peguis First Nation said in one incident a sociology professor presented a theory in class about why native people are more prone to alcoholism. The remarks hurt the native students in his class.[6]

Challenging Racism: Antiracist Education

> If you try to stop the story about racial politics, racial divisions, racist ideologies short of confronting some of these difficult issues; if you present an idealized picture of a "multicultural" or "ethnically varied" society which doesn't look at the way in which racism has acted back inside the working class itself, the way in which racism has combined with, for example, sexism working back within the black population itself; if you try to tell the story as if somewhere around the corner some whole constituted class enemy...you will have done absolutely nothing whatsoever for the political understanding of your students (Hall 1981, 68).

Critical curriculum theorists maintain that the school is not "innocent" of the contradictions of race, class, and gender (see, for example, Carnoy and Levin 1985, Connell *et al.* 1982, Wood 1985). Education is a political act and the role of the teacher should be that of an activist for democratic reforms in the school setting. Teachers should help students to better analyze and struggle against inequalities of power and resources in school and society (McCarthy 1990, 112). According to Connell et al.:

> Education has fundamental connections with the idea of human emancipation, though it is constantly in danger of being captured for other interests. In a society disfigured by class exploitation, sexual and racial oppression, and in chronic danger of war and environmental destruction, the only education worth the name is one that forms people capable of taking part in their own liberation. The business of school is not propaganda. It is equipping people with the knowledge and skills and concepts relevant to remaking a dangerous and disordered world. In the most basic sense...At the beginning of the 1980s, it is plain that the forces opposed to that growth here and on the world scale are not only powerful but have become increasingly militant. In such circumstances, education becomes a risky enterprise. Teachers too have to decide whose side they are on.

For schools and teachers, the challenge is to assist both educators and learners to achieve a new inclusive understanding of our social world and to address the issues of social and human development and, in particular, the issue of social justice and respect for the fundamental freedoms and rights of all peoples (Dei 1993, 37).

Antiracist education provides teachers and educators with an alternative approach to challenge conflicting expectations of our school system. The need for Canadian schools to serve the multi-ethnic community must be seen as an essential function of the school system. Antiracist education provides the opportunity to question the power relations in the school and society, it emphasizes the importance of personal experience and lived realities as source of knowledge, and explores the perspectives of different social groups in society (Dei 1993, Giroux 1988, Freire 1990). Antiracist education is the effort to counter forms of racism manifested in the education process. It seeks to identify and change institutional policies and procedures and individual behaviours and practices that may foster racism. Antiracist education is not a separate topic to be added to existing programs, rather it permeates all aspects of school work. It is education that challenges racism.

To challenge the cultural and historical biases of Canadian schooling, an inclusive pedagogy is required. For educators and teachers to find appropriate strategies for antiracist education, it is necessary to recognize the structures of inequality in our society and how power relations influence the structure and dynamics of race, ethnic, and gender relations. Antiracist education must be presented as political education to raise group and individual consciousness and to develop critical political thinking for meaningful change in society. It is an integral part of the curriculum.

Antiracist education is therefore presented as education that seeks to examine the structures of inequality in society. Schools should embrace antiracist education in its effort to further institutional change. By developing programs and a curriculum that emancipates, the school and the community can liberate both teachers and learners. Social justice for minorities will remain an illusion as long as existing curriculum prevails and our teaching practices remain unexamined.

Exercise

Co-operative Faces

The concept of a "square" may be difficult for younger children to understand and visualize. The human face is a far more basic and recognizable unit at this age.

Resources

Six large photographs (approximately A4 size) can be mounted on a stiff card. A mixture of races and sexes should be represented. The faces are cut into sections — nose, eyes, part of face, lips, chin, etc. The pieces are distributed among six envelopes so that each envelope contains at least one piece from each face.

Procedure

Six children sit around a table, and each is given an envelope. The children are told that they are to use the pieces in the envelope to make six faces. The game is not finished until all six faces are made. They may give any of their pieces to a group member who they think might need them, or they may place them in the centre of the table if they do not need them. Children may take pieces from the centre of the table (having a box in which these are placed helps them realize that these are being "offered" to the group), but may not take pieces from one another.

While Co-operative Faces is usually played with a "no-talking" rule, young children need to reason out loud, and being able to verbalize about the process facilitates their problem-solving abilities.

Potential

It is important to talk about exactly what happened. Children can be encouraged to talk about feelings they may have had — frustration, jealousy, possessiveness, how it felt to share, to complete the task, etc. In order to bring out the idea of the need for co-operation, the facilitator can ask the children what they would say to help others who were playing the game for the first time.

By using photos showing children of different races, children can also discuss how the faces differ, as well as how they are similar. It is interesting to make one list of similarities and one of differences, and to compare them. Which list is longer?

Variations

The children love to play this game with pictures of animals, or animal faces.[7]

Conclusion

Racial minorities, particularly Blacks and Natives, have not fared well in Canadian schools. In addition to harsh statistics indicating profound racial differences in achievement scores and drop-out rates, minorities also face severe problems of marginalization and alienation in schools. To explain problems of racial inequality in education and society, is a seemingly complex and intractable problem. However, in this chapter, it is argued that racism in Canadian society is pronounced and that schools have been slow to recognize that there are institutionalized practices that see immigrant children as inferior. Unless these practices are challenged, racial groups will continue to be oppressed. For this reason, it is proposed that fundamental changes in the school system and curriculum practices are needed. The curriculum must be reconstructed so that education will be inclusive.

Discussion Questions

1. What factors strengthen ethnic identity? What factors reduce the salience of ethnic identity in contemporary Canadian society?
2. What is the meaning and purpose of multiculturalism in Canada? Has the policy on multiculturalism been effective in reducing racial discrimination?
3. In spite of various initiatives, some groups are still subjected to racial discrimination. Can the school play a role to bring cultures together?

Notes

1. Stanley R. Barrett. 1987. *Is God a Racist? The Right Wing in Canada.* Toronto: University of Toronto Press.
2. S. Hall. 1988. "New Ethnicities." In *Black Film, British Cinema.* Edited by K. Mercer. ICA documents, 7 (27-31). London: ICA. p. 28.
3. *Edmonton Journal*, March 22, 1994, p. B3
4. Ibid, February 15, 1994, p. A11.
5. Benjamin Levin and Jon Young. 1994. *Understanding Canadian Schools: An Introduction to Educational Administration.* Toronto: Harcourt Brace & Company Canada, Limited. p. 85. Reprinted by permission.
6. *Edmonton Journal*, January 9, 1994.
7. Graham Pike and David Selby. 1989. *Global Teacher, Global Learner.* Kent: Hodder and Stoughton. pp. 168-9. Reprinted by permission.

References

Alladin, Ibrahim, and Bacchus, Kazim M., eds. 1991. *Education, politics and state in multicultural societies: An international perspective.* MA: Ginn Press.

Barth, F. ed. 1969. *Ethnic groups and boundaries: The social organization of cultural difference.* London: George Allen & Unwin.

Bolaria, Singh, and Li, Peter. 1985. *Racial oppression in Canada.* Toronto: Garamond Press.

Carnoy, M. 1974. *Education as cultural imperialism.* NY: David McKay.

Carnoy, M., and Levin, H. 1985. *Schooling and work in the democratic state.* Stanford: Stanford Univ. Press.

Changing Perspectives. 1992. *A resource guide for antiracist and ethnocultural-equity education.* All Divisions and OACS. Ontario: Queen's Printer for Ontario.

Connell, R. W., et al. 1982. *Making the difference: schools, families, and social division.* Boston: Allen Unwin.

Curtis, James, and Tepperman, Lorne. 1990. *Images of Canada: The sociological tradition.* Scarborough: Prentice-Hall Canada.

Decima Report. 1993. A report to the Canadian Council of Christians and Jews. Canadians' attitudes toward race and ethnic relations in Canada. November.

Dei, George J. 1993. The challenges of antiracist education in Canada. *Journal of Ethnic Studies* 25 (2): 36-51.

Depres, Leo A. 1975. "Ethnicity and resource competition in Guyanese society." In *Ethnicity and resource competition in plural societies*, ed. Leo A. Depres. USA: Mouton Publishers.

Driedger, Leo, ed. 1978. *The Canadian ethnic mosaic: A quest for identity.* Toronto: McClelland & Stewart.

Elliott, J. L., and Fleras, A. 1992. *Unequal relations. An introduction to race and ethnic dynamics in Canada.* Scarborough: Prentice Hall Canada.

Fanon, F. 1968. *The wretched of the earth.* NY: Grove Press.

Freire, P. 1990. *Pedagogy of the oppressed.* NY: Continuum.

Giroux, H. A. 1988. *Teachers as intellectuals: Critical studies in education series.* South Hadley, MA: Bergin & Garvey.

Gordon, Milton M. 1964. *Assimilation in American life.* NY: Oxford Univ. Press.

Hall, S. 1988. "New ethnicities." In *Black film, British cinema*, ed. K. Mercer, ICA documents, 7: 27-31. London: ICA.

———. 1981. "Teaching race." In *The school in the multicultural society*, ed. A. James and R. Jeffcoate. London: Harper & Row.

Hawkins, Freda. 1972. *Canadian immigration: public policy and public concern.* Montreal: McGill-Queen's Univ. Press.

Isajiw, W. 1974. Definitions of ethnicity. *Ethnicity* 1: 111-24.

Li, Peter. 1988. *The Chinese in Canada.* Oxford and Toronto: Oxford Univ. Press.

———. 1988. *Ethnic inequality in a class society.* Toronto: Wall & Thompson.

McCarthy, Cameron. 1990. *Race and curriculum: Social inequality and the theories and politics of difference in contemporary research on schooling.* United Kingdom: The Falmer Press.

McCarthy, C., and Crichlow, W., eds. 1993. *Race, identity and representation in education.* London: Routledge.

Mercredi, O., and Turpel, M.E. 1993. *In the rapids: Navigating the future of First Nations.* Toronto: Viking.

Newman, William N. 1978. "Theoretical perspectives for the analysis of social pluralism." In *The Canadian ethnic mosaic. A quest for identity*, ed. Leo Driedger. Toronto: McClelland & Stewart.

Ramcharan, Subhas. 1989. *Social problems and issues. A Canadian perspective.* Scarborough: Nelson Canada.

Rizvi, F. 1986. *Ethnicity, class and multicultural education.* Deakin, Victoria: Deakin Univ. Press.

Robertson, Ian. 1987. *Sociology*. 3d ed. NY: Worth.

Rodney, W. 1972. *How Europe underveloped Africa*. Washington, D.C.: Harvard Univ. Press.

Saram, P. A. 1991. "Multicultures and the state: A theoretical analysis." In *Education, politics and state in multicultural societies. An international perspective*, ed. Ibrahim Alladin and Kazim Bacchus. MA: Ginn Press.

Silverman, Robert, A., and Teevan, James, J. 1986. *Crime in Canadian society*. Toronto: Butterworths.

Smith, Raymond, T. 1966. People and change. *New World: Guyana Independence Issue*. Georgetown: New World Group Associates.

Smith, A. D. 1981. *The ethnic revival*. Cambridge: Cambridge Univ. Press.

van den Berghe, P. L. 1981. *The ethnic phenomenon*. NY: Elsevier.

Watt, David, and Roessingh, Hetty. 1994. Inclusion and language minority education: curricular implications. Faculty of Education, Univ. of Calgary.

———. 1994. ESL dropout: The myth of educational equity. Faculty of Education, Univ. of Calgary.

Weber, Max. 1968. *Economy and society*, ed. G. Roth and C. Wittich. NY: Bedminster Press.

Wood, G. 1985. "Schooling in a democracy: Transformation or reproduction." In *Multiculturalism as an educational policy*, ed. F. Rizvi Geelong, 91-111. Victoria: Deakin University.

Further Reading

For a short history of nonwhite immigration to Canada, see Ramcharan, Subhas. 1982. *Racism: nonwhites in Canada*. Toronto: Butterworths.

Li, Peter S., and Bolaria, Singh B., eds. 1983. *Racial minorities in multicultural Canada*. Toronto: Garamond Press.

van den Berghe, Pierre, L. 1978. *Race and racism: A comparative perspective*. USA: John Wiley & Sons.

York, Geoffrey. 1990. *The dispossessed: Life and death in Native Canada*. UK: Vintage.

2

RACISM AND NATIVE SCHOOLING: A HISTORICAL PERSPECTIVE

Syd Pauls

> *If Canadians are disturbed or shocked by revelations of racism in their society, that is as it should be. If they are surprised or puzzled by it however, that demonstrates an abysmal lack of awareness — undoubtedly fostered by our educational systems — of the less creditable aspects of Canadian history. (Hill)*[1]
>
> *Ormond McHague*
> Racism in Canada

Introduction

The education of Native people in Canada has been a source of tragedy and pain for the Natives and a source of shame for the rest of the country. Various factors have conspired against the Native people; the early explorers and settlers, who coveted the land and sought to remove the obstacle of Native possession of it; the churches, whose objective was the eradication of Native beliefs and the conversion to Christianity; and the government who wished to be rid of the promises made in treaties and thought that the way to do this was institutionalized genocide. None of these attempts have been completely successful, and today the Native people are rebuilding their self-concept and pride, practising their languages, restoring their traditional beliefs, and reestablishing their right to govern themselves. This will not be a simple task but the Native people are willing to make the necessary decisions and sacrifices. This chapter examines some of the historical factors that led to the marginalization of the Native people, and the kind of education system that developed for the Native children. The policy on Native education is also discussed and comments will be made on future policies and practices.

Institutionalized Racism

There are an estimated 5290 groups of aboriginal people in the world, with a total population of about 357 million. In Canada, there are 633 First Nations, with a total population of approximately 1 500 000 status Indians (Hitchcock 1994, 2-3). This figure does not include Metis or non-status Indians, who also consider themselves to be indigenous peoples. The meaning of "indigenous" tends to pose a semantic difficulty, since there are a variety of definitions being proposed, from simple self-declarations of individuals to definitions developed by institutions.

Definitions of Indigenous

> One United Nations study suggested four elements to be considered; (a) pre-existence, (b) non-dominance, (c) cultural differences and (d) self-identification as indigenous. The report went on to say that "The term indigenous applies to those people who are isolated socially or to marginal groups that have managed to preserve their traditions in spite of being incorporated into states dominated by other societies."
>
> The World Bank lists five elements in its definition of indigenous; (a) close attachment to ancestral territories and natural resources, (b) self-identification and identification by others as members of a distinct cultural group, (c) possession of an indigenous language, which is often distinct from the national language, (d) presence of customary social or political institutions, and (e) subsistence-oriented production systems.[2]

The World Bank definition seems to focus on historical elements and does not include the descendants of such people who may not have retained a separate language, a land base, or a subsistence economy but still consider themselves as indigenous. In many countries, including Canada, indigenous peoples have been subjected to cultural genocide directed at destroying the language, the political structures, and the economy of the indigenous people. Depending upon the relative success of these policies, certain indigenous groups may no longer qualify under the World Bank definition.

It may be useful to compare the indigenous people of Canada with the criteria given in both the UN and World Bank definitions. They occupied all of what is now Canada and were committed and attached to the land since it supplied their sustenance and livelihoods. They are no longer dominant, having been overcome by the sheer numbers of white people arriving in the country and by disease they brought with them. Even today, many indigenous people of Canada live on reserves, left-over remnants of their original lands, and follow a lifestyle incorporating their cultural and traditional roots, rather than "mainstream" Canadian values. The indigenous people also place importance on the retention of their various languages as a means of retaining a separate identity as Native people. Finally, the structure of government in Canada, the economic philosophy, and the educational system clearly reflect the dominant, rather than the indigenous, culture.

Genocide/Racism

The terms genocide and racism are often incorrectly used synonymously. Genocide is defined as; "the deliberate and systematic destruction of a racial, political or cultural group" (Davis and Zannis 1973, 28). It is often thought of as being a physical action characteristic of the Nazis' attempt to murder the Jews or the early English settlers' efforts to eliminate the Beothuks from Newfoundland. Genocide can also be defined as the destruction of a culture and, therefore, the society and the people that developed and were dependent upon that culture for survival.

Racism, on the other hand, is a belief in the innate superiority of one race or culture over another. In situations of colonization, the colonizers often resort to racist arguments to justify their occupation and control over the subjugated people. In fact, French philosopher Jean-Paul Sartre suggested that colonization cannot proceed without racism and genocide of the original peoples. In Canada this was certainly true, as the European colonizers saw traits in the Native people that they designated as inferior and that gave them the moral authority to impose their own version of civilization. Without such beliefs and the corresponding authorization for action that they implied, the European colonizers of Canada would not have been able to subjugate the aboriginal people. Racism is often intellectually disguised to make it more palatable, but the belief in the superiority of one group over another is a necessary characteristic.

The Canadian Context

In Canada, we like to believe that we, as a country, are less racist, more accepting of multiculturalism, and more open to accommodations designed to promote the retention of ethnic identity. How then, can the treatment that the Native people of this country have received over the past 400-500 years, since first contact, be explained?

Human Rights in Canada and Native People

> Nineteen ninety-three was billed as the International Year of the World's Indigenous People. It is in the nature of years and decades of this kind that countries try to put their best foot forward...both aboriginal and non-aboriginal Canadians continued to strive for more practical improvements. It nevertheless remains the position of our Commission that the plight of native Canadians is by far the most serious human rights problem in Canada, and that failure to achieve a more global solution can only continue to tarnish Canada's reputation and accomplishments.
>
> It is simply not possible to grapple with the many human rights issues that affect Canada's aboriginal peoples today without acknowledging how deeply they are rooted in two very different perspectives on our entire cultural and economic history.
>
> As a result, whether we speak of self-government or social services, land claims or employment equity, it is important not to think too simplistically. From the human rights standpoint it has been apparent for decades that much of the discrimination suffered by Canada's aboriginal peoples stems from a basic confusion about the nature of their equality with other Canadians. Paradoxically, despite the "special status" and segregation that are implicit in such instru-

ments as the Indian Act, these arrangements have failed to protect native people who remain on reserves from the encroachment of alien values; and they have led others to seek a place in the Canadian mainstream where they have virtually no protection at all. The task before us, therefore, is much more involved than merely rejecting the one-sided and paternalistic relationship that has hitherto been inscribed in law; what we have to do now is to bring about a truly serviceable partnership that does justice to the better elements of both traditions.[3]

The systemic and institutionalized racism that Native people in Canada face is evidenced in a variety of manners. Rates of unemployment, disease, suicide, incarceration, and substance abuse among Native people far exceed the national averages. This chapter will deal with another area in which Native people have traditionally experienced discrimination. The education that has been provided to Native people has been traditionally inferior and designed by the dominant society to complement the racist objectives of assimilation, and acculturation of the Native people.

Terminology

Before continuing, I would like to clarify the terms used when referring to the indigenous inhabitants of Canada. When Columbus landed in North America he was lost. He thought he was in India and therefore mistakenly referred to the people occupying the land as Indians. In fact, the peoples inhabiting North America were culturally diverse and there was no inclusive term that they used to refer to themselves. To some, Indian implies a legal definition that gives particular rights to a group of specific people as defined in the Indian Act, a piece of federal legislation. This definition is offensive to some, since it has nothing to do with how the people define themselves, and there are also other indigenous groups, such as the Metis and non-status Indians, who are excluded in the legalistic Indian definition.

The Indian Act definition is quoted at length in "Persons Entitled To Be Registered — Idem — Deeming provision 6" and it shows the frustrations indigenous peoples feel when dealing with this legalistic definition that purports to define who they are.

Persons Entitled To Be Registered — Idem — Deeming provision 6

(1)Subject to section 7, a person is entitled to be registered if:

(a) that person was registered or entitled to be registered immediately prior to April 17, 1985;

(b) that person is a member of a body of persons that has been declared by the Governor in Council on or after April 17, 1985 to be a band for the purposes of this Act;

(c) the name of that person was omitted or deleted from the Indian Registry or from a Band List prior to September 4, 1951, under subparagraph 12(1)(a)(iv), paragraph 12(1)(b) or subsection 12(2) or under subparagraph 12(1)(a)(iii) pursuant to an order made under subsection 109(2), as each provision read immediately prior to April 17, 1985, or under any former provision of this Act relating to the same subject matter as any of those provisions;

(d) the name of that person was omitted or deleted from the Indian Register, or from a Band List prior to September 4, 1951, under subparagraph 12(1)(a)(iii) pursuant to an order made under subsection 109(1), as each provision read immediately prior to April 17, 1985, or under any former provision of this Act relating to the same subject matter as any of those provisions;

(f) that person is a person both of whose parents are or, if no longer living, were at the time of death entitled to be registered under this section.

(2)Subject to section 7, a person is entitled to be registered if that person is a person one of whose parents is or, if no longer living, was at the time of death entitled to be registered under subsection (1).[4]

It can be readily seen that choosing an all encompassing term to refer to all of the original inhabitants of Canada, without offering offence to any, is a process fraught with danger. Many writers use the terms aboriginal, native, or Amerindian as encompassing terms and the word Indian to refer to those people recognized under the Indian Act. I have decided, arbitrarily, to use the term Native as the inclusive term for all indigenous peoples and have decided to use a capital letter to reflect the growing, renewed recognition of a sense of nationhood within the indigenous peoples of Canada. When I use "Indian," I am specifically referring to those people who are governed by the Indian Act. It is hoped that this arbitrary decision does not offend too many people.

History of Native Education

The history of Native education in Canada is not one in which either the Native or the dominant society can take much pride. "The history of formal education of Indians in Canada is marred by failure...for hundreds of years we have been victims of a colonial mentality...intent only on transforming us into 'their' culture. The results have been devastating" (Kirkness 1985, 1). It is clear that, from earliest times, the education system has been the tool selected to perform this transformation. "By far the most insidious systematic assault on Indian and Inuit culture is perpetrated by the imposed western educational system" (Davis and Zannis 1973, 127).

In all cultures and societies, formalized education or schooling has always had two purposes. One main purpose is to transmit specific knowledge or means of acquiring knowledge that the society has deemed to be necessary for the improved life of its citizens. The second purpose of schooling is to act as an instrument of socialization; to teach the attitudes, mores, and beliefs of the dominant section of the population. Paulo Freire (1983) stated this concept quite explicitly when he talked about the education system being designed to perpetuate the dominant/subservient relationship of oppressor and oppressed. (See "Education as a Means of Oppression"):

Education as a Means of Oppression

> The educator's role is to regulate the way the world "enters into" the students...since men "receive" the world as passive entities, education should make them more passive still, and adapt them to the world. The educated man is the adapted man because he is a better "fit" for the world. Translated into practice, this concept is well suited to the purposes of the oppressors, whose tranquillity rests on how well men fit the world the oppressors have created, and how little they question it.[5]

From early contact, the schooling that has been provided for Native people had the primary purpose of socialization and acculturation. European missionaries and settlers saw the Native people as passive recipients in need of knowledge, training, and direction from a more advanced civilization.

Early Missionary Schools

The early European arrivals to this continent could not have survived without the help of the Native people. They showed the explorers and settlers which plants and animals could be eaten, how to catch these animals, how to travel over the inland waterways and the snow-covered landscape, how to build shelters that would offer protection during the cold winters, and the various other skills necessary to survive. Without this help, the European occupation of North America would have been brief indeed.

Despite the fact that early European explorers could not have survived without the help of the Native people, the explorers and colonialists brought with them their own culture, religion, and standards of civilization. They were convinced that the Native way of life was inferior to the European one and that it was their duty to provide instruction and direction to the underdeveloped, savage, and heathen Native people. This ethnocentric belief found expression in religious zeal that the Europeans deemed to be the prerequisite for civilization. Missionaries soon established schools for Native people in the newly colonized area of New France. Schooling for Native people in Canada thus has a longer history than schooling for non-Natives. The missionaries were not much concerned with the development of intellectual processes of Native people; they were more concerned with getting Natives to adopt a Christian way of life and European ideas of civilization. Fisher (1992, 144-145) notes:

> Because the Missionaries did not separate Western Christianity and Western civilization, they approached Indian culture as a whole and demanded a total transformation. Their aim was the complete destruction of the traditional integrated Indian way of life.

Early Ethnocentrism

> Early settlers believed that they were at a more advanced phase of development as a society than the indigenous peoples they met in North America. It simply did not occur to them that a society could be advanced or complex in a different way despite the fact that settlers not only learned survival skills from the indigenous peoples, but also borrowed complex political ideas from them. It seemed obvious to the settlers that the "New World" was destined to become another Europe and that clearing the land for farming was an improvement over what had existed before. This understanding was interwoven with the belief that people unacquainted with the Christian gospel must be godless and therefore evil. Such a premise inspired fear of the "immoral" deeds the native people might inflict on white settlers, as well as missionary zeal to covert the Indian and improve their lives.
>
> It takes no leap of the imagination to recognize the dynamics already at work. Believing themselves to be culturally and morally superior, the settlers could justify individual and corporate actions to "improve" the land and "enlighten" the people. The benefit of getting aboriginal peoples to assimilate was to lessen the threat to European settlers and their way of life. The ability of Canadians to justify the innumerable documented acts of injustice against aboriginal peoples, on the grounds that European culture was "superior," is still a major stumbling block for native people seeking justice today.[6]

Since the language, religion, and culture of the Native people were bound into an integrated whole, the acceptance of a foreign religion meant the abandonment of their entire cultural background. The missionaries recognized this fact early on and worked for precisely that result.

One of the ways this was to be accomplished was to separate young status Indians from the "corrupting" influences of their parents. Residential schools, intended to indoctrinate young Native people into the European belief system and culture, were established. Educational concerns took a secondary and inferior position to this task of acculturation, assimilation, indoctrination, and cultural genocide.

Residential Schools

As the immigrant population in Canada grew, the government began to sign treaties with the Native people to obtain use of the land without the military struggles that occurred in the United States. One of the provisions that the Native people insisted be included in the treaties was a promise to provide schools and teachers on the lands reserved for them. The government quickly decided that it would be more economical to provide education for Natives by entering into partnerships with existing religious organizations, rather than operating its own schools (Dickason 1992, 333). The federal government participated in the establishment of schools with the proviso that "the schools be operated so far as possible by missionaries, who had already demonstrated their commitment to 'civilizing' Canada's Indians" (Barman 1986, 6).

The government reasoned that the Native people were doomed to disappear, if not physically as a race, then culturally as a people. They were, therefore, anxious to accelerate this process and the religious organizations seemed the ideal instruments. The churches had already demonstrated their intention of "civilizing," Christianizing, and acculturating Native people; and the government simply expanded their mandate. As Hodgson (1992, 103) states, "One of the most insidious tools of assimilation was the residential school system. Set up and run primarily by churches on behalf of the federal government, the residential schools, in effect, formalized family breakdown as a matter of national policy."

The residential school model was chosen since it seemed the best way of isolating young Native people from their communities and indoctrinating them with European values. The residential schools went through several metamorphoses. One reincarnation was the industrial school, where the purpose was to teach useful skills, rather than too much education. It was assumed that Native students were incapable of higher learning and, therefore, the best that the school could do was to provide a low-level skill that the students could use to gain a minimal living in the white economic structure. Students in these schools would normally spend only a half day in classrooms and the remaining half days and evenings in agricultural pursuits or learning a trade. Many of these schools became sources of cheap labour for surrounding farmers, and the unpaid work of the students supported the infrastructure of the school. Tasks in the laundry, in the kitchen, the making and repairing of clothing, farming, and care of livestock were commonly assigned to students.

Many Native people who have survived the residential school system do not have fond memories of the "civilizing" process they endured. By taking children away from their families and forbidding the use of Native culture or languages the churches hoped to extinguish Indianess (Kirkness 1985). According to Smith (1993, 42) "The church run schools were all in business for just one reason — to drive a wedge between the students and their culture, to turn Indians into budding young Christians trained in the work ethic." Haig-Brown (1988) provides examples of the "civilizing" process that have been related by survivors of the experience:

> The elimination of language has always been a primary stage in a process of cultural genocide. . . (a student) was physically punished for speaking Tsehaht: they pushed sewing needles through his tongue, a routine punishment for language offenders.
>
> At the residential school we were not allowed to speak our language; we weren't allowed to dance or sing because they told us it was evil. It was evil for us to practice any of our cultural ways.

It may be difficult, in this time of liberal ideology and emphasis on the importance and integrity of the family and the individual, to understand how such a mass imprisonment of young people could occur. It is also equally difficult to understand what the long-term ramifications of such an organized attempt at cultural genocide might be. The account in "An Image of the Residential School Experience" may make these difficult concepts, as well as the pain and frustration that the Native people feel to this day, easier to understand.

An Image of the Residential School Experience

> Imagine what it would be like if all the white Canadian five-year-old children were moved to Japan, under Japanese guard, and they all had to live there until they were fifteen to twenty years old. Imagine also that they had to speak Japanese, learn Buddhism, participate in all Japanese customs, and never speak their mother tongue. They would not be allowed to participate in any Canadian practice or ceremony during their years in Japan.
>
> Imagine that your children had to be pulled from your arms and taken to Japan, not to be seen for months, years or perhaps ever. Imagine that all your children were taken. Would you not feel an agonizing feeling of failure that you could not even protect your children? Would you not feel a loss of hope? Would you not feel a deep, deep loneliness? Would you not fear for their safety? Would you not worry about who would teach them the family rituals, especially if your whole social system was built on the family and ceremonies? How could you cope? What if three successive generations were moved to Japan in this way? What would be left of your culture and language or of the meaning of your whole social system?
>
> What would you do if you were a child being removed from your parents' arms? Would you scream, "Mom, help! Mom help!"? Would you feel, "They should have stopped them from taking me"? What would you feel if you arrived in that big building where there were people speaking a funny language and when you spoke the language you knew, you were hit and told to speak in that strange language? What if your culture taught that your hair was part of your spirit, and the strange people cut off all your hair and scrubbed your head with something that burned your scalp to get rid of "lice"? What if you were bathed in a public washroom? What would you do with the shame? What would you do if you saw your brother or sister and you ran to them and were hit for speaking to them?[7]

The residential schools have left a devastating legacy. Children spent long periods of time away from home and were constantly being told what to do and think. As a result, generations of Natives have grown up not having developed the self confidence to cope with an independent existence in adulthood. "Residential schools have had a traumatic impact on Aboriginal children and family life and account for many of today's problems of violence, addiction, loss of culture and loss of self esteem" (Royal Commission on Aboriginal Peoples 1992, 3). Kirkness (1992, 12) states that the residential schools deprived generations of Native people of the knowledge of their own identity and Indianess. They have left a legacy of cultural conflict, alienation, poor self-concept, and lack of preparation for independence, for jobs, and for life in general. Cardinal (1969, 55) says that a primary consequence of the residential school system was to "turn the child against education, preventing him from seeing or appreciating the benefits of a real education." Finally, Smith (1993, 42-43) provides this damning summary of the residential school system:

> Children were wrested from their families once they reached school age and sent to spend 10 months of every year in grim institutions where they slept in big dormitories, were often beaten for speaking their own language...They were separated from their brothers and sisters and spent as much time working the school farms as they did in the classrooms. Entire generations were alienated from their language, the richest part of their culture...The children of the residential school era emerged unsure of just who and what they were — Indian by race, Christian reform school by training, and often utterly incapable of fitting into either world.

Federal and Integrated Schools

In the late 1950s, the federal government finally realized that the residential schools were not doing the job intended for them. Not only had the Native people not disappeared but there were more of them; and because the residential schools did not have a high level of academic concentration, there were more poorly educated Native people. The government, prompted by reports and studies, and by the Native people themselves, finally decided that they would open and operate schools on reserves for Indian people and would arrange with provincial governments to contribute to the education of Native people living off reserves. It is important to note that the government did not change its policy of assimilation but merely changed the agents charged with promoting assimilation from religious institutions to a federal department or to provincially operated schools.

The on-reserve schools were often problematic. Often, Indian Affairs simply took over the operation of a residential school but the staff and program remained unchanged. In some cases, they built inferior quality schools on reserves to house programs that, by their own admission, were not comparable to provincial programs. In many of these schools the staff were uncertified and the program was heavy with repetition and rote memorization. The texts and materials used were riddled with anti-Native messages. The Native communities had no say in the hiring of teachers, the evaluation of program or staff, or the types of curricula that were used in the schools.

About the same time that Indian Affairs started to open schools on reserves, they also began to enter into long-term tuition agreements with the provinces. They were convinced that their own on-reserve schools would be a temporary measure and that soon all Native students would attend provincial schools. This was part of the overall strategy of forcing Native people to adopt European culture and abandon their own language and culture. To make this easier, the federal government negotiated master tuition agreements with the provinces without the knowledge or consent of the Native people. The provincial schools often saw the Native students as a means to obtain tuition dollars from the federal government and they were more interested in the number of students than the educational program provided for them. They were not obliged to design or offer any special programming to meet the needs of Native students; indeed the expectation was that by exposing Native students to the same provincial curriculum they would be forced to give up their claims to any special status and to abandon their language and culture.

Government Policy of Acculturation

Statements made by early Canadian politicians regarding Indians are indicative of the goal of the government to forcibly assimilate and acculturate Canada's Native population. In 1874, Sir John A. MacDonald introduced the original Indian Act, stating:

> Indian children should be taken away from their parents so as to eliminate their barbarian influence and expose the children to the benefits of civilization. The teacher has been sent out as an educational missionary to introduce cultural changes in Indian societies. (Green 1990, 36)

Alexander Morris, who negotiated many of the numbered treaties in Western Canada, as cited in Frideres (1993, 2), said, "Let us have Christianity and civilization to leaven the masses of heathenism and paganism among the Indian Tribes," and Duncan Campbell Scott, the deputy superintendent of the Indian department from 1913 to 1932, stated, "Our objective is to continue until there is not a single Indian in Canada that has not been absorbed into the body politic, and there is no Indian question" (Smith 1993, 38). Scott also attempted to outlaw many of the traditional ceremonies and customs that were essential to the survival of the Indian cultures. Attempts were made to outlaw the Potlatch on the West Coast and the Sun Dance on the Prairies. The belief was that the lack of these ceremonies would accelerate the disintegration of the Native culture and thus the absorption of the people into white "civilized" society (Francis 1992, 99-101).

Although the rhetoric has been modified over time, the federal government policy of assimilation has remained intact.

Government Policy of Assimilation

> This policy of assimilation — bringing aboriginal Canadians into the mainstream of Canadian life — has been the cornerstone of "Indian policy" since Confederation. It was behind the outlawing of traditional ceremonies, the creation of reserves and the promotion of permanent communities, the residential school system that tore families apart and the land claim settlements in which individuals were paid cash for forfeiting their rights as aboriginal people. It was also behind the government's bias towards individual welfare payments rather

> than support for community self-sufficiency. Assimilation policy is an expression of both racism and genocide. It is racist to view aboriginal life on the land as inferior to the settler farming culture. It is genocide to forcibly remove aboriginal people from their land or stand in the way of their communal development, thus destroying their existence as a people.[8]

The common thread that ran through all of the incarnations of Native schooling is the fact that the policy of assimilation and acculturation remained constant. It was disguised in a variety of ways, but the underlying intention was the cultural genocide of the Native people. In the residential and Indian Affairs schools, Native students were told that their ancestors were savages, their religion was pagan, their language was primitive, and the only way they could become truly human was to adopt the white man's ways. In the residential schools they were physically punished for speaking their own languages and in the integrated schools they were laughed at and ridiculed if they tried to speak a Native language. Reference to, or participation in, any cultural or traditional ceremony was forbidden in the residential schools and depicted as heathen and barbaric in the integrated schools. The texts and materials that they studied projected and reinforced these negative stereotypes until the Native students either withdrew or began to accept these falsehoods.

The White Paper

The Liberal government of Pierre Trudeau introduced a White Paper in 1969 that called for a change in the way in which relations were conducted between the federal government and status Indian people. Essentially it was the same assimilation policy that had been followed by Canadian and pre-Canadian governments, but this White Paper differed in that it openly stated the objective of assimilation and talked of ending the special-treaty status and the treaties with the Native people. It justified these measures under a Liberal philosophy that concentrated on the rights and participation of individuals, rather than collectives.

Jean Chrétien, the Minister of Indian Affairs at the time, clearly stated the government's beliefs (Chrétien 1969, 6-9): "True equality presupposes that the Indian people have the right to full and equal participation in the cultural, social, economic and political life in Canada...that services come through the same channels and from the same government agencies for all Canadians and that, separate but equal services do not provide truly equal treatment."

The White Paper proposed the ending of treaties and the complete transfer of responsibility for Indians from the federal government to the provincial governments. It also proposed the abolition of the Department of Indian Affairs, allocation of reserve lands to individual ownership, and the abolition of Indian status. This may be seen as an attack on the social and cultural fabric of the Native people. The continuation of the Native way of life received a further setback.

The Minister went on to say that (Chrétien 1969, 11): "The treaties which were signed were of minimum importance and that the promises that they contained were minimal or had already been discharged. The significance of the treaties in meeting the economic, educational, health and welfare needs of the Indian people has always been limited and will continue to decline...these treaties [will] be reviewed to see how they can be equitably ended."

The effect on education for Native peoples was immediate and far reaching. Until 1969, the residential schools had been quietly fading away and the education of reserve Indian students was conducted in day schools built and operated by the Department of Indian Affairs and off-reserve Native people were "integrated" into the provincial schools. The goals of the government were unchanged from the past: integration, assimilation, and cultural genocide of the Native people. The only difference was that this objective was now to be accomplished through the provincial-school system, rather than by the religious institutions.

By openly stating the government's objectives, the White Paper provided the catalyst for the Indian leadership to redouble their efforts to build provincial and national organizations through which they could lobby for their own proposals. In 1972, they responded with their own position paper, entitled *Indian Control of Indian Education.* As a result of this so-called Orange Paper, published by the National Indian Brotherhood (NIB), most First Nations now operate their own schools on their territories. There are still a large number of status Indians who attend provincial schools, particularly at the secondary level.

Indian Control of Indian Education

> The past practice of using the school committee as an advisory body with limited influence, in restricted areas of the school program, must give way to an education authority with the control of funds and consequent authority which are necessary for an effective decision making body. The Federal Government must take the required steps to transfer to local Bands the authority and the funds which are allotted for Indian Education.
>
> The local Education Authority would be responsible for:
>
> - budgeting, spending, and establishing priorities;
> - determining the types of school facilities required to meet local needs; e.g. day school, residence, group home, nursery, kindergarten, high school;
> - directing staff hiring and curriculum development with special concern for Indian languages and culture;
> - administering the physical plant;
> - developing adult education and upgrading courses;
> - negotiating agreements with provincial or separate school jurisdictions for the kind of services necessary for local requirements;
> - co-operation and evaluation of education programs both on and off the reserve;
> - provide counselling services.

> Training must be made available to those reserves desiring local control of education. This training must include every aspect of educational administration. It is important that Bands moving towards local control have the opportunity to prepare themselves for the move. Once the parents have control of a local school, continuing guidance during the operational phase is equally important and necessary.[9]

Racism in Today's Native Schooling

Although the era of the residential schools is past, the thinking and the policies behind the establishment of the residential schools remains. The policy of the government is still one of assimilation and acculturation of the Native people. In the schools that Native people currently attend there are still manifestations of this racist attitude, particularly within the provincial-school system.

Cultural Considerations

Historically, the cultural attitudes and beliefs of the Native students have been misinterpreted by the provincial schools and non-Native teachers. White society values eye-to-eye contact as a sign of confidence and trustworthiness, and therefore expects students to look teachers in the eye. To Native people, eye-to-eye contact between young people and older people is considered disrespectful, and students are expected to show respect by looking down or avoiding the gaze of persons in authority or who are worthy of respect. This simple trait has often been interpreted by white teachers as an indicator that the student is not trustworthy, guilty of something, or simply not paying attention. The result is that the Native student is more likely to be sanctioned in some way.

Many Native students have been raised to believe that the good of the collectivity is more important that the good of the individual. An individual who publicly demonstrates superior ability is likely to be seen as showing off and not worthy of respect. When this student is placed in an "integrated" classroom, the natural reticence to display individual ability is taken as a sign of a lack of intellectual capacity and the student is classified as less advanced than the rest of the class. Native students also prefer working together in groups and sharing their ideas. In a classroom where only individual work is expected, they are seen as not doing well or as being more interested in chatting with their neighbour than doing their school work.

Learning Styles

In traditional Native societies, it was the elders of the community who taught the young. They tended to teach by demonstration and repetition, on an individual basis, and allowed the learners plenty of practice. Conversely, in some white schools the emphasis tends to be on group instruction at specific times and minimal practice. Instruction tends to be oral, rather than demonstrative, and students are expected to rely upon aural, rather than visual input.

Native students tend to look at the world in a different way than white students do. Native thinking is not linear, in the sense that there is a cause-and-effect relationship for everything. Native students tend to think more globally and seek connections and relationships with their learning. Usually, in white classrooms, information is presented in a linear format and subjects are discussed in discrete time periods. Teachers do not emphasize the connections between their learning and their life experiences, and expect students to make them on their own. For Native students, who are used to thinking globally, this is often impossible.

Bias

These cultural characteristics, while general in nature, put the Native students at an immediate disadvantage when they come to the white school. The fact that these characteristics are not valued and are often discouraged leads the student to devalue their own culture. As a result of the factors discussed above, when Native students come to a provincial school they are immediately subjected to an institutionalized form of racism. It is assumed that if they come from a First-Nation education program that they must have been exposed to an inferior education. Therefore, they are placed in a grade one or two levels below the one from which they came. Also, it is assumed that Native children have learning difficulties, so many are placed in sheltered-environment classrooms designed for students who are severely learning disabled. In this way, Native students are kept out of the main school population and the school jurisdiction can apply for additional funds to meet the "special education" needs of the students. It is not suggested that all school divisions deliberately diagnose incorrectly Native students for financial gain, but there are instances where this has happened. In many cases, the incorrect diagnosis is the result of the misinterpretation of the cultural factors listed above. Regardless of why this error occurs, the effect on the students is the same. Native beliefs and customs are deemed to be inappropriate or detrimental, and they are forced to accept that a set of alien beliefs is superior to their own.

The use of standardized tests and measures of intelligence are often not applicable for Native students. These tests are culturally and linguistically biased against Native students, who may not have the same experiential background as the group on whom the tests are normed. The misinterpretation and misapplication of these tests often leads to the (incorrect) placement of Native students in special-education environments.

Curriculum Development

Although the provinces have progressed considerably in scrutinizing curriculum for racist content, many subtle elements of racism still remain. The discrete format in which the information is presented, as discussed above, is one of these. Many references or stories with a Native setting show past and present Native society as static, quaint, and picturesque, rather than vibrant, modern, and adaptive. The effect on Native students is minimal, since they know that is not the way it is; but the effect on non-Native students is to reinforce inaccurate stereotypes of Native people.

Curriculum modification programs, materials development, and the teaching of Native languages are some ways that provincial jurisdictions are slowly starting to incorporate Native cultural needs into their programming. Often, this takes the form of a special addition to a provincial curriculum or a specific program called Native Studies. It is doubtful that by setting Natives apart from the regular curriculum, as a separate subject, that these programs are doing much good for the image of Native people in today's society. What is necessary is the incorporation of aspects of the Native cultures into all subject areas.

The Elders' Interpretation of Treaty

> It was said that not one piece of timber, not one stone was given up to the government. The only thing which was included in the bargaining was those portions of land where something could be sown by the white man.
>
> Elder Lazarus Roan
>
> The commissioners were not to take the game animals, the timber, nor the big lakes — that was for the Indians' means of survival. Also anything underground would not be given up, only six inches, enough for settlers to grow crops. "If anything is discovered below the surface of the land it will be towards your benefit" the commissioner said.
>
> Elder Fred Horse.[10]

Conclusion

In conclusion, I will make some observations on future considerations for Native schooling in Canada. The reversal of the effects of 500 years of racist policy will not happen overnight. The Native people themselves have accepted many of the racist stereotypes of themselves and, as a result frequently suffer from low self-esteem and negative feelings about themselves and their culture. There are two areas that should be examined more closely: First-Nation schools, and self government and land claims. Both are equally important for any discussion on future Native schooling.

Since the Orange Paper in 1972, First Nations have been slowly taking control of their own education systems on their own territory. The Metis in Alberta are doing the same under the self-government arrangements currently being negotiated. These schools often use the provincial curriculum, but modify it to suit the local needs of the students. They are also careful to exclude materials that are biased against Native people. The schools are also hiring more Native teachers, so that students have positive role models to follow. The use of a Native language, either as a subject or as the language of instruction, is also increasing and the teaching of the Native culture is also being implemented.

These schools for status Indians are still funded by the federal government and must contend with meddling from federal bureaucrats, limited funding, the lack of appropriate support service for teachers and the still deeply held, if not often stated, belief of Indian Affairs that the only way for Natives to "succeed" is to attend provincial schools.

Despite the development of First-Nation controlled schools, there are still many Native people, both First-Nation community residents and other Native people, who attend provincial schools. As the First Nations are becoming more astute and aware of what is going on, and as they continue to take over more of their own schooling, they are negotiating tuition agreements that force the provincial school divisions to provide programming more suitable for their children. They are also increasingly demanding a say in their children's education through representation on provincial boards of education.

The development of self-government, where Native people are struggling to reassert control over their own lives and destinies as people is also a positive step to reversing the damage of the racist policies of the government. Native governments will restore the pride of Native people and will provide the positive role models that young Native students need.

Settlement of land claims and the provision of a land base for economic development is another positive step necessary to restore Native people's belief in themselves. When treaties were signed, the elders who signed them believed that they were only giving up the use of the land for farming. They agreed to allow settlers to use the top six inches of the ground for agricultural purposes. However, they believed that the flora and fauna of the land remained theirs and that they had not given up title or ownership or any of the resources of their country.

The settlement of the outstanding land claim issues and the establishment of an economic base, as well as a system of resource-revenue sharing, are imperative if Native people are to rebuild their societies and cultures.

Obviously, much remains to be done, and it is only by examining racist attitudes and consciously changing practices and attitudes can the situation be rectified and the Native people restored to an honoured place in Canadian society.

Discussion Questions

1. Racism against Native people in Canada has been recognized by many agencies over the past many years. Yet the problem remains. What can you do to build a more open and tolerant society that would allow Native people to participate more fully?
2. Recently, the Royal Commission on Aboriginal Peoples and the Federal Government agreed that Native self government is an inherent right, and that only the mechanisms need to be worked out. Collect information on Native self government and relate these developments to Native education.
3. Imagine that you are a Native student attending a provincial elementary school. What problems might you expect to face in the classroom?
4. Trace the historical development of the relationship between Europeans and Native people using an economic perspective. Attempt to explain the change in the relationship from mutual beneficial partnership to a superior/subservient relationship characterized by negative stereotypical concepts of Native people.

Notes

1. Quoted in Ormond McHague. 1991. *Racism in Canada.* Saskatoon: Fifth House.
2. R. K. Hitchcock. 1994. International human rights, the environment and indigenous peoples. *Colorado Journal of International Environmental Law and Policy. Endangered peoples: Indigenous rights and the environment.* Niwot, CO: University Press of Colorado. pp. 1-22.
3. Canadian Human Rights Commission. *Annual Report, 1993.* (ISBN 0-662-60236-6). Ottawa: Ministry of Supply and Services Canada, 1994. p. 20. Reproduced with permission of the Minister of Supply and Services Canada, 1994.
4. D. L. Hawley. 1986. *The Annotated Indian Act,* 2d ed. Toronto: Carswell. pp. 12-3. Reprinted by permission of Carswell — a division of Thomson Canada Limited.
5. P. Freire. 1983. *Pedagogy of the Oppressed.* New York: The Continuum Publishing Company. pp. 62-63.
6. J. Schouls Olthuis and D. Engelstad. 1992. "The Basic Dilemma: Sovereignty or Assimilation." In *Nation to Nation: Aboriginal Sovereignty and the Future of Canada.* Edited by D. Engelstad and J. Bird, Concord, ON: House of Anansi Press. pp. 22-7. Reprinted with the permission of Stoddart Publishing, Don Mills, Ontario.
7. M. Hodgson. 1992. "Rebuilding Community after the Residential School Experience." In *Nation to Nation: Aboriginal Sovereignty and the Future of Canada.* Edited by D. Engelstad and J. Bird, Concord, ON: House of Anansi Press. pp. 101-12. Reprinted with the permission of Stoddart Publishing, Don Mills, Ontario.
8. Olthuis, J. Schouls and D. Engelstad. 1992. "The Basic Dilemma: Sovereignty or Assimilation." In *Nation to Nation: Aboriginal Sovereignty and the Future of Canada.* Edited by D. Engelstad and J. Bird, Concord, ON: House of Anansi Press. pp. 22-7. Reprinted with the permission of Stoddart Publishing, Don Mills, Ontario.
9. National Indian Brotherhood. 1972. *Indian Control of Indian Education.* Ottawa: NIB. Reprinted with permission.
10. R. Price. ed. 1980. *The Spirit of the Alberta Indian Treaties.* Montreal: Institute for Research on Public Policy.

References

Barman, J.; Hebert, Y.; and McCaskill, D., eds. 1986. *Indian education in Canada: Volume 1: The Legacy.* Vancouver: Univ. of British Columbia Press.

Cardinal, H. 1969. *The unjust society: The tragedy of Canada's Indians.* Edmonton: Hurtig.

Canadian Human Rights Commission. 1993. *Annual report.* Ottawa: Minister of Supply and Services.

Chrétien, J. 1969. *Statement of the Government of Canada on Indian Policy.* Ottawa: Queen's Printer.

Davis, R., and Zannis, M. 1973. *The genocide machine in Canada: The pacification of the North.* Montreal: Black Rose Books.

Dickason, O. P. 1992. *Canada's First Nations: A history of founding peoples from earliest times.* Toronto: McClelland & Stewart.

Fisher, R. 1992. *Contact and conflict.* 2d ed. Vancouver: Univ. of British Columbia Press.

Francis, D. 1992. *The imaginary Indian: The image of the Indian in Canadian culture.* Vancouver: Arsenal Pulp Press.

Freire, P. 1983. *Pedagogy of the oppressed.* NY: Continuum.

Frideres, J. S. 1993. *Native people in Canada: Contemporary conflicts.* Scarborough: Prentice Hall Canada.

Green, C. 1990. Coming of age: Native education in the 21st century. *Education Canada* 30 (1): 35-9.

Haig-Brown, C. 1988. *Resistance and renewal: Surviving the Indian residential school.* Vancouver: Tillacum Library.

Hawley, D. L. 1986. *The Indian Act: Annotated.* 2d ed. Toronto: Carswell.

Hitchcock, R. K. 1994. International human rights, the environment and indigenous peoples. *Colorado Journal of International Environmental Law and Policy. Endangered peoples: Indigenous rights and the environment.* (1-22). Niwot, CO: Univ. Press of Colorado.

Hodgson, M. 1992. "Rebuilding community after the residential school experience." In *Nation to nation: Aboriginal sovereignty and the future of Canada*, ed. D. Engelstad and J. Bird. 101-12. Concord, ON: Anansi.

Kirkness, V. J. 1985. Indian control of Indian education: Authority and responsibility for progress. Paper read at Western Social Sciences Association Conference, Fort Worth. ERIC Document Reproduction Services no. ED 271-7.

Kirkness, V. J., and Selkirk-Bowman, S. 1992. *First Nations and schools: Triumphs and struggles.* Toronto: Canadian Education Association.

National Indian Brotherhood 1972. *Indian control of Indian education.* Ottawa: NIB.

Price, R., ed. 1980. *The spirit of the Alberta Indian treaties.* Montreal: The Institute for Research on Public Policy.

Royal Commission on Aboriginal Peoples. 1992. *Overview of the First Round.* Ottawa: Queen's Printer.

Schouls, T.; Olthuis, J.; and Engelstad, D. 1992. "The basic dilemma: Sovereignty or assimilation." In *Nation to nation: Aboriginal sovereignty and the future of Canada*, ed. D. Engelstad and J. Bird, 12-27. Concord, ON: Anansi.

Smith, D. 1993. *The seventh fire: The struggle for aboriginal government.* Toronto: Key Porter.

Further Reading

Readers interested in issues involving Native people may wish to take advantage of a number of publications dealing with these issues. As the discussions over self-government and the problems of racial discrimination are addressed there will be an increased body of literature discussing Native issues. Publications that the reader may want to examine are:

Asch, M. 1988. *Home and Native land: Aboriginal rights and the Canadian Constitution.* Scarborough: Nelson Canada.

Assembly of First Nations (AFN). 1988. Tradition and education: Towards a vision of our future: A declaration of First Nations jurisdiction over education. *Canadian Journal of Native Education.* Edmonton: University of Alberta.

Krotz, L. 1990. *Indian country: Inside another Canada.* Toronto: McClelland & Stewart.

Meili, D. 1991. *Those who know: Profiles of Alberta's Native elders.* Edmonton: NeWest Press.

Mercredi, O., and Turpel, M. E. 1993. *In the rapids: Navigating the future of First Nations.* Toronto: Viking.

Shorten, L. 1991. *Without reserve: Stories from urban Natives.* Edmonton: NeWest Press.

Weaver, S. M. 1981. *Making Canadian Indian policy: The hidden agenda.* Toronto: Univ. of Toronto Press.

3

BLACK/AFRICAN-CANADIAN STUDENTS' PERSPECTIVES ON SCHOOL RACISM

George Dei

> *Among many champions of racial equality there is a tendency to see black people as a homogeneous mass and to implicitly assume that they are so different from any other group in society that the standard variables do not apply to them. With the exception that the stereotypes this creates are benign rather than malign, this differs little from the racist approach.*[1]
>
> *M. Fitzgerald*
> Political Parties and Black People

Introduction

In this chapter, I deal with an aspect of racism in schooling that focuses primarily, but not exclusively, on the practice of exclusion. I am concerned with the individual, as well as institutional, processes of "othering" and constructing "otherness," and the marginalizing effects on some students. I am also concerned with the processes of decentring the experiences, histories, and cultures of minority groups in the Canadian school setting. In my opinion, these are the fundamental issues and challenges confronting education in multi-ethnic societies. They also constitute the processes of youth alienation from school and help explain why some students may lack a deep sense of identification with, and connection to, their schools. These issues go beyond a simplistic Black/white dichotomy or duality in the discourse on race relations and conflict in the school setting.

The discussion examines real and perceived individual aspects of racism and sexism, as well as other oppressive and discriminatory practices that structure and organize public schooling in the Canadian context. Among the issues examined are students' concerns about low teacher expectations of some youths, social labelling and stereotyping in the schools, inter- and intra-group conflicts among students, and biases in the school curriculum and the classroom pedagogy of some teachers. It is argued that students' views on school racism, whether real or perceived, constitute legitimate grounds and concerns for all educators to take seriously if we are to address the fundamental issues of educational equity and the "inclusive" school environment. Educators need to interrogate the ways in which racist ideas become entrenched in the institutional structures and practices of schooling.

Racism and Schooling

It is now a cliché to say that racism has a long history in human society. The history of events encompassing early European trade and missionary contacts with non-European peoples, the systematic introduction and enforcement of varied human enslavement, and the advent of colonialism are well-documented cases of social relations among peoples. Today these historical events and the processes of racializing human groups continue to reproduce themselves in what can aptly be described as "globalization of racism" all the world over.

Within the Euro-American context, it can be argued that no institution of society has been able to escape the charges of racism. It is acknowledged by some critical educators and students that racism and other forms of discrimination constitute significant factors in the school experiences of many youths (Hidalgo et al. 1990, Kelly 1988). But there have been, and even, disturbingly, in some quarters today, continue to be, attempts to deny race as a factor in youths' schooling and education. This has either taken the form of the "colour-blind" approach to schooling or the conventional liberal attempts to question the intellectual validity and meaning of the race concept. All this in the face of studies, particularly in the United States, that show that race does have significance in school and that many minority students who "succeed" at school have done so at the expense of a negation of their racial identities. Fordham (1988), for example, has talked about racelessness as a factor in Black students' success, to the extent that high-achieving Black students pay a price for their academic and school success by a disidentification with their Black/African cultures. What such studies point out is that "race matters" in youth schooling and education.

While race itself is a contested notion, we cannot deny the reality of the racialized societies in which we live today (Figueroa 1991). There is always a reluctance on the part of many us to talk about race issues. And yet, we are all implicated, in one way or another, in the issues of racism. We have to be able to confront and deal more openly with the tension and contradictions in discussing race and racism in our schools. We should be able to speak more openly about the fit and the inconsistencies between institutional values and attitudes and institutional behaviour.

But race and racial identity is not the only site of struggle in the schools or in the wider society. Social relations are based not only on race, but also on gender and class. This means that we need to broaden our definitions of racism in schools to include a critical integrative perspective by which we would be able to examine the relational aspects of social and cultural differences (race, class, sex, gender, language, religion, origin) and the power dynamics that are constituted around notions of difference and diversity.

In our society, how difference is named, constructed, legitimized, negotiated, and acted upon is cardinal to the understanding of race and antiracism issues in schooling and education (see also McCarthy and Crichlow 1993). Acknowledging and understanding difference is to problematize Euro-Canadian cultural hegemony, where the dominant group's norms and values define "difference" and also organize the structures within which the delivery of education takes place.

As an educator researching in the Canadian public school system, I am greatly perturbed by the marginality and depersonalization of, particularly, the experiences of so-called students of colour (Brathwaite 1989, James 1990, Board of Education 1989). There is a culture of dominance, in which the voicelessness and silencing of students is disheartening to the critical observer. It is interesting, and at the same time, also frustrating, to try to understand how our schools engage some students, while at the same time disengaging others (Solomon 1992, James 1994). Many students are caught in a struggle to escape social labels and categories that repeatedly oversimplify the complexities of students' lived actualities.

There is a racial, cultural, and gender "othering" of students. For example, in the schools the social construction of "deviance" fits patriarchal relations of schooling. Arguably, dominant discourses of some youths in the wider society define the meanings that many educators bring to representations of the students in their schools. Disaffected students complain about the in-school and out-of-school environment and what they perceive as a lack of opportunities to realize their dreams and ambitions.

For minority students particularly, the nuances of their shifting identities and intersecting marginalities in the schools are exacerbated by the failure of the educational system to recognize that students enter their classrooms with a reservoir of cultural and political knowledge, expertise, and understanding of their social conditions. There is the non-acknowledgement of many students' historical and cultural knowledge and understanding of their world. Minority youths, who have been victimized by racial and discriminatory incidents, continue to suffer through the tendency of some teachers, educators, and administrators (whether in their individual attitudes or through the use of curriculum texts and classroom pedagogy) to attribute these problems to the student culture or family upbringing. This is the classic approach of "blaming the victim" or using the culture-deficit model to explain social phenomena (Cashmore and Troyna 1982; 1993). For example, Black and other minority youths are blamed, whether as individuals or as a group (culture), for the problems of schooling. Few educators critically interrogate the patriarchal structures that govern schooling and the delivery of education.

At the same time, many leave unquestioned the white middle-class norms and values that continue to represent the standards by which all other school cultures are measured. Crichlow (1994, 8), for example, recently questioned why school authorities often see students' cultural departures from white middle-class norms and values as aberrations, cultural deprivations, and deficits, rather than as "signifying a complex dynamics of social difference."

In discussing the school "problems" of minority youths, educational researchers have generally adopted a combination of two theoretical approaches: cultural differences theories, where educational "problems" are attributed to a mismatch between the school's culture and language and those of the student (Willis 1977, Giroux 1983); and structural inequalities theories, where educational "problems" are attributed to the status of a particular minority or social class group within the larger society (Bowles and Gintis 1976, Bourdieu and Passeron 1977, Apple and Weis 1983, Oakes 1985). While these two theoretical perspectives are valuable, they do not help us to fully understand why some groups appear to transcend barriers more successfully than others, or how the patterns of adaptation and barriers to equality vary both within groups among minority groups (Ogbu 1987, Haw 1991, Brah and Deem 1986). We need to understand and appreciate the forces behind some students having to assimilate the dominant culture of the school to excel (Razack and Dei 1994).

In this paper, I employ a critical, antiracism approach to understanding Black/African-Canadian students' concerns about racism in schooling. The approach will draw attention to the need for a critical analysis of the institutional structures within which the teaching, learning, and administration of education take place in the schools. The antiracism approach is a critique of the dominant hegemonic discourse about race relations and multiculturalism in the schools, based on the idea of a simplistic tolerance of other people and their cultures, while at the same time leaving intact the unequal power structures of society (Thomas 1984, Lee 1985, 1994 and Dei 1993). The antiracism approach seeks the appropriate centrality of race and the intersections with class, gender, sexuality, and ethnicity in the schooling processes of the youth. It focuses on what the issues of difference and diversity are and how they should be mediated in the school system to ensure successful educational outcomes for all youth.

In recent years, a growing number of educators and administrators have acknowledged the pedagogic need to confront the challenge of diversity and difference in Euro-Canadian/American society and the urgency for an educational system that is more inclusive and is capable of responding to minority concerns about public schooling. It is argued that public schools are part of the institutional structures sanctioned by society and the state to serve the material, political and ideological interests of the state and the economic/social formation (Apple 1981). It is important then that strategies designed to respond to issues about race and minority education address questions of systemic inequalities and explore alternative and viable approaches to education.

In the focus on the issues of race, representation, and identity in schooling, my intention is to uncover school practices that illuminate the adaptation and resistance patterns of Black/African-Canadian students in the school system. For example, it is important not only to know how Black youths respond to the school, but also how the school itself responds to them. This would call for an exploration of how school policies restrict the educational opportunities of Black students. A critical examination of the issue may help provide an understanding as to why some students are engaged with school, while others are disengaged from it.

Currently, there are major, legitimate concerns about the quality of education and academic excellence. Unfortunately, some appear to be unaware that these issues cannot be tackled without a simultaneous emphasis on educational access and social equity for ethnocultural minorities. We believe educational practices of "inclusion" to be those that promote school success among all students, but particularly among minority groups (Razack and Dei 1994).

Methodology

This chapter is based on a three-year study that began in May, 1992, to examine Black students' experiences in a Canadian inner-city public school. The main learning objective has been to examine how the experiences of Black/African-Canadian youth in, and out of, school can inform our understanding of the problem of students becoming disengaged and eventually dropping out. With the help of graduate students, I interviewed more than 200 high-school students (Black and non-Black, including white students), both individually and in focus groups, about their school experiences, and for their views and perceptions on student disengagement and dropping out of school.

Students selected for the study came largely from four Ontario high schools, although some school drop-outs were also interviewed, as well as a small, random sample of students from various Toronto schools. School teachers, administrators, and Black/African-Canadian parents were also interviewed, in part to cross-reference students' narratives, and also to get their sense of the issues concerning public education and students' engagement and disengagement from school.

The major sample from the four high schools included male and female students from general- and advanced-level programs in Grades 10 and 12. The criteria for selecting Grade 10 students at high risk of dropping out include below-average marks, poor attendance, and inadequate accumulation of credits (Ziegler 1989, Waterhouse 1990). Grade 12 students provided information as to why they stayed in school and how the system has worked for them. In a few cases, difficulty in getting students from these two grades led us to include students from Grades 9 and 11. But we have generally focussed on the total credits accumulated as an important criterion in the grade selection of students. Apart from these interviews, the project also includes an ethnography of the school (e.g., observations of school culture, work roles, gender roles, as well as student-peer and student-teacher interactions, and classroom activities). I have sat in on classroom discussions, and hung around school compounds and hallways to observe the varied interactions that take place in the daily life of a school.

In the following pages, I will address students' individual and group perceptions of discriminatory and unequal treatment at school, and I will situate students' accounts within the wider context of the structural barriers in the culture(s) of schooling as they implicate Black students' engagement and disengagement from school.

Teacher Prejudice of Students

Black youths know of the efforts that schools are making to address systemic barriers to educational equity. But students generally think that not much has been done so far. When asked what they want to see changed about their schools, they point to discriminatory, and sometimes racist, practices of certain individuals at school. In fact, students often cite racist behaviour and attitudes as reasons for disliking particular teachers and school staff.

Students perceive some teachers and administrative staff as making racially offensive remarks. When asked to elaborate on their assertions, Black students would recall specific incidents that are indications of teacher attitudes toward, and expectations of, students. While both Black and non-Black students complain about the attitudes of some teachers, it seems the issue is central to the Black youths' perception of the school system. Jean (a pseudonym) is in the Grade 12 advanced-level program in her school. Citing the case of a particular teacher noted by other Black peers, she complains about how a teacher's attitude can turn off the student and disengage him or her from school:

> I find her attitude is just all wrong for teaching really. She constantly puts us down and I, you know, I know, she has about she has a lot of classes. She's got Grade 10, 9, 12, and OAC classes and I think of people from all her classes and they constantly tell me how she puts them down. The same thing that she does in our class I'm the kind of person who asks a lot of questions and I've done, I've done well in math up until this year. This year my grades are really going down and I think a lot of it has to do with her; it's just that attitude I really like to ask questions. That's how I learn and I think I should be allowed to ask questions in school because I don't understand something then you know I want to. I'll ask a question and she'll turn it, she'll manipulate the question in such a way that I answer my own question and then she says to me you didn't really need to ask that question I don't want you to ask any questions if you don't need to...And then I try to counteract by saying but I really didn't understand and she says, well if you don't understand maybe you shouldn't be in enriched math. Maybe you should go to (mentions name of school) and take a course in plumbing. She goes, you guys aren't very intelligent are you? You know with her little accent it's really it's horrible, She should not be able to treat us like that I mean that's not...there are a lot of students in our class who were in my math class last year and the difference in the grades that we're getting this year and the grades...we got last year is tremendous...(24/01/93).

In a focus-group interview with eight Black youths, students expressed the opinion that a small number of teachers exist in their schools who make attending and learning worthwhile. As one male student puts it:

> Some teachers, some teachers really make you feel good, 'cause I have had teachers tell me, "Don't fool around because you're going somewhere," you know? And that kind of feels nice, because white teachers tell me that...But not all. It's a selected few (DF/2/D4).

Clearly, if there is one area in which students show much emotion and anger when discussing unfavourable school experiences, it is the low expectations that some students claim certain teachers hold about Black youths. Students explain such low teacher expectations as part of the deeply held beliefs about people who are nonwhite. In interviews, students would cite particular teachers making fun of students and making students "feel dumb." Low teacher expectations add to the bitterness students feel about the deprivileging of their knowledge and the experiences they bring to the school. Canadian-born Leah left high school prematurely, but later enrolled in a community college. She talks about the existence of racism in the school system and its effect on the student:

> As far as I'm concerned, I think everybody has a bias. Everybody. And racism is so, it's so strongly prevalent. It, it's, if you think about it, it is enough to literally turn your stomach. It is, racism is a very strong force that exists within the system, and it, it does too much damage...(Interviewer: You mean in the school?) I mean we have to understand teachers are people, too. And there are a lot of teachers out there who simply just do not like Black people. There are teachers out there who do not like whites, or Orientals. And you'll be surprised; you'll have your hand up for days...and you will not be answered. And you could have attained a 98 and simply get a 54 because of your colour...or whatever that one's bias may be. You'd be surprised. Oh yeah, all the time. All the time. As far as I'm concerned, I have never been given the credit that I deserve. But I know one day I will get it (11/26/92).

Labelling and Social Stereotyping of the Youth

The deleterious impact of teachers' low expectations of students cannot be overemphasized. Students believe that part of the problem they have to deal with as Black youths is social labelling and stereotyping. One female student in a focus-group discussion attributed the problem of low teacher expectations to societal stereotyping of Black people, emanating from the media and public discourse:

> I think it all follows a stereotypical pattern. Like, since they see Black people are always portrayed negatively in the media and stuff, they tend to address them differently because of that (DF/2/D4).

Black students, particularly those born in the Caribbean, complain about the social labels of the Black male as a trouble-maker, violent, and criminal. Students speak of the tendency for some educators to prejudge them on the basis of established stereotypes before coming to know them (students) as individuals (Sleeter 1994, 8). Other students, in their narratives, make an easy and unproblematic connection between social labelling and the systemic categorization of Black youths in the school system. Nisha, who is 17 years old, is classified a gifted student in her high school. When interviewed, she had just finished the Grade 11, advanced-level program, and was attending summer school to get her OAC English. I remember vividly when, at the end of our interview in my office, she asked to borrow my copy of Patricia Hill Collins' book, *Black Feminist Thought*. Nisha talks about the perception that some teachers (and students) have of general- and basic-level students as those who are not serious and most likely run into trouble at school, and the impact on Black youths, who are disproportionately represented in these programs (see Radwanski 1987):

> I think that they're [students in basic- and general-level program] discouraged and they feel like they can't make a difference...it's like

> they can't learn or they feel like they're stupid or you know. I think they feel...like that they're different that they can't learn or they're stupid. A lot of people were told that they were stupid in elementary school, especially a lot of my friends and they just feel well they hear it so much it's like a what — self-fulfilling prophecy you know. You just hear it all the time and their family doesn't say anything like no you're not and so they just say ok I'm not smart I can't do it...(06/27/92).
>
> Some students believe they are constantly being watched by school authorities and they feel that their actions and behaviours are often misconstrued. A few students use the example of hanging out in the hallways and the wearing of hats at school to stress how they are socially constructed as the "bad guys." In another focus-group discussion we asked students (in the presence of a female Black teacher) about our observation of some students hanging out in the hallways. The students feel white teachers are unduly intimidated by, and particularly suspicious of, Black students hanging out on the hallways. One student, defending the use of hallways for socializing, argued "we're not doing anything bad, they just...Because we're Black they think we're doing something bad..." (DF/1/D3).

A male student added:

> If you're walking down the hallways, and there's only you and somebody else, the principal'll come up to you in person and tell you you're not supposed to be in the hallways, right. And then they'll bring up something done and try to accuse you of doing that thing (DF/1/D3).

Internalized Racism: Inter- and Intra-Group Racial Conflicts at School

Students' discussions about inter- and intra-group conflicts at school show how many Black youths have themselves internalized the racist codes of society. This is revealed in a focus-group discussion when students talked about shadism, Black students who "act white," and "whites who want to be Black." In the following segment of a focus-group discussion, while students relate many aspects of racism to lack of education, plain ignorance, and disrespect of Blacks by non-Blacks, they also point to disrespect and disunity within the Black community itself. Students concerned about Black unity complain about prejudiced and negative comments made by Black students about other Black colleagues. A critical reading of students' accounts reveals the myriad forms of intra- and inter-group racism, one that has to do with distancing between *self* and *other*, and between *us* and *them*. This discriminatory culture is influenced in large measure by the specificity of students' locations in the school. In some cases, language use and having different accents become powerful markers. Students feel Black unity, respect, and understanding of Black culture and history are essential if the community is to deal effectively with the problems of social racism. See "Who Is Black...How Much?"

Who is Black...How Much?

[This is part of a conversation with students who are expressing forms of racism that exist among peer groups.]

Interviewer: Talking about racism, right, I listened to some of the tapes and somebody, I don't know whether it was this school, but there were some people who were talking about, "Oh, Sheila, Georgina, oh, she's not Black enough. She acts white."

Male: Wishy washy. (laughter)

Female 3: Why do they have to be white wash anyway? Why can't they be their self? I can't stand those people.

Interviewer: Do you know some people in the school here who are that way?

Male: Oh, yes. (laughter)

Interviewer: Talk about it, I mean, I want to hear about it...

Female 4: Another thing too, why does, like, some people, and you're a Black person calling them, "Oh, he's too Black." Like, anyways...

Female 2: Yeah, I know. Shadism, thank you.

Male: Oh, yeah, too Black.

Female 2: Thank you. (laughter)

Interviewer: Are you always talking about skin colour, or is it something else?

Male: Skin colour. Skin colour.

Female 3: Well, yeah.

Female 2: And it could be the way that you act, too.

Female 4: Or, something like, if you turned out the light, you'd never find that person, the way how he's Black? All that stuff.

Female 2: Shadism.

[multiple voices]

Male: You know what, sometimes they're just joking when they say that, it's just a joke.

Female 2: But the thing is, it shouldn't be a joke.

Female 3: It shouldn't be a joke.

Female 2: That's the thing, it shouldn't be a joke.

Male 2: But you've laughed a lot.

[laughter]

Female 3: I don't. The thing is, Black people have to learn to respect each other, you know.

Male: Stick together.

Female 3: And not make fun...

Female 2: Before we get (along with) other cultures...

Female 3: They don't stick together, you know. They just make fun, they even make fun with a white person at a Black person.

Female: Yeah.

Male: If I had a [inaudible]

Female 2: And that's why other races don't come to respect us, because if we can't, you know, have that kind of respect among ourselves, how...

Female 3: And if they were teaching, all these, like, teaching all of us, even the whites, like, more about Blacks, they wouldn't come acting like just the clothes that we wear and that. Because most of them they only thing they think of us is, like, the clothes or the talk. Like, Jamaicans, they make fun of Jamaicans, like, "Ya, man."

Male: Yeah.

Female 3: You know?

[multiple voices]

Male: And they don't know what it means.

Female 3: I always get mad at this guy, because he keep on saying those Jamaican...I told him that that's not the only thing about Black people, that's not the only thing about Jamaicans, you know? I mean, they should probably teach them some more, they would have an understanding of how we are, you know?

Male 2: Like, they are more into the white stuff.

Male 1: Also, they should know about African things.

Interviewer: Describe it.

Male: Things they do.

Female 3: Character.

Female 4: All their friends.

Female 3: Or Black people aren't good enough for them, they're better than Black people.

Male: Yeah.

Female 3: I think that's really what...

Female 4: Sometimes, it don't matter how white you look, sometimes you have a little bit of Black in you. You are Black, so, you're Black, they act Black, they talk Black, but acting like they're white. (laughter)

Female 4: I hate those people.

Interviewer: What's "acting like white"?

Female 4: They just act like white people, you know, like they're white. You know, they walk with, they only have white friends, you know, they listen to white people music, they don't know nothing about Black people music, they talk about that nonsense and don't let it [?rave] you and all like this, you know. They just "act white." (laughter)

Female 3: And then you have the white people who try to act like...

Male: Uhhhh.

Female 4: I hate them people, too.

Male: You hate everybody, man.

Female 3: I find that so offensive because they don't know anything about it. They think, oh, clothes, you know, this and that, and they think, well, I'm Black like you. They get a tan and, "Okay, I'm almost like you, now."

Male: "Ooh, I want to look like them."

Female 3: I mean, that's offensive.

Male: Yeah, that's the thing I can't understand. Why do these white people...

Female 2: Disrespect Blacks.

Male: No, no, they disrespect Black people the most ways.

Female 2: And then they want to tan.

Male: And then they want to tan their skin.

Female 1: That's what I want to know. [laughs][2]

What emerges from this conversation is how students attribute some importance to the power of self and group definitions in dealing with the social issues of racism. They speak about knowing oneself, one's culture, and one's history as a starting point to building one's inner self, as well as collective strength. For this to be possible, students argue that schools have to be more inclusive in terms of representing the diversity of human experiences to all students. The school's failure in this educational task contributes to a lack of understanding of, respect for, each other among students, and the tendency for some students to develop a false sense of superiority over others. For a few students, the school's inability to deal with issues of race and racism can lead them to dwell on other concerns that a critic may describe as superficial, (e.g., the students' references to white people's tanning).

For some students, such discussions as in "Who Is Black...How Much?" about who is Black, or not Black enough, constitute a constant struggle to maintain individual self and group cultural identities. Many times, students' actions do come into conflict, even with their peers. Nisha, the gifted student, cannot understand Black students who are prejudiced and speak negatively about other students, particularly their Black female friends. In response to a question about who her best friend is at school, she reveals inner pain that perhaps students think she may not be "Black" enough. Her words reflect enormous pressures of discrimination that the young female student experiences that could possibly lead to a student disengaging from school:

> ...my best friend is Filipino actually but I used to have a whole bunch of Black friends but I just noticed a lot of my Black friends...it's like I can't keep my Black female friends. I mean one minute they're my friend and the next minute they're all talking about me and everything so that's one thing about me. (Interviewer: What do they say about you?)...well I found out because of Michael (boyfriend)...he hangs around with the Black guys, and the Black guys and Black girls stick together. After I leave with my best friend after school, they all talk and he told me like they talk I used to have green contacts, oh you know and (long) black hair (or)...hate people who think they're white and...try to have their contacts and everything...and they used to write on my locker, oh you green-eyed so on and so on, or they might say oh she's showing off her hair it's in that you know or she's so cool you look good you know ha ha and stuff. So I had my hair back and then they say she thinks she's so sophisticated with her hair back...so it's really stupid. (06/27/92).

Sharon, a Grade 12 student, provides further insight into how students sometimes have to negotiate their individual self and group cultural identities within the school. She speaks about how she came to join a Black Heritage Club in her school. Joining the club did not come easy, as she recalls:

> ...I remember when somebody, when this person called me an Oreo, I was like, "What does that mean?" Like, I'm asking Black friends that I have "What does Oreo mean?" and then they told me like, "you're only Black on the outside, but you're white inside." And I was like "Oh, really." So, I think, from just that one remark from my fellow Black sister, actually got me interested in the Black Heritage Club. I was always interested, but not fully (11/15/92).

Sexism

Students also point out they have to contend with sexist and discriminatory behaviour in the schools. Black female students, in particular, point to very offensive language often directed at them. They refer to name-calling and sexist jokes conveyed by their male peers, sometimes through the use of a non-Canadian vernacular/dialect that many school authorities may not easily comprehend. As one female student asserted in a focus-group discussion, "some of these Black guys, they treat the Black girls really rudely…(saying)…"Bitch" (DF/2/D4). Other students speak about males bragging about their women and calling them "Baby, girlie…," or saying, "Hi, sexy." A female student talks about the disrespect of a male colleague whose advances she shunned at school:

> …You think you look too good, because when I call to you, you don't want to come to me." That's what the guys think, the girls will answer them when they call them, "Pss, Pss"…You could say, "Excuse me," but, "Pss," that's not her name. You don't…[laughter]…You don't see that written on her clothes, you know" (DF/1/D3).

Another female referred to what is generally seen as a popular male refrain, "I've been watching you all night…Your legs must be tired, because you've been walking through my mind all night…[laughter]." When asked for a response, a male student affirmed his colleague's concerns and condemned the attitude of his peers:

> It's just their attitude, okay, I'm sorry, because if you see a nice girl and you…or you just hiss at them, they're not no [inaudible] where you gotta say, "Excuse me, I want to talk to you," or something like that. If you give them the rude way, they'll cut at you and then they'll just jump at you. They'll jump…(DF/1/D3).

Generally, female teachers interviewed attest to this charge and are frustrated about the problem. Language-code switching becomes a powerful tool to engage in sexist, as well as homophobic conduct. Deborah, a designated "at-risk" student, talks about sexism being "…subtle in the school system…" and that "not all students may be aware of it." She talks of one particular incident involving a fellow Black student:

> Jokes towards women…well, I never got any. Well, I did get one and I thought it was really rude. And I just looked at him, I guess funny, because people say I have this look, [laughter] and when I give them the look, they mean, you shouldn't try it or something like that, and he said something to me. It was after school, and I was working on a presentation for physics, and he goes, "Hey babe," and he said something like, "I want to sex you," and I was like…" (01/29/93).

Nisha also points out that there is sexism in the schools, most often directed against female students and particularly Black females, through name calling and sexist jokes from their male peers. But she also makes a connection between sexism and Black male stereotyping, and particularly, about the enormous pressure to live up to a macho image in which Black male youths find themselves:

> I think Black guys have it worse. I do because they pick on those Black guys. They really, really do, ha ha ha, the teachers and all the fights. People come to fight the Black guys and you have to act like

> you want to fight even if you don't want to fight you have to fight and you're pushed to just do sports. You really see if a Black guy is smart they don't admit it, like they don't want to talk about it...[so] they [Black males] just want to just do enough to pass, to be like the rest of their friends just wear the clothes and that's it. I think again...they say ok if you're Black and you're smart it's usually female...not male — it's awful." (06/27/92).

It is important to point out that these instances of prejudicial, sexist and discriminatory treatment on the basis of one's race and gender constitute sources of emotional and psychological conflicts and other health distress for many Black students.

Race, Representation, and Identity in Schooling

The issue of Black representation in the school curriculum is fundamental to developing an inclusive school environment. It is no exaggeration to say that Black students are generally critical when discussing the Canadian school system, particularly the fact that not all world experiences are represented in classroom discourses and academic texts. At the core of the issue of Black identity is the well-articulated concern that there are gaps in curricular content. Black contribution is not included with enough sophistication and generality to reassure Black students that their race and the achievements of their ancestors are respected (Daenzer and Dei 1994). Black youths find the absence of Black experience in the school curriculum content as one form of unequal and discriminatory treatment at school.

From Marlo, a participant in a summer-jobs program funded by the provincial government, one learns how the Black student may find it difficult to identify with the school:

> When I was going to school the teachers focussed on European history, European this...Alexander Graham Bell discovered this and when you sit in a classroom full of twelve white people and all you hear is white this white that you think, so what am I here for. Right! A lot of times you think it's a lot of shit you know, a lot of bullshit so you don't find it that interesting — you just sit down and you ok Alexander this and George Washington this but at the same time the teacher could always say well this came from the Caribbean and this came from Africa and just or this came from Germany and kinda add everyone's input...have German inventors and African inventors and so on but when school system that I know...focussed on just white European and that's it — nothing more and they don't tell you about great African stuff or...Indian or East Indian — there's nothing like that, so a lot of the students that are minorities...don't feel interested or are left out...it's just you in a corner of the room (06/08/92).

Another student in a focus-group discussion speaks about racial bias in classroom text:

> Like, some things they make you read, I mean, no one's concerned about you, I mean, what are you reading the book for? Tell me why, I

> don't know. It have no meaning, and then, these English teachers, they never give you a Black book to read, they're always something white. They're always something white (DF/2/D4).

Many Black youths also make a direct connection between the problem of student disengagement and the lack of representation of Black role models in the schools. Students want to see more Black and minority teachers in the Canadian school system. However, a few students are quick to add that having Black teachers would not necessarily make a major difference, unless there are also other fundamental changes in the school system. In fact, these few talk about "...Black teachers who are not really Black." Students who feel that a teacher's race should not be an issue in education concede that it is a good idea to have teachers from different racial backgrounds in the schools. Many see the Black teacher as an important role model, and a few speak about the likelihood of the teacher having a social perspective with which they can identify.

When Mary was interviewed, she had dropped out of school the previous year, but was planning to go back. Her parents were born in the Caribbean. She was born in Montreal, and speaks fluent French. She points out the importance of a Black teacher, just like a Black school counsellor, having a perspective on matters in her school that she can relate to:

> Maybe the student will relate to the teacher better, because maybe they are from the same background or they [inaudible]. I find if, I had a teacher who was Black and it was easier for me to talk to her, because my other teacher I couldn't do it...I guess it makes a lot of difference, like, especially if you have a counsellor come from your own country, religion and everything, it's good, because they, like, if it's like a white counsellor and a Black kid, the white counsellor is going to try to put himself in the kid's place, but it's impossible, she's not Black. If you have a Black teacher, it's more easier for her — a Black counsellor, it's more easier for her to put her in her kid, in her situation and try to solve it and give me some ideas as related to us...(07/30/92).

In focus-group discussions, many students speak about the importance of having Black teachers. One female student, while pointing out that "...some Black teachers do not care..." nevertheless staunchly defends the need for Black teachers, given (as she says) "the experiences Black students have to go through":

> She'll know what you're going through, because mostly all Black teachers understand what you're going through right now. But the white ones, they just want you to be in class and do your work, and if you don't get it done they'll be up on your case for the rest of your time. But the Black students, they know what, like, they know what you're going through and how you're feeling, and if you can't get that thing done they'll be there to guide you through the whole way (DF/1/D3).

Conclusion

No doubt some critics may argue that these accounts are merely students' perceptions of racial prejudice and unequal treatment at school, with which other groups in the same school setting (e.g., white students, teachers, administrators) may not necessarily agree. However, this does not negate the students' perceptions of events and school structure. In fact, the existence of such perceptions should be cause for concern for every educator and school administrator. The questions that need answering are — why and how have students formed such ideas? For many students, perceptions are the reality.

The narratives of Black/African-Canadian youths show how the dynamics of social difference shape and implicate the processes and experiences of public schooling. On both analytical and practical levels, students' accounts bring to the fore the dilemma of searching for an appropriate centrality of the experiences, histories, and cultures of the diverse student body in curriculum and classroom pedagogical practices, to facilitate youth learning. Black youths are concerned about the school's ability (in the sense of social discourse, texts, and classroom pedagogy) to misrepresent, negate, and devalue some experiences, while at the same time recognizing others. Our current public school system is a long way from dealing comprehensively with the qualitative value of justice and educational equity, and systematically addressing the questions of race, identity, and representation in education. This is not to deny that our educational institutions are beginning to confront the challenges of diversity, particularly the relational aspects of social difference. This is also not to belittle the efforts of many well-intentioned teachers and school administrators working steadfastly to address the concerns of minority students, parents, and community workers about the structure of public schooling in Canada. The fact is that educators and administrators need to explore *how* and *why* some students still harbour negative feelings about school, despite current efforts to face up to some of the challenges of providing education in a multi-ethnic society.

On the matter of race and racism in school, this study points to the necessity of moving beyond a simplistic Black/white duality. The language and discursive practices of the students themselves about their school experiences provide examples of the myriad forms of racism and discrimination in the schools. Black students' racial politics and interpretations, as discerned from focus-group discussions of school racism, have practical implications in terms of how the youth understand and struggle for social and educational equity. Students' accounts reveal an understanding of the structural and material constraints that both inhibit and facilitate their school progress and eventual "success." Evidently, many students explain race and racism at school with references to larger societal structures.

To deal with the concerns expressed by students, educational institutions and school administrators should increase current efforts to develop race and antiracism policies. Antiracism educational strategies should aim at the inclusion of minority students into the mainstream culture of the schools. I see antiracism strategies as an effective way of addressing the disempowering aspects of public schooling, particularly for minority youth, in Canadian society. An understanding of the impact and consequences of racism on individuals, groups and society is crucial to the antiracism project in the schools. Our schools require new forms of education that have social and political relevance, and have meaning to our students and the communities in which we live. In more practical terms, antiracism education can be pursued as an action-oriented educational strategy for institutional and systemic change to address the issues of racism and the interlocking systems of social oppression.

As I have argued elsewhere (Dei 1994), the pursuance of the goals and ideals of antiracism education means educators and students must be prepared to cross boundaries into different territories and to create spaces to engage in dialogue with each other for genuine social change and transformation. Our conversations must critically interrogate ourselves and our societies. We must engage with each other well beyond the dictates and confines of a "politics of the moment."

To deal with the issues of racism, educators have to openly discuss the concept of race in their classroom teaching. For many, this will initially require antiracism teacher-training in relation to minority cultures and social knowledge. Such teaching will have to focus on students', teachers', and educators' understanding of how race or social position has an implication in the personal dedication to the institution in which one works. It is also important that educators, teachers, administrators, or students understand how racial, class, and gender identities are implicated in ways of knowing, and of knowledge itself. Teachers have to challenge their students to enrol in the "culture of success" not in the "culture of failure" as manifested in the youth engagement in sports and athletics, rather than academics.

There is also the need for a school curriculum and classroom pedagogy that aim at spiritualizing the youth in their learning processes. Learning should be an emotionally felt experience for the youth (wa Thiongo 1986, 17). Educators should help students ground their learning in an appropriate cultural context, by drawing on the connections between the student's body, mind, and soul. If racism is to be effectively dealt with, then students must be able to spiritualize the whole educational environment and make the necessary connections between individuals, groups, and a higher moral order.

As a society, we should aim at providing youths with a comprehensive education about themselves and their societies. It is on this basis that academic excellence will emerge. It is important for Canadian educators to educate Black/African youths about their Africanity by affirming Black/African traditional values and cultural patterns in the school system. Knowing about African cultural values and traditions can be an important buffer against racism. More importantly, it can provide students with the requisite coping and surviving skills and serve as significant sources of youth empowerment to deal with the competitiveness and the rugged individualism that arguably are the hallmarks of the Eurocentred school system.

Antiracist teaching must reflect and account for diversity and difference in society. Such teachings should move beyond a mere narration of difference to responding meaningfully and concretely to differences in society (Greene 1994, Valli 1994). Educators must join the cause of students' empowerment by evoking and affirming students' own knowledge, voices, and experiences as a necessary condition to rupturing the status quo. Students should be able to talk about how they see the societies in which they live and how they make meaning of the everyday occurrences around them. A teacher's classroom pedagogy must cultivate a safe atmosphere for students to talk back and forth with participants on the issue of racism and other forms of social oppression, and how they impede students' learning, and the realization of the educational project as a whole. Teachers should critically use their own cultures and those of their students as pedagogical tools.

In concluding, I will reiterate that there is the need for classroom teaching to recognize the power of lived experience, experiences of difference, and the relevance of what is taught and learned to the material conditions of everyday existence in society (Greene 1994). Teachers should be prepared to engage in issues-oriented teaching, to teach about resistance, to recognize social oppression, institutionalized inequality, and to act conscientiously to address and remove such injustices in society. This, to me, is the primary purpose of education, to create a just society for all through the enhancement of individual and group capabilities. The issues of race and racism are significant subject matters in the education of youths, particularly, in multi-ethnic societies. Race continues to have much currency in contemporary society. Educators cannot shield their responsibility to investigate how the societal systems of domination and subjugation are mediated in the processes of schooling and delivering education. Putting power relations at the centre of schooling requires an interrogation of how knowing, learning, and understanding our world happen in the schools.

Discussion Questions

1. Discuss how racism manifests itself in the school setting.
2. What roles can students play in the struggle for antiracism organizational change in schools?
3. The dynamics of social difference is such that to understand the full social effects of race students must also comprehend the ways in which all other forms of social oppression interact (race, class, gender, and sexuality). Discuss.

Notes

1. M. Fitzgerald. 1984. *Political Parties and Black People*. London: Runnymede Trust.
2. George Dei.

References

Apple, M., and Weis, L. 1983. "Ideology, and practice in education: A political conceptual introduction." In *Ideology and practice in schooling*, ed. M. Apple and L. Weis. Philadelphia: Temple Univ. Press.

Bourdieu, P., and Passeron, J. C. 1977. *Reproduction in education, society and culture*. Beverly Hills: Sage.

Bowles, S., and Gintis, H. 1976. *Schooling in capitalist America*. NY: Basic Books.

Brah, A., and Deem, R. 1986. "Structural racism or cultural difference: Schooling for Asian girls." In *Just a bunch of girls*, ed. G. Weiner. Milton Keynes: Open Univ. Press.

Brathwaite, K. 1989. "The Black student and the school: A Canadian dilemma." In *African continuities/L'Heritage Africain.*, ed. S. Chilingu and S. Niang, 195-216. Toronto: Terebi.

Crichlow, W. 1994. *Black studies: A curriculum of inclusion: Selecting literature for Black preschool learners in today's society paper.* Toronto: OISE.

Daenzer, P., and Dei, G.J.S. 1994. *Issues of school completion/dropout: A focus on Black youth in Ontario schools and other relevant studies.* Ontario Royal Commission on Learning.

Dei, G.J.S. 1994. Introduction: anti-racist education. *Orbit* 25 (2): 1-3.

———. 1993. *The examination of high dropout rate among Black students on Ontario Public Schools.* Preliminary report submitted to Ontario Ministry of Education and Training, Toronto.

———. 1993a. The challenges of anti-racist education in Canada. *Canadian Ethnic Studies,* 25 (2): 36-51.

Figueroa, P. 1991. *Education and the social construction of 'race'.* London: Routledge.

Fordham, S. 1988. Racelessness as a factor in Black students' success: Pragmatic strategy or Pyrrhic victory. *Harvard Educational Review* 58 (1): 54-84.

Gibson, M. A. 1988. *Accommodation without assimilation. Sikh immigrants in an American high school.* Ithaca: Cornell Univ. Press.

Giroux, H. 1983. *Theory and resistance in education: A pedagogy of opposition.* MA: Bergin & Garvey.

Greene, M. 1994. Beginnings, identities and possibilities: The uses of social imagination. Paper read at American Educational Research Association meeting, 4-8 April, at New Orleans.

Haw, K. F. 1991. Implications of gender and race — a problem for teachers? A review of emerging literature. *Educational Research* 33 (1): 12-21. Spring.

Hildalgo, N.; McDowell, C. L.; and Siddle, E. eds. 1990. Facing racism in education. Reprint series no. 21. *Harvard Educational Review.*

James, C. E. 1994. I don't want to talk about it. *Orbit* 25 (2): 26-9. Toronto: OISE.

———. 1990. *Making it.* Oakville: Mosaic Press.

Kelly, E. 1988. *Racism in schools: New research evidence.* Tessa Cohn: Trentham Books.

Lee, E. 1985. *Letters to Marcia.* Toronto: Cross-Cultural Communication Centre.

McCarthy, C., and Crichlow, W., eds. 1993. *Race, identity and representation in education.* NY: Routledge.

Oakes, J. 1985. *Keeping track: How schools structure inequality.* New Haven: Yale Univ. Press.

Ogbu, J. U. 1985. Variability in minority school performance: A problem in search of explanation. *Anthropology and Education Quarterly* 18 (4): 312-34.

Sleeter, C. 1994. Multicultural education, social positionality, and whiteness. Paper read at American Educational Research Association meeting, 4-8 April, at New Orleans.

Solomon, P. 1992. *Black resistance in high school: forging a separatist culture.* NY: SUNY Press.

Thomas, B. 1993. *Racism and education: Research perspectives.* Toronto: OISE Press.

———. 1984. Principles of anti-racist education. *Currents* 2 (3). Toronto: Urban Alliance on Race Relations.

Toronto Board of Education. 1988. *Education of Black students in Toronto: Final report of the consultative committee.*

Troyna, B., and Cashmore, E. 1993. *Introduction to race relations.* Boston: Routledge & Kegan Paul.

———. 1982. *Black youth in crisis.* Boston: Allen & Unwin.

Valli, L. 1994. Trusting relations, preservice teachers, and multicultural schools. Paper read at American Educational Research Association meeting, 4-8 April, at New Orleans.

Waterhouse, P. 1990. *Qualitative research on school leavers: Summary final report.* Ottawa: Employment and Immigration Canada, and Statistics Canada.

wa Thiongo, N. 1986. *Decolonizing the mind: The politics of language in African literature.* London: James Currey.

Willis, P. 1977. *Learning to labour: How working class kids get working-class jobs.* Westmead, England: Saxon House.

Ziegler, S. 1989. Dropout prevention. *Scope* 4 (3). Toronto Board of Education.

Author Notes

I am thankful for the assistance of many graduate students at the Ontario Institute for Studies in Education during various phases of the research project with Black/African-Canadian youths. I am particularly grateful to Deborah Elva, Gabrielle Hezekiah, Josephine Mazzucca, Elizabeth McIsaac, Thato Bereng, Anita Sheth, and Bobby Blanford. Financial assistance for the study has been provided by the Ontario Ministry of Education and Training and the Social Science Research Council of Canada (SSHRC).

In the project, the term Black is used by self-definition. In this paper, I use Black and African interchangeably to denote all students who are of African descent and consequently call themselves as such.

Further Readings

Anti-racist education: Working across differences. 1994. Special Issue of *Orbit* 25 (2). Toronto: OISE.

Gill, D.; Mayor, B.; and Blair, M., eds. 1992. *Racism and education: Structure and strategies.* Newbury Park: Sage Publications.

May, S. 1994. *Making multicultural education work.* Toronto: OISE.

4

BEHIND THE IVY WALLS: RACISM/ANTIRACISM IN ACADEME

Augie Fleras

For our schools to do better than they do we have to give up the belief that it is possible to create the conditions for productive learning when those conditions do not exist for education personnel. (Sarason)[1]

M. Fullan
The New Meaning of Educational Change

Introduction

Racism is commonly assumed to be a widespread if somewhat under-discoursed aspect of university life. Campus racism is expressed in diverse ways, from the personal and intentional to the systemic and institutional, with varying levels of intensity and intent in between. Yet data in support of these assertions remain largely impressionistic or media-hyped, often reflecting uncritical acceptance of common-sense or polemics. This paper will address the lacuna in our knowledge by examining the rationale behind this under-theorized state of affairs. It is argued that racism in the ivory towers may be institutionally pervasive, but efforts at renewal and reform continue to be marred by underestimating the "political" dimensions of any restructuring. Current concessions may have sharpened a commitment to inclusiveness and equity; nevertheless, further progress in improving minority-university relations may prove glacial in pace without bolder antiracist initiatives. Topics for discussion include, (a) the magnitude and scope of campus racism, (b) underlying rationale, (c) manifestation and impact, (d) solutions in progress, (e) levels of resistance, and (f) proposals for radical reform. Both primary and secondary data are employed (including existing surveys and reports as well as interviews with select officials) to explore the politics of ivory-tower racism from the perspective of problem and solutions.

"Above the Fray?"

It's taken as axiomatic that racism is a pervasive feature of Canadian institutions. The magnitude and scope of this racism, as well as its intensity and intent, are expressed in different ways. Yet its impact tends to be the same, regardless of *who, what, why,* or *how*. People of colour are "put down" or "put in their place" in a society that professes multiculturalism but doesn't always match practice with piety (Fleras and Elliott 1992).

Educational institutions are no exception to this rule. Both primary and secondary schools have been criticized as sites of racism and discrimination, in effect sullying Canada's reputation as pacesetter for progressive social change. Considerable energy has gone into the design and implementation of appropriate policies; since 1992, for example, school boards in Ontario have parlayed antiracist and ethnocultural equity programs into everyday practice (Ministry of Education and Training 1993). By contrast, post-secondary initiatives for mainstreaming diversity have been inconsistent at best and nonexistent at worst. Terms such as racism continue to be bandied about, without much concern for rigour or consistency. Few empirically valid studies that isolate the components of campus racism are available: those that do tend to be methodologically flawed or driven by ideology rather than social science (Ontario Federation of Students [OFS] 1991, O'Neill and Yelaha 1994). Even fewer are capable of framing questions for answers commensurate with the gravity of the problem.

In other words, the problem of campus racism is often ignored or under-theorized — despite initiatives for mandating cultural diversity or curbing racial harassment. Policies and programs tend to be motivated by a preference for crisis management or public relations, rather than minority grievance resolution. Face-saving solutions are proposed on the basis of largely anecdotal evidence, subject to varying interpretation and vulnerable to second guessing. This seeming indifference to campus racism beyond the symbolic or token cannot be taken lightly. Rather than being "above the fray," as popularly depicted, colleges and universities are no less susceptible to racism than other institutions (Exum 1980, OFS 1991). Refusal to confront these realities not only interferes with problem solution; it also superimposes conflict over co-operation as a preferred strategy. Such myopia may deprive students of the skills to deal with diversity in a global market economy. It also excludes minority students from full and equitable participation because of the dampening effect from a "chilly" post-secondary climate.

This paper examines the myths and realities that shape and define the parameters of racism at post-secondary levels. The magnitude and scope of campus racism, as well as its properties and consequences, are analyzed and assessed, along various dimensions of theory and practice. While there is nothing especially novel in acknowledging ivory-tower racism as an under-theorized subject for study, with potentially sinister effects for healthy race relations, such an assertion does underscore the complexity of the problem for solution. This paper also explores the politics of antiracism at a time when universities are grappling with an identity crisis in response to the demands of diversity and change. Acceptance or rejection of an antiracist agenda is shown to vary with competing perspectives on post-secondary education, either as agency of social action or centre of higher learning. The mainstreaming of diversity along the corridors of privilege and power will remain as elusive as ever, this paper concludes, without a wholesale restructuring of university rules, roles, and responsibilities. Five key questions are central to the content and organization of this argument.

First: Is there a problem with respect to racism on Canadian campuses? Are all racial incidents by definition racist, either in intent or in consequence? How do we know; who decides; and where can we find out? Collecting relevant data on the magnitude of campus racism would appear essential for the application of appropriate solutions.

Second: How is this problem manifested? Is it confined primarily to interpersonal levels and everyday interaction, or embedded within institutional structures? Is it possible to measure racism according to reliable criteria? The fact that terms such as prejudice, harassment, and discrimination are employed randomly in conjunction with racism not only complicates the process of defining the problem; it also nullifies proposals for solution.

Third: Why does the problem exist? To what extent does responsibility for campus racism reside in individuals, rather than institutions? The distinction is critical: Historically, universities evolved as bastions of white (male) privilege, with a supportive array of Eurocentric assumptions, structures, and operations. That alone should alert stakeholders to the perils and politics associated with institutional accommodation.

Fourth: What has been accomplished to date with the problem of racism? Are solutions piecemeal and ad hoc, or are they comprehensive in design and implementation, with increasing emphasis on structures, rather than personal attitudes? How effective are reactive versus proactive strategies? The success of antiracist initiatives will depend on how diligently racism is addressed rather than on the total elimination of racial incidents and racist structures — surely an impossible task in an environment so political and competitive. Invariably, antiracist proposals generate controversy and backlash; in doing so, they expose the shrinking middle ground between those who dismiss reforms as a menace to higher learning and those who endorse a more inclusive, less discriminatory environment (Northfield 1993). This dialogue also secures a starting point for re-assessing the roles and responsibilities of higher education in a pluralistic and changing society.

Fifth: What are the barriers to effective antiracist implementation? What options exist to curb campus racism without repudiating the virtues of academic freedom and standards of excellence? Where is the balance between quality and equality, between freedom and inclusion? Everyone agrees that racism is a problem; there is less consensus regarding a solution, in part because of failure to accurately define the problem, in other part because of entrenched resistance. The ideal of an antiracist university that is both inclusive and equitable is offered as solution to the identity crisis confronted by higher education.

Responses to these questions are varied and open to dispute; yet confronting such issues can no longer be dismissed as an option or luxury. The legitimacy of all institutions is being put to the test and contested by post-modernist discourse for radical change. Post-secondary education is no exception to this rule for accommodating diversity through removal of discriminatory barriers. To date, most concessions have looked upon antiracism as a device for cooling out "troublesome constituents" through conflict management or damage control. But recent initiatives have experimented with proactive measures for revising existing social arrangements and hidden agendas. Still, there is doubt whether antiracism principles can penetrate the armour of an essentially political environment. It also remains to be seen whether higher education can muster the will and resources to empower all university personnel with the right to be free from racial discrimination, as well as the right to flourish in a supportive environment where each can "pursue their common purposes without fear of injustice, indignity, or bodily harm" (Queen's 1991, 2).

Campus Racism: From Ivory Tower to Concrete Jungle

The demographic revolution of the past twenty years has had a disquieting effect on post-secondary schooling. The composition of the student body has been irrevocably altered; classrooms are increasingly complex and demanding, because of diversity and change; and university operations can no longer abide by conventional rules, roles, and responsibilities (Price 1993). Yet research on higher levels of education has not garnered as much interest as anticipated (Smith 1991). Even less attention appears directed at issues related to campus racism and antiracism; although, some universities have undertaken a comprehensive examination of race relations as a prelude to action, while others have proceeded directly to the policy and programs stage (McGill 1994).

Compare this complacency with the clamour over the diversity agenda (from multiculturalism to political correctness) on American campuses (Hughes 1992, Berger 1993, Dickman 1993). On the one hand, traditionalists fear that unbridled multiculturalism will deprive students of exposure to basics or the classics, with a corresponding decline in shared values and national unity. Pandering to diversity may also scuttle the autonomy of the modern university, they argue; it may also encourage a retribalization of university campuses, repudiate those values central to higher education, and ignite a massive delegitimation of post-secondary education (Berger 1993). On the other, critics welcome the opportunity for inclusiveness as part of a broader struggle for control over public culture (Kessler-Harris 1992, Hayes-Bautista 1992, Winkler 1992). The debate in Canada has yet to reach comparable proportions; nevertheless, awareness levels are escalating (Smith 1992).

Magnitude and Scope

A variety of sources furnish a glimpse into campus racism. University publications (policy statements or calendars) are one source; another consists of eye-witness reports by victims or observers. Several survey studies also exist as a basis for assessment and analysis (Ramcharan,1991). In 1986, York University conducted a comprehensive study on race relations involving 1300 students, with 26 percent of the sample non-white. Only 3 percent stated that they had experienced racism on campus, with verbal harassment singled out as the prime violator. About 10 percent of the sample were thought to possess potentially racist attitudes. The subsequent establishment of a Centre for Race and Ethnic Relations at York — reportedly the first of its kind in Canada — has provided a much needed database. Thirty racial incidents were reported between 1988 and 1990; 56 between 1990 and 1991; 58 between 1991 and 1992; and 68 between 1992 and 1993. These figures are comparable to results elsewhere: for example, the University of Guelph recorded 90 complaints following the appointment of a Human Rights Commission officer in January, 1993 (University of Guelph 1994).

The University of Western Ontario presented another study in 1989 (UWO 1989). Of the approximately 800 respondents, 9.1 percent acknowledged they were victims of at least one actual or perceived incident of racism, most commonly involving jokes or slurs. Nearly 200 had witnessed one of 261 racial incidents on campus in the previous year. The majority of incidents occurred in classrooms, with residences and cafeterias following behind in frequency. Students were involved in 80 percent of the cases. In the first year of operation ending in June, 1992, the Race Relations Office at UWO handled 36 racial complaints, with verbal abuse among students the main culprit (UWO 1993). Only one incident of racial violence was recorded. Finally, the University of Windsor completed a study that capitalized on a randomly selected sample of 100 visible minority students (Ramcharan 1991). The findings were ambiguous: On the negative side, 15 percent of the sample acknowledged the existence of racist attitudes and racial discrimination on campus. Many also believed that racial and ethnic minorities were more likely to receive inferior or unequal treatment. On the positive side, 70 percent reported no personal experiences of racial intolerance on campus, whereas 60 percent did not believe that faculty or staff favoured whites over nonwhites. In its most recent annual report, the University of Windsor reported 22 race-related complaints for the year ending June 30, 1993 — a figure not entirely inconsistent with recorded incidents elsewhere.

Some tentative conclusions can be drawn from these surveys. Statistics related to the number of overt racial incidents on campus can be misleading: First, the numbers themselves may say more about the survey instrument than about campus racism. The recording of an incident as race related is not necessarily proof of racism; it may reflect interpersonal conflict that happens to involve racially different groups. Nor does a formal complaint automatically authenticate the validity of an accusation. Second, there may be a strong tendency to under-report racial incidents — partly from fear of reprisal or from being branded a malcontent. Minorities may be discouraged from coming forward with legitimate concerns because of worries that a complaint could be dismissed as frivolous if not upheld (McGill 1994). Visa minority students may prefer not to report racial incidents, even when directly confronted, for fear of revoking their visa status or compromising academic standing (Ramcharan 1991). Many whites are still incapable of recognizing racism in its varied forms, let alone in reporting it to proper authorities, while minorities may prefer the security of confiding among themselves (University of Guelph 1994). Third, the numbers themselves are not necessarily an accurate barometer of social pathologies. Increases in reported incidents may convey a greater willingness to report racial violations, rather than any lapse in the social fibre of society. Lastly, numbers cannot possibly convey a victim's humiliation or sense of betrayal. Minorities routinely encounter mistrust or hostility, in addition to distorted perceptions and polite put-downs, all of which combine to intensify feelings of isolation or exclusion (OFS 1991). Unless victimized themselves, few can appreciate either the pain inflicted by racist graffiti or the paralyzing fear imposed by hate groups and racist literature. Even seemingly harmless pranks or a thoughtless remark can create psychological distress every bit as emotionally devastating and socially debilitating as open bigotry (Stern 1992).

In sum, racism continues to be perceived and experienced as a campus menace — despite a dearth of supporting statistical data. Universities have shown a reluctance to substantiate charges of campus racism, preferring instead to rely on hearsay or existing surveys for fearing of fanning dormant hostilities, sparking unflattering publicity, or incurring minority wrath over yet another "body count" (Queen's 1991). Discrepancies between perception and numbers may involve divergent views of racism: For whites, racism consists of discriminatory incidents by misguided persons; for minorities, racism is about power within institutions. Evidence also suggests that minorities are unlikely to be directly victimized by blatantly racist actions. Openly racist platforms find little public acceptance or political support in Canada (Adam 1992). Polite racism is a different story, however, and minorities may experience a general discomfort because of innuendo or put-downs over their presence on campus (Ramcharan 1991). The concepts of a "chilly" working climate and "glass ceilings" have been amply documented elsewhere with respect to gender relations (Kanter 1977).

Proof or Perception?

Are Canadian campuses racist? Are levels of discrimination and harassment equivalent to national proportions? These are not idle questions since racism is portrayed by many as intrinsic to higher education, thus self-evident and beyond debate (Queen's 1991, York 1993, UWO 1993). Obviously much depends on how we define racism and its correlates, prejudice, harassment, and discrimination. National surveys indicate that perhaps 15 percent of all Canadians are hard-core racists with unabashed resentment of minorities. Most Canadians entertain some prejudicial attitudes toward minorities, despite a reluctance to openly articulate such misgivings in public (Henry and Tator 1985, Reitz and Breton 1994). Dislike of minorities is not necessarily proof of racism per se; it may more properly reflect a predisposition related to stereotypes ("unwarranted generalizations") or ethnocentrism ("cultural arrogance"). Nor do prejudicial attitudes automatically produce discriminatory actions, much less evolve into racist doctrines.

The capacity to compartmentalize and conceal is especially evident at post-secondary levels. Those with advanced education are commonly perceived as more socially astute than the general public. Personal enlightenment and intellectual growth could account for any differences. No less compelling, however, is the acquisition of conceptual skills with which to disguise personal dislike. Exposure to academic discipline provides students with the social savvy to think through a political point of view before blurting out potentially embarrassing statements. These tactics in concealment and evasion are empowering in that they equip post-secondary students with the option of appearing progressive, rather than coarse or untutored (Hacker 1993). They also confirm, as Harry Arthurs (1993) observes, that universities are not necessarily "republics of reason" that equitably distribute freedom and equal standing regardless of who or what is involved (University of Guelph 1994).

In addition, surveys are limited in what they can reveal. Tallying the number of racial incidents, both witnessed or experienced, is amenable to measurement by quantification: So too is the under-representation of targeted minorities in positions of employment. People's responses to questions about attitudes and opinions can also be quantified. Yet the validity of these responses is questionable, since respondents are known to conceal and evade when commenting on racial issues — even with complete strangers — in an effort to bolster a veneer of sophistication (Hacker 1993). Surveys are incapable of "quantifying" the dynamics or complexities behind these "empirical facts" — particularly when behaviour departs from explicitly stated norms. Nor can they hope to unearth the layers of systemic bias within higher education. Overt bigotry may be less problematic than social arrangements or hidden agendas that marginalize minorities while robbing many of the "comfort zone" necessary for academic success.

Mass media may also inflame perceptions of campus racism. The inner logic and operating imperatives of a profit-oriented industry may distort the social construction of media reality (Fleras 1991). Reality is further fractured by framing issues along the lines of conflict or confrontation (Zerbisias 1994). Social issues may be hyped out of proportion by splicing together isolated and unrelated incidents into a national pattern of crisis proportions (Fleras 1994). For example, an article that appeared in the *US News* (Stern 1992) bemoaned the pervasiveness of racism on American campuses. Of the 3300 colleges and universities, a total of 250 had reported an incident of ethnoviolence between 1986 and 1991. Admittedly, this figure cannot take into account the large number of unreported incidents; arguably, even a single incident is one too many in terms of personal pain. Yet to assert racism as a rampant epidemic on American campuses on the basis of skimpy evidence not only glosses over the problem, but also trivializes the impact of these incidents when they occur.

To sum up, the contours of campus racism continue to elude social scientific inquiry. Evidence to date can be interpreted in different ways when judged by available data. Campus racism is neither the epidemic some make it out to be, nor is it an inconsequential blip on some distant horizon. Even a middle ground is strewn with perils: According to Harry Arthurs (1993), it makes sense to distinguish between ideological racism and the beleaguered actions of a pressured budget official without the discretionary funds to finance a minority program. For policy purposes, a deliberate attempt to incite a race riot must be separated from the idle banalities of locker room banter. Otherwise, the indiscriminate mixture of the obscene with the annoying, of hate versus ignorance, may discredit the very constituency under consideration. Provoking an antiracist backlash may also diminish the suffering of those truly victimized by racist or discriminatory actions. Many are equally concerned by the lack of empirical data in this area. Such an omission exerts even more pressure for decoding the pillars of racism — prejudice, harassment, and discrimination — for each demands a unique response.

Dimensions of Campus Racism

Canada may have a reputation as a progressive society in the management of race and ethnic relations. But institutional racism was once a chronic and inescapable component of Canadian society (Elliott and Fleras 1991). Minorities were routinely barred from even partial participation in mainstream institutions. Predictably, they were subjected to verbal and physical harassment without much chance of recourse or reprisals. Similarly, campus racism was openly expressed against Jews or African-Canadians through racial slurs or institutionalized in discriminatory practices such as entry restrictions and quotas.

Overt displays of racism are socially unacceptable at present: This injunction applies to institutions or interpersonal relations. Institutions can no longer openly discriminate against minorities, lest they attract negative publicity or incite campus chaos. Racially motivated crimes ("hate" crimes) are likely to be punished more severely than

by those who ought reasonably to know that such attention is unwanted (UWO 1993). In the words of Monique Shebbeare (McGill 1994, 6), harassment involves:

> [t]he abusive, unfair, or demeaning treatment of a person or group of persons that has the effect or purpose of unreasonably interfering with a person's or group's status or performance or creating a hostile or intimidating working or educational environment...

As is the case with discrimination, harassment constitutes an abuse of power that need not be overt or directed at a specific target to negatively affect another persons work, study, involvement, or well-being (Waterloo 1994). Discrimination by harassment — ranging in scope from innuendo and name-calling to pin-ups and open threats — is now covered under laws and human rights codes.

Racism

Racism is subject to varied meanings (Elliott and Fleras 1991). Some define it as a belief that race shapes the intellectual, moral, and social characteristics of people, and that certain races are inherently inferior because of these negatively valued attributes (Waterloo 1994). Any dogma or activity that diminishes others unjustly and justifies (rationalizes) discriminatory treatment by reference to race is considered racist (OFS 1991). Others define racism as the power held by one group or individuals that encourages dominance, control, and superiority over another on the basis of select characteristics pertaining to appearance, intelligence, or moral worth (University of Guelph 1994). Some racist behaviour is unplanned and unpremeditated, but expressed in isolated acts at irregular intervals, because of individual impulse or insensitivity. Other racist behaviour is neither spontaneous or sporadic: It is manifest instead through patterns of racial discrimination and racial harassment that reflect broader patterns of oppression, built into the structures of society and backed by sanctions of power and authority (University of Guelph 1994). Racism can also be intentional or unintentional, and its presence detected by its effects in excluding minority decision-making, marginalizing minority participation, or suppressing minority knowledge as irrelevant.

As with discrimination, different types of racism can be discerned (Elliott and Fleras 1991). Redneck racism represents a deliberate and conscious effort to deny or exclude; polite racism is more subtle and indirect; institutional racism consists of socially sanctioned put-downs; and systemic racism entails consequences that are inadvertent, but exclusionary and real. In general, the discourse on racism has become more complex in recent years. The concept has stretched to encompass any system of inferiority involving domination or control. The focus of racism has shifted away from a "thing" created by contact between individuals, to an awareness of social arrangements that bolster white privilege at the expense of minority realities (UWO 1993). Intent and consciousness are less important than context and consequence in evaluating the racist dimensions of even well-meaning actions. The notion of equality and its relationship to racism has also undergone a conceptual overhaul. Racism once meant denial of equality because of race or colour. ("No minorities need apply here." "Sorry, the job's been taken.") The racist label is now applied to those situations that deny colour relevance in deciding who gets what in the competition for scarce resources. ("We treat everyone the same around here.") This implies that equality is not equivalent to colour-blind formal rights before the law. A genuine equality must take differences into account to be any substantive value for minorities.

The Nature of Ivory-Tower Racism

As the secularization of society escalates, colleges and universities have displaced churches and traditional family structures as the purveyors of core values and community standards (Chesler and Crowfoot 1989). But post-secondary institutions are no less regressive than mainstream institutions when they confront the confusing and often contradictory nature of Canadian race relations (Hick and Santos 1992). Racial injustice within the ivory towers is secured by official policies and practices, incorporated into structures and operations as normal or necessary, and sustained through ideologies that rationalize inequities as aberrations from otherwise fair and open system of competition (Chesler and Crowfoot 1989). Yet campus racism is anything but incidental or accidental, much less individual or attitudinal. Nor is it "idealist" in the sense that underachievement stems from cultural differences, with its implicit commitment to blame the victim as a central explanatory variable (Hick and Santos 1992).

Defining the Nature of Campus Racism

> (F)or the liberal professor...racism connotes conscious acts, where there is an intent to hurt or degrade or disadvantage others because of their colour or ethnicity...He does not consider the all white or predominantly white character of an occupation or institution in itself to be racism. He does not understand the notion of covert racism, that white people maintain a system of racial oppression by acts of omission, indifference, and failure to change the status quo. The Third World definition of racism...focuses on society as a whole and on structured relations between people rather than on individual personalities and actions. From this standpoint, the university is racist because people of colour are and have been systematically excluded from full and equal participation and power — as students, professors, administrators, and, particularly, in the historic definition of the character of the institution and its curriculum.[2]

The sheer invisibility of systemic racism renders it difficult for whites to recognize the institutional inequities that confront people of colour. Those from the dominant sector are often oblivious to the privileges and social advantages associated with "whiteness" as the preferred norm and taken-for-granted standard (McIntosh 1988). The patterns of entitlement that flow from white privilege frequently operate without conscious intent; as a result, even those who are attuned to racial injustice find it difficult to isolate structural barriers, let alone to act with fairness. Nevertheless, the consequences of well-intentioned organizational actions — or inaction — can be racist in impact when perpetuating the Eurocentric character of post-secondary institutions.

In short, the true nature of ivory-tower racism is neither sporadic nor random; nor is it restricted to the aberrant minds and deranged actions of a few social misfits. White-supremacist doctrines rarely find a receptive climate at universities. The openly racist typologies of Philippe Rushton, or blatant sexism of Matin Yaqzan were vociferously rebuked by students and faculty; yet some defended their right to articulate such assertions. Racist slurs and jokes, in addition to washroom graffiti, continue to be a problem, but are increasingly subject to censure or sanctions. Such defamatory statements may not spring from explicit racism; nevertheless, in a society where "race matters" they have the effect, however inadvertent, of reinforcing a racist status quo.

Campus racism is not so much about what happens but more about what doesn't happen because of entrenched white (male) privilege (Drakich et al. 1994). Both Eurocentric and viricentric values tend to prevail with respect to underlying assumptions, organizational structure, operating principles, reward systems, and intended outcomes. Consider only the process of normal social science as a typification of a "white-man's world." Both Dorothy Smith (1979) and Sylvia Hale (1993) claim that social-science discourse involves the imposition of explanatory patterns on data through abstract conceptual models, logical concepts, and objectified language. The virtues of objectivity and detachment supersede those of the personal or experiential as a basis for university scholarship. Theories of race, class, ethnicity, and gender, as well as the relationship between them, are couched in abstractions that assert the primacy of one variable over others in shaping social position. Such abstract empiricism not only ignores minority lived-in realities; it also promulgates support for the status quo (Hale 1993). In brief, ivory-tower racism is subtle and nondescript, yet pervasive and systemic, in upholding patterns of white privilege. Such unobtrusiveness makes racism that much more difficult to identify and isolate, let alone to challenge and eliminate.

Coping with the Crisis

Charges of racism in the ivory towers have elicited responses ranging from denial to whole-hearted agreement. Few, however, would doubt the reality of campus racism, even if its intensity and tone are subject to dispute. Many would also agree that individuals should be free from racial discrimination for reasons unrelated to ability or skills (CAUT 1994). Towards that end, many universities have instituted harassment codes and discrimination policies to conform with provincial Human Rights Codes. To be sure, designating responsibility for action to specific officials or offices does not ensure follow-up or implementation (McGill 1994). Nevertheless, there is consensus that as long as people agree on the problem and the objectives, solutions will fall into place (Queen's 1991, 3) Such optimism is to be admired, but may be misplaced; nevertheless, consensus is growing around proposed solutions to improve minority-university relations.

Response: REactive and PROactive

Post-secondary institutions have conceded the ineffectiveness of ad-hoc responses to racist incidents. Impromptu solutions are prone to magnify tensions, rather than dampen hostilities. The consequences can be fatal, notably in situations where the administration is accused of foot-dragging or is ineffective in censuring those accused of racism. Convention dictates that reaction by senior administration must be incisive and immediate. Indecisiveness may invoke additional grievances or media-monitored hostilities, in some cases to the point of paralyzing an entire campus (Stern 1992). Failure to act quickly toward zero tolerance can escalate a crisis by fostering an impression that antiracism has less priority than pandering to contented alumni. To avoid either chaos or institutional paralysis, two types of response mechanism have been evolved (Stern 1992).

First and foremost are *reactive* strategies that concentrate on crisis management through damage control and conflict resolution. Rules and procedures are put in place to deal with racist incidents as expeditiously as possible for preservation of campus peace and order. Reactive response plans consist of rehearsed contingency measures about what to do in an emergency, and who should do it. Formal mechanisms are instituted to ensure open lines of communication and grievance resolution. Resource persons are appointed to provide advisory and consultative services for students in need. Recruitment of committee members from a cross-section of the campus may assist in planning policy and procedures for worst case scenarios. As a last resort, disciplinary codes are implemented to punish offenders and deter would-be offenders.

The second type of response consists of *proactive* measures for prevention and problem-solving. Universities across the country have conducted research and drawn up plans to identify and solve the problem (Gray 1993). Formal positions have been instituted such as Race Relations Office or Human Rights Committee as a means of grievance resolution or conflict mediation. In conjunction with these support committees are formalized mission statements that denounce campus racism. Among the universities and colleges to examine their environments for racism are: Dalhousie, Ryerson, Queen's, Simon Fraser, the University of Western Ontario, and the universities of Guelph, Windsor, Winnipeg, and Victoria. For the most part, the recommendations (see "Recommendations for Improving Race Relations on Campus") from these reports tend to follow a similar script by focusing on proposals related to policy, offices, committees, admissions, hiring and rewards, equity measures, and complaint procedures (Queen's 1991, UWO 1993, McGill 1994, O'Neill and Yelaha 1994).

Recommendations for Improving Race Relations on Campus

(a) Facilitate the participation of members from under-represented groups at institutional levels of decision-making. Foster equity in terms of recruitment and hiring, in addition to appointment, promotion, and tenure. Review all procedures, policies, and practices to ensure they are free of systemic bias. Indicate that those in positions of authority are answerable for failure to implement race-relations programs, or improve employment opportunities that are exempt from inappropriate barriers.

(b) Encourage the entry of aboriginal and minority students through more flexible admission requirements and removal of hidden barriers in the recruitment process. Institute minority-hiring goals within certain time frames for improving employment equity opportunities at the level of minority representation, access, and equitable treatment.

(c) Include non-Eurocentric perspectives and minority concerns across the entire post-secondary spectrum, from governing bodies to classrooms, curricula, resource centres and libraries, ethics, and research. Accommodate minority religious observance with scheduling demands. Construct minority-friendly student and support services as well as a classroom climate consistent with Canada's multicultural principles.

(d) Investigate complaints. Reduce incidents of discrimination and racism on campus by dealing firmly with violations through consultation or counselling in addition to formal or informal resolution. Recommend corrective action. Ensure persons in authority assume responsibility, and are accountable for actions that violate the spirit of antiracist initiatives.

(e) Foster a supportive university climate for work and study that is free of discrimination and racial harassment. Introduce race relations awareness education for all university members. Provide skills training programs that assist in handling or preventing racial problems. Pursue positive community relations.

(f) Design workshops to assist departments in promoting an environment free of discrimination or harassment. Establish appropriate procedures for implementation of race relations programs. Publicize an awareness of complaint procedures and disciplinary channels that are universally accessible, free of reprisals from peers or authority, and complainant-friendly without discrediting due process.

Universities appear to be moving in the right direction. Policy and mission statements are increasingly commonplace — nearly twenty documents were in place by late 1993 (Gray 1993) — with a broad array of chairs, committees, advisors, and offices for advising, consulting, monitoring, recommending, and initiating disciplinary action. The scope of these offices is varied: Some prefer a general harassment or nondiscriminatory model (OISE, Victoria, and Simon Fraser); others a human rights and/or ethical behaviour format (Alberta, Waterloo); still others a solely antiracism and race relations format (York, Toronto, and UWO); and yet still others an equity and proactivity format (Queen's) (Gray 1993, McGill 1994). Even stand-alone initiatives, such as the University of Guelph's Race Relations Office are integrated into a more comprehensive human rights program. All share certain outlooks in common; namely, a desire to uphold the right for all members of the university community to study or work in an environment free of discrimination or harassment. Most are also convinced of the need to educate students and staff about racism — its causes and consequences as well as manifestations and solutions (CAUT 1994).

Admittedly, the effectiveness of these offices and policies is open to conjecture: Chesler and Crowfoot (1989, 42) concede that effectiveness depends on their location within the academic structure. Access to resources is no less critical, as Chesler and Crowfoot observe in "How Effective Is the Human Rights Program?"

How Effective Is the Human Rights Program?

> If its creation is not reflected in the mission or goal statement of the university we understand it as an "add on" rather than a basic change in the organization's direction. If it is a staff office/position rather than a line office/position we understand that there is little authority or power connected with it. If it is located solely in the central administration and not also represented in each sub-unit of the system we know it is likely to be isolated from the places where critical decisions are implemented. If it is charged with dealing with social relationships and not with pedagogical and curricular change we understand it strikes at the margin but not at the heart of the academic enterprise. If it cannot influence (through incentives) the institution's research program and faculty review and promotion processes we understand it will not carry significant intellectual power. And its students (especially students of colour) are not invited in its formation staffing and ongoing functioning we understand it will unlikely to reflect their unique experiences of racism in the university and their visions of how things might be different (Chesler and Crowfoot 1989, 42).

There are additional risks; the establishment of offices may help individual victims, but it also increases the chances of psychologizing racism, rather than galvanizing support against the systemic, but asymmetrical, power relations in society that are reproduced in the ivory towers (Carniol 1991, Hick and Santos 1992, also Bartolome 1994). In other words, despite a spate of administrative concessions and reforms, the question remains, as baffling as ever: How willing are universities to go the antiracist route, given its potential to provoke or partition?

Towards Antiracism

Two styles prevail in accommodating diversity within schools: multicultural and/or antiracist (Fleras and Elliott 1992). Multicultural education refers to a philosophy for celebrating differences. It consists of activities or curricula that promote an awareness of diversity in terms of its intrinsic value to minorities and/or society at large (Ministry of Education and Training 1993). The aim of multicultural education is largely attitudinal, that is, to enhance sensitivity by improving knowledge about cultural differences. Strategies are varied, spanning the spectrum from "museum" approaches to immersion programs.

Antiracist education differs from multicultural education. Antiracism is a position that repudiates racism as a legitimate point of reference for debate within the academic agenda. By contrast, the term, nonracism "tolerates" racism as an optional perspective for analysis or point of debate (Queen's 1991). While nonracism is merely intolerant of racism in practice, antiracism seeks to actively eradicate racism through awareness, challenge, and confrontation. Antiracism is concerned with the identification and removal of discriminatory barriers, both personal or systemic, as a basis for redefining minority-majority relations. According to the antiracist platform, minority underachievement is not caused by cultural differences, nor will cross-cultural understanding contribute to any fundamental change. The behavioural and structural components of racial inequality are emphasized instead for improving minority status. Particular attention is devoted to the power and privileges that sustain racism through institutional policies, practices, and procedures (Ministry of Education and Training 1993). Figure 4.2 compares multicultural education and antiracist education.

Multicultural and Antiracist Education: Comparisons and Contrasts

Two styles of antiracist strategy can be discerned: one is directed at modifying individual behaviour, the other at the removal of discriminatory structural barriers through institutional reform.

Personal

"Personal" antiracism concentrates on behaviour modification through education and training. Ideally, all members of the university, from students to staff, should be enrolled in intergroup training workshops. Race-relations workshops for incoming students are proposed as part of their orientation. Faculty and administration, as well as support staff, are expected to receive ongoing training as part of their condition for permanent employment (Stern 1992). The content under these educational modules can vary. At a minimum, however, all initiatives must begin with the notion that "race matters." While most concur that minorities are disadvantaged, few understand the advantages of white privilege as the standard and ideal (McIntosh 1988). Fewer still can appreciate how white privilege actively contributes to minority disadvantage. The emphasis is on how people interpret their realities in different ways, with the result that

FIGURE 4.2

Multicultural and Antiracist Education: Comparisons and Contrasts

	Multicultural Education	Antiracist Education
Focus	Culture	Structure
Objective	Sensitivity	Removal of Discriminatory Barriers
Concern	Ethnocentrism	Systemic Racism
Scope	Ethnicity	Race
Outcome	Understanding Equality	Personal

no one perspective holds a monopoly on truth. Attention is devoted to the principle and practice of diversity as a legitimate component of Canadian society, with an equal right to compete for scarce resources without sacrificing their differences or experiencing put-downs. Finally, all individuals should be encouraged and empowered to take a stand when they encounter racism.

Institutional

The second set of antiracism strategies looks to dismantle the structural basis of campus inequality. The burden is shifted toward the systemic grounds of racism through removal of the discriminatory barriers. Selection and recruitment procedures as well as rules for promotion and reward are scrutinized for hidden bias to ensure an open and accessible campus. Values and practices that historically have propelled the ivory towers are monitored, but are irrelevant in a changing and diverse context. The concept of academic freedom is one such issue, as are notions related to Eurocentric curricula and blanket assessment routines for students of colour. University policies and programs are reassessed to ensure they not only reflect local demographics, but also encompass minority realities and values as legitimate components of the post-secondary enterprise (see Shenk 1994). These two-pronged antiracist initiatives sound plausible in theory; their implementation may be another story.

> If we want to stamp out racism on campus we had better understand university politics (Arthurs 1993, 7).

From the UN to Canada's Charter of Rights to Ontario's Human Rights Code, there is universal acceptance that individuals should be free of racial discrimination (McGill 1994). In theory, policies and procedures exist for shielding minorities from discrimination and racial harassment. Many concur with the principle of antiracism and employment equity as a step in the right direction. In practice, however, rhetoric often outstrips the reality. Such a discrepancy is not surprising: A topic as controversial and politically charged as reinventing the university is likely to attract its share of ambivalence or hypocrisy, if not outright hostility (Lyons and Farrell 1994). Antiracist initiatives have been denounced as irrelevant in the absence of empirical proof of a "problem." They have also been criticized as a misallocation of scarce resources, unnecessarily inflammatory or divisive, and unbecoming to a university enterprise. The concept of ethnocultural equity is equated with reverse discrimination because of its alleged preference for individuals on grounds other than merit, credentials, or open competition. Even proactive motives are suspect: An antiracist campaign may spring from motives for damage control or empire-building, rather than for compassion or justice. Similarly, policies and procedures may have been introduced primarily for staying one step ahead of various compliance laws. The absence of enforcement measures may also foster the impression of a commitment that is long on platitudes, but short on action or results.

Paradigm Clash

Discussions about racism and antiracism invariably lead to debate about post-secondary education and its relationship to society. Put simply, universities at present are experiencing a crisis of *identity* because of growing uncertainty over roles and responsibilities in a rapidly changing and increasingly diverse world (Price 1993). The very legitimacy of the post-secondary enterprise is threatened by mutually opposing forces. On one side are those who prefer the notion of the university as an ivory tower of intellectual repute, largely removed from the cultural upheavals on the outside. On the other side are those who prefer a refurbishing of the university to foster progressive change and advance minority causes. For the sake of argument, these positions divide into social action and higher learning.

Social Action

Adherents of social action argue that the mission of higher education should be overtly political, with objectives directed at nothing less than the transformation of society. Universities are portrayed as agents of progressive change, rather than intellectually neutral sites (Martin 1993). Learning for learning's sake is secondary to empowering students for social engagement and political struggles. The pursuit of self-esteem and identity politics is no less paramount, and accorded preferential status. Everything from curricula to teaching is channelled into the pursuit of radical egalitarianism, in large part by unmasking the tyranny of rational inquiry as socially constructed and political in its own right. The salience of race, class, and gender as a basis of knowledge is reinforced instead (Carty 1991). Cognitively binding standards of scholarship have been abandoned as irrelevant and immoral because of their positivist connotations. In the words of Chesler and Crowfoot (1989, 22):

> A particular (positivist) version of the scientific method has also come to dominate university life and the scientific curriculum — physical, biological, and social. In the search for the authority and expertise of universal principles grounded in empirically established facts, whole systems and their elements are subject to positivist and reductionist methods, whereby phenomena are taken apart into their constituent elements and then reconstructed. Distance and detachment is maintained between the knower and the (to be) known. Emotion or intuition or preference (now seen as bias), rather than being seen as potential rich and productive forces in human inquiry, are generally shunned and depreciated.

A different set of criteria are proposed instead as a basis for the collection and analysis of knowledge, namely, the advancement of minority causes. Abstracted empiricism, with its separation of object from subject as a preferred mode of inquiry, is rejected in favour of the subjective and the experiential as well as the intuitive or emotive (Berger 1993). This denial of objective knowledge as legitimate or apolitical is indeed subversive; it may scuttle careers by removing the intellectual props supporting higher education.

Higher Learning

Opposed to this position are those who uphold the traditional university's premise — uncovering the foundations and conditions of objective truth (Martin 1993). Institutions of higher learning are viewed as apolitical, neutral organizations whose primary purpose is to equip students with the knowledge and skills for diverse modes of rational inquiry (Martin 1993, Sleeter 1991, Mukherjee 1993). True scholarship is not political, in other words, and the study of Western civilization is not intended to promote a partisan agenda but to educate students through academic and cultural standards that flow from objectively determinable values or transcendent universal truths (McIntyre 1993).

The knowledge enterprise is constructed around a positivist ideology. The virtues of objectivity and detachment as a basis for universal scholarship supersede those of the personal or experiential. Even the social world is described and analyzed according to the logic and methods of natural science. This commitment to "instrumentally technocratic rationality" culminates in an empirical analytical method of inquiry based on quantifiable objective facts and neutral observation (Darden 1990, 6). Competing truth claims are sorted out by rationally organized process of knowledge, including: definition, collection, testing, organization and typology, verification, and argument and revision (or true until further notice) (Berger 1993). Figure 4.3 compares higher learning with social action.

Academic Freedom vs. Higher Learning/Social Action

The principle of academic freedom is central to the post-secondary enterprise. Other values pale by comparison, as the CAUT confirmed when it adopted its Policy Statement on Academic Freedom in 1977 (McGill 1994, 12-13):

> The common good of society depends upon the search for knowledge and its free exposition. Academic freedom in universities is essential to both these purposes in the teaching function of the university as well as in its scholarship and research...Academic members of the community are entitled, regardless of prescribed doctrine, to freedom in carrying out research and in publishing the results thereof, freedom of teaching and of discussion...in a manner consistent with the scholarly obligation to base research and teaching on an honest search for knowledge."

For many, the centrality of academic freedom as a foundation principle is beyond contention (Berger 1993). A capacity to pursue impartial truth and value free knowledge without fear of reprisals is seriously compromised without guarantees of noninter-

FIGURE 4.3

Perspectives on Post-Secondary Education

	Higher Learning	Social Action
Mission	Intellectual	Political
Mandate	Objective Knowledge	Social Change/Transformation
Style	Value Free	Value Laden
Objective	Truth	Egalitarianism

ference by intruders or do-gooders. Certain restrictions apply, of course: academic freedom does not extend to persons but to the nature of things they do (study, research, teach, and debate) — subject to commonly accepted scholarly standards (Waterloo 1990, 1). Nevertheless any moves to "muzzle" (de Toro 1994, 15) are fiercely resisted as a threat to academic freedom and institutional autonomy. Rightly or wrongly, academics bristle at being told what to do, particularly in matters related to social equity or social engineering — as demonstrated by the recent uproar over the Ontario's government's proposed "Framework Policy Regarding the Prevention of Harassment and Discrimination in Ontario Universities" (CAUT 1994). The formation of the Society for Academic Freedom and Scholarship, with nearly 300 members from across Canada, endorses the right of faculty to conduct classes or to do research as they choose, and to speak freely on or off campus (Granatstein 1994).

The philosophical underpinnings of higher academe are now being contested. Transformationists criticize the principle of academic freedom as a self-serving excuse to tolerate eccentricity or the right to offend — even when results are fatal (Wolf 1994). Whereas academic freedom may once have been rooted in ideology (content), its boundaries have shifted to a personal level (conduct). On too many occasions academics hide behind academic freedom as a smoke screen to defend practices that have little in common with academic issues (McGill 1994). This freedom of expression can also be manipulated to silence or scorn minorities who dare challenge the preferred academic canon. In some cases, these slurs and put-downs are flagrant and deliberate; in others, they are inadvertent and unconscious, yet no less powerful in impact.

Reaction to antiracism can be couched in arguments that correlate with responses to academic freedom (Drakich et al. 1994). Opponents appear to be polarized: On one side, antiracist initiatives are viewed as restrictive of free expression; on the other, unfettered freedom can inflame racism. Yet, debating this issue by standing firmly on one side or other is unnecessarily polarizing. Such a stance may improve the quest for clarity or certainty, but often at the expense of balance and compromise (Throne 1994). In the case of free expression, such freedoms are important. However, they cannot override human rights or condone the right to harass, intimidate, or interfere. Nor can they deny similar freedoms to others by creating environments inappropriate to work, study, or participation (Dalhousie 1989, Waterloo 1990, Queen's 1991). All freedoms carry responsibilities, in other words, and universities will eventually concede that academic freedoms neither exist in a vacuum nor prevail in a social utopia of perfect equality. Rather, they must be assessed against the realities of unequal *context* and *consequences* of actions that disempower or ostracize.

Overlapping Realities

This clash of paradigms is beginning to resonate throughout academic corridors. Institutions of higher education have accumulated a unique set of assumptions and practices related to the knowledge enterprise. As self-appointed repositories of cognitive rationality, universities tend to endorse reason and science, rather than race or gender, as a basis for knowledge or truth. This endorsement of the intellectual status quo, of course, is no less political than the transformationist's demand for change, only more implicitly so. To be sure, space is furnished for disagreement and skepticism as preconditions for intellectual discoveries. Yet, the boundaries of intellectual dissension, with its commitment to agree to disagree, are often restricted to conventional canons of normal science.

Universities and colleges are now confronted by the postmodernist paradox: They must preserve academic freedom without trampling on minority rights for inclusion in a racist-free environment (Drakich 1994). Post-secondary institutions are compelled to create environments in which people of colour can enjoy the freedom to study, teach, and conduct research, within the context of higher learning. Yet endorsement of antiracism must be reconciled with equally valid principles such as due process and academic freedom (Arthurs 1993). Efforts to reconcile mutually exclusive, yet seemingly valid, perspectives may compel a rethinking of the university enterprise. Instead of providing autonomous space for the calm cultivation of rational thought and analysis, as widely claimed, higher education is better viewed as a complex and complicated political system where policies on race relations shift from benign neglect to clumsy expediency, rather than from constructive logic or moral compassion (Arthurs 1993). Unless a balance can be found that combines the analytical with the subjective, the transformationists with the objectivists, the inclusionists with the elitists, then the resulting clash of opposing paradigms will signal the demise of the modern university as we know it (Berger 1993). Depending on one's political stripes, that scenario may be good, bad, or both.

Mainstreaming the Ivory Tower

As institutions of higher learning, universities are expected to comport themselves in an exemplary fashion. They are looked upon as bastions of enlightenment; yet many are saddled with the responsibility for spearheading progressive social change. Their mission and objectives related to teaching and research must somehow connect historical virtues with contemporary realities (Proceedings 1993). Whether the universities can meet this challenge without capitulating to conflicting demands will hinge on how effectively they re-examine contemporary roles and responsibilities.

Universities are increasingly committed to inclusiveness and equity, despite dwindling resources and anticipated resistance. Many have moved away from a position of exclusion — with its denial ("There's no problem here."), or resistance ("What do these people want?"), or tokenism ("What more do they want?") — to that of inclusion through acceptance of equity measures (Mukherjee 1993). Solutions have tended toward moderate reforms such as additional courses or sensitivity training, all of which provide a temporary departure from conventional norms, but do not disrupt institutional structures, curricular content, academic freedom, standards of merit, and hierarchies that shore up entrenched interests.

Evidence is mounting that minorities want institutional and meaningful inclusion, rather than token acceptance at the margins of higher learning (McIntyre 1993). Attempts to address campus racism through inclusiveness will require the cooperative efforts of all stakeholders — from president to custodian, from students to staff, from boardrooms to classrooms — by way of forums, presidential statements, and campus debate (Stern 1992). Responding to this challenge will entail both political will and financial muscle, at a time of fiscal restraint and minority assertiveness. It will demand personal courage for speaking out against racism in all its nuances. Compromise or commitment will be sorely tested in balancing the apparent clash between quality and equality, and freedom and inclusiveness. This restructuring process is not intended to fragment or needlessly diversify higher education. Rather, the aim is to create a post-secondary culture in which diversity can flourish as a legitimate component of the university system, without repudiating the principles that animate higher education and propel its mission (Arthurs 1993).

Toward Inclusiveness

The struggle for equity and inclusiveness has scored impressive victories along other fronts. Canadian universities and colleges have demonstrated a capacity to improve access and create opportunities for students and faculty with disabilities (Hill 1992). Many have heralded the provision of specialized support services, not as "special measures" or preferential treatment, but as "equivalent" measures for levelling out the playing field. A similar line of reasoning can be applied to university-minority relations. For what is at issue here is a recognition that people of colour confront equally disabling conditions with respect to access, participation, and outcome. The barriers are not physical to be sure, but social or cultural, yet no less real and inhibiting of life-chances. As is the case with other targeted minorities, the push for access and minority opportunity cannot be dismissed as a luxury or frivolous option. The competitive edge and financial security associated with university credentials in a restricted labour market has seen to that.

The issue of campus racism and antiracist universities raises a host of questions about the form and function of post-secondary education for the twenty-first century. A shared set of values and common culture would appear critical in addressing the identity crisis confronting contemporary higher education. Yet the question looms ever larger: Who will participate in redefining the role and responsibilities of post-secondary education, and whose interests will they serve (Banks 1992)? Inclusiveness is one key in the reconstruction process. Racism itself is a social and cultural phenomena, as well as a political and economic issue, and must be confronted accordingly, namely through creation of a political culture intolerant of exclusion or inequities (Arthurs 1993). Antiracism is not merely an add-on that can be compartmentalized or isolated, then dusted off for public relations or crisis intervention. Rather, the incorporation of antiracism as a philosophy and practice is potentially revolutionary, with its promise to radically redefine the entire university enterprise from teaching to tenure. Such a reinvention will prove formidable in a political environment, where diverse interests compete for scarce resources. Despite costs and disruptions, the benefits from this struggle will be worthwhile with respect to post-secondary institutions, both inclusive and equitable, in a world that is increasingly global in outlook and postmodernist in practice.

Conclusion

The main highlights in this chapter are: (a) Post-secondary institutions are experiencing a rethinking of conventional roles and responsibilities in respond to the demands of a changing and diverse world. Issues related to racism and antiracism are inseparable from the emergent crisis of identity at post-secondary levels. (b) Campus racism has not received the attention it deserves — partly because of inflated expectations about higher education as centres of reason and tolerance, and partly because of narrow-minded notions about racism. (c) Our understanding of ivory-tower racism is undermined by a lack of available data. Albeit meagre and restricted in application, several surveys suggest that direct racism against identifiable targets is infrequent. Racism on campus tends instead toward the systematic as it pertains to structure, function, and process. (d) The term campus racism is an omnibus category that incorporates prejudice (stereotypes and ethnocentrism), racial discrimination (polite, rednecked, institutional, and systemic), and harassment. Each of these may be a manifestation of racism; all, however, contribute to the perpetuation of the "business-as-usual" mentality. (e) Universities have responded to the challenges of campus racism by establishing a variety of policies, committees, fact-finding missions, and programs. Both reactive and proactive measures show promise in improving the social climate, but have also proven difficult to implement for political reasons. (f) Antiracist initiatives may furnish the key to a more inclusive and equitable university enterprise. Antiracism and multicultural education differ from each other in terms of assumptions, objectives, and outcomes. These differences are contentious, however, since antiracism threatens not only white privilege and power, but also the foundational premises of higher academe. (g) The contemporary crisis in higher education can be rephrased as a paradigm clash between advocates of higher learning versus those of social action. Debates over the pros and cons of academic freedom in an inclusive university provide a conceptual hook for sorting out conflicting issues. (h) The "mainstreaming" of diversity into the ivory towers will not materialize without a struggle. Nevertheless, such inclusion is no longer an option or luxury if post-secondary institutions hope to sustain their legitimacy in the face of increased diversity and globalizing changes.

Discussion Questions

1. Racism appears to be a problem of multidimensional proportions at post-secondary levels. Explain the nature of campus racism by looking at its properties and characteristics.
2. Universities have responded to the challenges of diversity and change through a series of measures, both reactive and proactive. Describe several of these initiatives, with particular emphasis on antiracist measures. Indicate why antiracist moves may not be warmly received in a conservative institution.
3. There is an identity crisis in higher education that reflects a certain degree of confusion over contemporary roles and modern responsibilities. Explain what is meant by this. Pay particular attention to the debate between social action versus higher learning perspectives as it relates to antiracism and academic freedom.

4. In terms of this article on ivory-tower racism, what is the problem with respect to post-secondary education; what are the proposed solutions; and what are the prospects for success in light of existing barriers?

Notes

1. Quoted in M. Fullan. 1991. *The New Meaning of Educational Change*. Toronto: OISE Press.

2. Robert Blauner. 1972. *Racial Oppression in America*. New York: Harper and Row. pp. 276-8.

References

Adam, Heribert. 1992. "Ethnicity, nationalism and the state." In *Beyond multicultural education: International perspectives*, ed. Kogila A. Moodley, 14-22. Calgary: Detsilig Enterprises.

Arthurs, Harry. 1992. Keynote Address. National symposium for university presidents on institutional strategies for race and ethnic relations at Canadian universities, 2-4 February, at Queen's University.

Banks, James A. 1992. "A curriculum for empowerment, action, and change." In *Beyond multicultural education. International perspectives*, ed. Kogila A. Moodley, 154-70. Calgary: Detsilig Enterprises.

Bannerji, Himani; Carter, Linda; Dehli, Keri; Heald, Susan; and McKenna. eds. 1991. "Introduction." In *Unsettling relations: The university as a site of feminist struggles*. Toronto: Women's Press.

Berger, Brigitte. 1993. Multiculturalism and the modern university. *Partisan Review*. 516-30.

Blauner, Robert. 1972. *Racial oppression in America*. NY: Harper & Row.

CAUT. 1994. CAUT calls on Ontario Gov't to withdraw "framework." *CAUT Bulletin ACPPU*. June.

Carniol, Ben. 1991. The way we respond can become an issue. Paper read at Remedies for Racism and Sexism Conference, University of Western Ontario, London.

Carty, Linda. 1991. "Black women in academia: A statement from the periphery." In *Unsettling relations: The university as a site of feminist struggles*, ed. Himani Bannerji et al. Toronto: Women's Press.

Chesler, Mark A., and Crowfoot, James. 1989. *Racism in higher education 1: An organizational analysis*. Program in Conflict Management Alternatives (PCMA) Working paper no. 21. November. Place of publication unknown.

Dalhousie. 1989. *Breaking barriers: Report of the task force on access for Blacks and Native Peoples*. September.

Darder, Antonia. 1990. *Culture and power in the classroom: A critical foundation for bicultural education*. Critical Studies in Education and Culture Series, ed. Henry A. Giroux and Paulo Freire. NY: Bergin & Garvey.

Dickman, Howard. 1993. *The imperiled academy*. Transaction Publishers.

de Toro, Fernando. 1994. Ontario's zero-tolerance policy or the end of academic freedom: Between the reign of intellectual terrorism and university cleansing. *CAUT Bulletin ACPPU*. June.

Elliott, J. L., and Fleras, A. 1991. *Unequal relations. An introduction to race and ethnic dynamics in Canada*. Scarborough: Prentice Hall Canada.

Exum, William H. 1980. Plus ca change...? Racism in higher education. Paper read at Annual Meetings of the American Psychological Association, 2-6 September. Toronto: OISE.

Fleras, A., and Elliott, J. L. 1992. *Multiculturalism in Canada: The challenge of diversity*. Scarborough: Nelson Canada.

Fleras, A. 1994. "Doing what is workable, necessary, and fair. Multiculturalism in Canada." In *Contemporary political issues*, ed. Mark Charlton and Paul Barker, 25-40. Scarborough: Nelson Canada.

———. 1993. "From culture to equality: Multiculturalism as ideology and policy." In *Social inequality in Canada*. 2d ed, ed. James Curtis, Edward Grab, and Neil Guppy, 330-52. Scarborough: Prentice Hall Canada.

———. 1991. "Beyond the mosaic. Racial minorities and the mass media in a multicultural society." In *Communications in Canadian society*, ed. Benjamin D. Singer, 344-67. Scarborough: Nelson Canada.

Gray, Kathy. 1993. *Racism policies. Memorandum to Canadian Universities Employment Equity Network.* September 10.

George Brown College. 1990. *Race and ethnic relations policy.* January.

Granatstein, J. L. 1994. Universities strangled by "PC" politicians. *Canadian Speeches: Issues of the Day*. July 2-8.

Hacker, Andrew. 1993. "Diversity" and its dangers. *New York Times Review of Books*, 21-5. October 7.

Hale, Sylvia. 1993. "Using the oppressor's language: A study of women and development." In *Human rights: Issues and trends*, ed. Abdul Lodhi and Russell McNeilly, 167-78. Toronto: Canadian Scholars Press.

Hayes-Bautista, David E. 1992. Academe can take the lead in binding together the residents of a multicultural society. *The Chronicle of Higher Education*. October 28.

Henry, Frances, and Tator, Carol. 1985. "Racism in Canada: Social myths and strategies for change." In *Ethnicity and ethnic relations in Canada*. 2d ed, ed. Rita M Bienvenue and Jay E. Goldstein, 321-35. Toronto: Butterworths.

Hill, Jennifer Leigh. 1992. Accessibility: students with disabilities in universities in Canada. *The Canadian Journal of Higher Education* 22 (1): 48-67.

Hughes, Robert. 1992. The fraying of America. *Time*. February 3.

Kanter, Rosabeth. 1977. *Men and women of the corporation*. NY: Vintage.

Kessler-Harris, Alice. 1992. Multiculturalism can strengthen, not undermine a common culture. *The Chronicle of Higher Education*. October 21.

Lyons, Christopher, and Farrell Mona. 1994. Teaching tolerance. *McGill Journal of Education* 29 (1): 5-14.

Martin, Jerry. 1993. The postmodern argument considered. *Partisan Review*: 638-46.

McGill University. 1994. *Anti-racism and race relations.* Prepared by Monique Shebbeare. McGill's Equity Office. July.

McIntosh, Peggy. 1988. *White privilege and male privilege: A personal account of coming to see correspondences through work in women studies.* Working paper no. 189. MA: Wellesly College, Centre for Research on Women.

McIntyre, Sheila. 1993. Backlash against equality: The "tyranny" of the "politically correct." *McGill Law Journal/Revue de Droit de McGill.* 38 (1): 3-63.

Ministry of Education and Training. 1993. *Antiracism and ethnocultural equity in school boards. Guidelines for policy development and implementation.* Toronto.

Montgomery, Moses, and MacDonald, M. G. 1991. Human rights and race relations policy in Canadian universities and colleges. *International Education Magazine*. 22: 8-16.

Mukherjee, Alok. 1993. "Educational equity for racial minorities and the school: The role of community action." In *Human rights: Issues and trends*, ed. Abdul Lodhi and Russell McNeilly, 135-44. Toronto: Canadian Schools Press.

Ng, Roxanna. 1989. "Sexism, racism, nationalism." In *Race, class, gender: Bonds and barriers*, ed. Jess Vorst. Toronto and Winnipeg: Between the Lines and the Society for Socialist Studies.

Northfield, Stephen. 1993. No middle ground. *The London Free Press*. March 20.

O'Neill, Brian. J., and Yelaja, Shankar A. 1994. "Multiculturalism and postsecondary education." In *Ethnicity and culture in Canada: The research landscape*, ed. J. W. Berry and J. A. Laponce, 483-506. Toronto: Univ. of Toronto Press.

Ontario Council of Regents. 1992. *Report on harassment and discrimination in Ontario colleges of applied arts and technology.* May.

Ontario Federation of Students. 1991. *Whitewashed: Institutional racism in Ontario post-secondary education.* Toronto.

Price, Christopher. 1993. Schools of thought. *New Statesman and Society*. August 20.

Proceedings. 1992. National symposium for university presidents on institutional strategies for race and ethnic relations at Canadian universities. Report of a symposium, 2-4 February, Queen's University.

Queen's University. 1991. *Towards diversity and equity at Queen's: A strategy for change.* Final report of the principal's advisory committee on race relations. *Queen's Gazette Supplement.* April 8.

Ramcharan, Subhas; Chacko, James; and Baker, Roxanne. 1991. *An attitudinal study of visible minority students at the University of Windsor.* Windsor, Ontario.

Reitz, Jeffrey, and Breton Raymond. 1994. *The illusion of difference: Realities of ethnicity in Canada and the United States.* Toronto: C D Howe Institute.

Shenk, Margot. 1994. The role of librarians in the inclusive university. *CAUT Bulletin ACPPU.* June 12.

Sleeter, Christine E. 1991. *Empowerment through multicultural education.* Albany: SUNY Press.

Smith, Dorothy. 1979. Using the oppressor's language. *Resources for Feminist Research.* Special Publication no. 5: 10-8.

Smith, S. 1991. Report. Commission of inquiry on Canadian university education. Ottawa. Association of Universities and Colleges in Canada.

Smith, Bobbi Jo. 1992. Curbing racism on campus. *Campus Scene*: 12-5.

Stern, Kenneth S. 1992. Battling bigotry on campus. *USA Today Magazine.* 58-62. March.

University of Guelph. 1994. *Final report of the president's task force on anti-racism and race relations.* Summer.

University of Toronto. 1994. *First report of the race relations and antiracist initiative office.* April.

University of Western Ontario. 1993. Report of the race relations policy review committee. *Western News Supplement.* September 16.

———. 1989. *Survey of race relations at the University of Western Ontario.*

Waterloo. 1990. *University of Waterloo policy: Ethical behaviour.* June 5.

———. 1994. *Discrimination and harassment. A student's perspective: An educational package for students.* Lisa DuCharme. Office of Ethical Behaviour and Human Rights.

University of Windsor. 1993. Fourth annual report. July 1, 1992-June 30, 1993. *Ombudsperson and Race Relations Officer.* September 8.

Winkler, Karen J. 1992. Race, class, gender in American studies: "Mantra" or new conception of the field. *Chronicle of Higher Education.* November 25.

Wolfe, Morris. 1994. Dr. Fabricant's solution. *Saturday Night*, 11-8, 56-9. July/August.

York University. 1993. Fiscal Report, August 1992 to August 1993. *Centre for race and ethnic relations.*

———. 1986. *Report of the committee on race and ethnic relations.*

Zelmer, A., and Johnson, N. 1988. International students in higher education. *Canadian Journal of Higher Education.* 18 (3).

Zerbisias, Antonia. 1994. Media accused of inflaming conflicts of language and race. *Toronto Star.* May 30.

Further Reading

Generally speaking, little is available for students who want to read more about campus racism. Some of the best material is not readily accessible, although it may be obtained directly from the appropriate organization or agency. In particular, I recommend the various Task Force Reports on Race Relations and Anti-Racism such as those conducted at Queen's, Guelph, and McGill (see reference list for more details). Also recommended is

Subhas Ramcharan's study of minorities at the University of Windsor, as are the Proceedings from a National Symposium for University Presidents on Race and Ethnic Relations held at Queen's in 1992. Harry Arthur's keynote presentation alone is worth the cost, and should be mandatory reading for anyone connected to post-secondary schooling. The same ringing endorsement applies to Peggy McIntosh's article, *White Privilege, Male Privilege.*

In terms of published material, I endorse the article by Brian O'Neill and the late Shankar A. Yelaja, with its comprehensive look at multiculturalism and higher education. For those interested in a more radical perspective on multiculturalism and education in general, *Beyond Multicultural Education. International Perspectives*, edited by Kogila A. Moodley's: Calgary: Detsilig Enterprises 1992 is commendable; so too is Alok Mukherjee's fine article in *Human Rights: Issues and Trends* by Abdul Lohdi and Russell McNeilly, Toronto: Canadian Scholars Press 1993. Few should have difficulty accessing material on American campuses: Highly recommended is Brigitte Berger's excellent article in the *Partisan Review*.

PART II

Race, Identity, and Curriculum

INTRODUCTION

Educational literature has dealt with the race question in a slippery way. There are various omissions and generalizations. The race question has to bring forward challenging questions about unequal power relations; whose knowledge it is, and how it is transformed. This section addresses some of these questions. By looking at the curriculum, a broader explanation of how knowledge is defined and transmitted is examined. The discussion challenges the way the curriculum represents and constructs race. The blind spots and omissions are exposed by going beyond the traditional approaches, which treat minority failure as pathological. The essays in this section seek to take the discussion away from these approaches to one that questions unequal relations in schools and how minority/dominant relations are defined in educational settings and in society.

Chapter Five, by John Anchan and Lenore Holychuk, and Chapter Six, by Ingrid Johnston, look at the biases and stereotypes in the curriculum. Biased textbooks tend to misrepresent peoples and cultures. Anchan and Holychuk examine elements of the Alberta curriculum to highlight the changes that have been made to accommodate an antiracist education. They argue that the Alberta curriculum allows teachers the possibilities for addressing cultural diversity in a more objective way. However, to overcome xenophobic tendencies, textbooks and other curriculum materials must be examined critically for their content, which is just what Johnston does. She analyses literature texts for biases and her analysis indicates that students are not taught how to examine cultural and racial biases in what they read. Students are passive learners and they are not encouraged to engage critically the ideological assumptions they read in texts.

In Chapter Seven, Terrance Carson argues that the classroom has become international and it is now difficult to separate local issues from global ones. The school population reflects the cultural diversity that exists in Canada. However, racism is still a pressing concern. Immigrant and minority children are subjected to racial discrimination in schools. They live a very traumatic existence. Carson proposes that the international classroom can create possibilities for closer global understanding.

The chapters in this section are:

Chapter Five: Dealing with Racism and Cultural Diversity in the Curriculum (John P. Anchan and Lenore Holychuk)

Chapter Six: Point of View in Literary Texts: A Perspective on Unexamined Racist Ideologies in the High-School English Curriculum (Ingrid Johnston)

Chapter Seven: Racism and Reality in the International Classroom (Terrance Carson)

5

DEALING WITH RACIAL AND CULTURAL DIVERSITY IN THE CURRICULUM

John P. Anchan and Lenore Holychuk

> *Educational reformers commonly err by treating the system of schools as if it existed in a social vacuum.*[1]
>
> *S. Bowles and H. Gintis*
> Schooling in Capitalist America

Introduction

To an extent, previous textbooks have ignored the multicultural aspect of North America. Despite some claims that the arrival of immigrants to Canada from non-European countries is a recent phenomenon, the opposite is true. From the Chinese railroad workers, to the Black slaves escaping from the United States, not to mention the various autochthonous peoples, who have lived here long before the arrival of the white people, people of colour have long been a part of Canada. And yet, for a long time, textbooks and other media in the West have ignored or denied the existence of people of different ethnic backgrounds, races, and cultures. Some curriculum developers who are aware of this problem have attempted to include and recognize the presence of what Marx and Engels called "peoples without history" (Larrain 1989, 57).

Bias in Art Books

> Title of the first chapter in the twelfth edition of E.H. Gombrich's classic study *The Story of Art* 1972, 'Strange Beginnings; Prehistoric and Primitive Peoples.' Chinese artists from whom "we must not, of course, expect any portraits of real landscapes..."[2]

The role of the school as an agent of cultural transmission, of values and beliefs of the dominant culture, has been explicated through various dialectic discourses among educators. One criticism aimed at the hidden curriculum contends that biased textbooks tend to ignore or misrepresent people of other races and cultures. While textbooks have changed over time, these changes are still in evolution and teachers who are aware of such realities in life can go beyond the limitations of the prescribed curriculum in developing a program containing elements of antiracist teaching. This chapter will look at the Alberta Curriculum as a case study for its promising flexibility in allowing teachers to infuse elements of antiracist education in their classroom teaching. It will also be argued that a teacher who is culturally sensitized to issues of racial and cultural diversity can use the curriculum to his or her own advantage.

Unlike clearly defined objectives in a multicultural education in the school curriculum, the Alberta curriculum does not identify antiracist education as a mandated plan of action. Despite critics who suggest that such a curriculum lacks clear objectives and undermines the goals of an antiracist education, the Alberta curriculum does offer the freedom for conscious and willing teachers to engage in a language of possibility, which would include elements of an antiracist educational agenda. In describing the use of this language of possibility, we will offer examples from selections from children's literature. Constructivist theories of learning have helped to recently shape two programs of studies, Social Studies and Language Learning. While neither program describes an antiracist education, both offer opportunities for teachers and students to address issues related to racism.

Theoretical Underpinnings

According to Brazilian educator Paolo Freire, no education can be considered neutral or apolitical. Many critics have identified and deplored racism, prejudice, misconceptions, and stereotyping in books and other published materials. Bias in academic materials and school textbooks, including children's literature and learning materials, have also been subject to such criticism. As one writer notes, "Prejudice in print is not new...Much writing is candidly subjective...[and] there is no such thing as an unbiased book [*sic*]" (Klein 1985, 1). Despite these limitations, one can find the possibilities to transcend such constraints. By examining the school curriculum in Alberta, we will highlight the changes that have taken place over time and we will offer specific examples from selected materials to emphasize the opportunities available for teachers. While racist bias in school textbooks has not been altogether eliminated, the Alberta curriculum has recognized the changing nature of the Canadian population, and the curriculum has undergone considerable changes towards an antiracist education. Though multicultural education has developed into a recognizable area, elements of antiracist education in school curriculum are still in the process of being recognized and developed. Besides the attempts to eliminate ignorance and misconceptions about other cultures and groups of people, the migration of people from different cultures to Canada has caused educators to reconsider how they understand people who are different from them. Nevertheless, antiracist education remains relatively undiscussed. Racial diversity and cultural diversity have attracted common interests and yet, the stereotypes seen in textbooks and other media sources have not changed. The dualities we tend to define, such as civilized vs. uncivilized, developed vs. undeveloped, modern vs. primitive, rich vs. poor, believers vs. heathen, and us vs. them or other, have long been due for critical questioning. Textbooks that present races and cultures with this "otherness" are heavily laden with the liberal understanding of the exotic, unfamiliar, esoteric, mystical, and strange groups of people who live in "interesting" situations. The liberal-technocratic paradigm tends to be friendly and also paternalistic, in contrast to the transformative paradigm, which emphasizes critical analysis that explores the structural complexities of problems and issues. To overcome xenophobic tendencies, textbooks and other media sources must attempt to present the significance of cultural and racial diversities. Fear of the unknown and misconceptions about other races can manifest in the form of racism. Racism, in its various forms of expression, needs to be identified and dealt with. This leads us to the question — what is racism?

According to Klein (1985, 4), any book that "imprints a racist image on the reader's mind" could be considered racist in its approach. Benedict (1968, 98-99) defines racism as:

> The dogma that one ethnic group is condemned by Nature to hereditary inferiority and another group is destined to hereditary superiority. It is the dogma that the hope of civilization depends upon eliminating some races and keeping others pure. It is the dogma that one race has carried progress with it throughout human history and can alone ensure future progress...Like any belief which goes beyond scientific knowledge, it can be judged only by its fruits and by its votaries and its ulterior purposes...Racism, therefore, like any dogma that cannot be scientifically demonstrated, must be studied historically.

Bias in Children's Books

> The primary school reading support material *Here are the Brick Street Boys* (1974), ends with an explicit picture of the caricatured stereotype cannibals complete with bones through their noses, round a pot in which is simmering the hated football referee.
>
> Teachers have also taken strong exception to the *Bangers and Mash* series because of the illustrations of the black family. The publishers, Longmans, argue that all pictures are cartoons, and that the white families are caricatures also. But it is the manner in which the Blacks are caricatured that is racist: their lips are grotesquely thickened and their noses spread virtually from ear to ear. Cartoons, like comics, by their very nature emphasize differences; once an element of ridicule is added, the resulting treatment of ethnic minorities is inevitably racist.[3]

From the "anthropo-sociologists" Broca, Lapouge, and Ammon, who carried out anthropometric measurements in the last half of the nineteenth century, to the "social engineers" of eugenics who derived motivation from social Darwinism ("survival of the fittest") that led to scientific racism, to the more recent "Final Solution," of Hitler, the existence of racism in one form or another has marred the history of humankind (Benedict 1968, 118-120). It is now well known that Charles Darwin's study evolved into the idea of biological determinism and in the 1880s, his cousin, Francis Galton, created the field of eugenics for the "improvement of the human race" (Selden 1988, 52). In the course of history, self-proclaimed intellectuals have made racist proclamations under the guise of academic research. These have filtred and manifested in their simplistic forms in school textbooks. And to include such misconceptions in the curriculum that constitutes a plan of experiences for the learner is immoral and heinous. Before discussing this topic further, a brief note on the usage of the word curriculum is necessary.

The Curriculum

The word curriculum has been used in a variety of ways. It has been used to mean (Hass and Parkay 1993, 2):

- a school's written courses of study and other curriculum materials;
- the subject matter taught to the students;
- the courses offered in a school; [and]
- the planned experiences of the learners under the guidance of the school .

The word curriculum has its root in the Latin word *currere*, and its study involves the "investigation of the nature of the individual experience of the public" (Pinar 1975, 400). What is the importance of curriculum in the process of transaction of learning? It has been argued that "those who control the curriculum also control most of the society's institutions and utilize the curriculum to reflect their social and cultural reality...Aspects of that reality include the rational, historical, political, and cultural bases for that social control [*sic*]" (Collins 1993, 201). And the cultural reality of those in power might be, as is most often the case, subject to a personal reality that does not represent the reality that the powerless perceive. For example, the idea that racism is a validated scientific concept based on rationality can be presented as a part of objective knowledge. As Klein (1985, 90) notes, "Science is taught as being objective, neutral and value free. Yet, because science developed in the West at a time when racism was entrenched in society, it upholds that racism within the discipline." Thus, teachers, curriculum developers, publishers, children, and parents have to remind themselves that textbooks are not neutral or value free. To understand the experience of the public, the curriculum developer has to be aware of assumptions and personal biases. As Castnell and Pinar (1993, 6) note, the educator has to remember that, "Knowledge is rarely politically neutral or disinterested. School knowledge communicates — not always explicitly, of course — assumptions regarding many features of human life. Moreover, it communicates that which we choose to remember about our past and what we choose to believe about the present."

The curriculum by itself does not have an influence on how one understands ideas and develops attitudes and beliefs. The notion of the hidden curriculum has been explored by many theorists, but besides the importance of what is being taught, the influence of a number of other factors cannot be denied. As Apple (1985, 150) observes, "The view that [textbooks] reflect an ideology of dominant groups in society may be too mechanistic and simplistic, since the text, as well as other cultural products, is a result of complex interactions mediated by economics and social structure."

Yet, what is being taught and how it is being taught, are important considerations for an educator. A decontextualized, superficial, and uncritical curriculum can only damage the principles of an education that is unbiased. The curriculum is only effective if it allows the teacher the flexibility and opportunity to provide a language of possibility. An effective teacher is aware of the so-called hidden agenda in a hidden curriculum and circumvents weak elements contained in such a curriculum. A curriculum that defies flexibility does not provide the teacher opportunities to innovate. Criticizing such curricula, Aoki (1992, 18) notes that, "We are less naive today. But still we see about us efforts that place teaching in a gray box, if not a black box, wherein teachers are mere facilitators to teaching built into programmed learning packages. These are teacher-proof packages wherein the preference is for noncontamination by teachers' presence. This is akin to a technological understanding of teaching whose logical outcome is the robotization of teaching: schools in the image of Japanese automobile factories, heaven forbid!"

Besides developing curriculum, choosing textbooks and the way teachers improvise on what is available become important decision-making processes in an antiracist education. In choosing textbooks, one must, "Avoid books which equate the white man with 'civilization,' those with philanthropical approaches to other people, or which reduce *all* non-western societies to the exotic, the primitive or the quaint" (Klein 1985, 17-8). To achieve the goals and objectives of an antiracist educational process, a sensitive teacher would be aware of the limitations and possibilities of using a given resource book.

The Antiracist Curriculum

What does an antiracist education curriculum look like? In an antiracist education curriculum, the attempt is to focus on eliminating racial intolerance, racial injustice, and racial inequality. Besides avoiding ethnic and race stereotyping, textbooks have to address issues such as social stratification and equality of opportunity. The antiracist curriculum does not only enable the teacher to address such vital issues but provides opportunities to empower students of diverse cultures by recognizing their languages, histories, and existence. Describing such an antiracist curriculum, Swartz (1988, 6) notes, "A curriculum which values diverse cultures in an equitable way is self-affirming...It makes a statement to students about the importance of their present and future roles as participants and contributors to society." In containing a more accurate representation of minority groups, an "inclusive curriculum" establishes a greater understanding and awareness of diverse cultures. Such a curriculum would recognize what Foucault calls the "subjugated knowledges" of the minorities and "resurrect these subjugated knowledges" (Welch 1985, 25). The history that has been "buried or disguised" and knowledges that have been qualified as inferior to the dominant definitions of scientificity, knowledges regarded as primitive by mainstream intellectuals, must be allowed the right and freedom to express themselves (Foucault 1980, 82-3). This resurrection of buried history and knowledges, and the expression of silent voices is necessary in a language of possibility. The lack of prescriptive rigidity makes the Alberta curriculum more flexible and hence provides an opportunity for innovative and sensitive teachers to include issues of racial concerns. Since the curriculum offers this flexibility, it is possible for teachers to make their teaching inclusive and antiracist in approach. We shall now explicate how this flexibility in a language of possibility has the promise to achieve the goals of an antiracist education.

A Language of Possibility

For those who believe learning is more than the prescription and acquisition of specified ideas, there exist opportunities within a flexible curriculum for discovering a language of possibility. As students and teacher act upon these opportunities, possibilities develop for meaningful and engaging learning to occur. This requires teachers and students to move past a literal understanding of the curriculum to a stance of meaning-making where learning is the result of dynamic connections developed between the curriculum and student life (Giroux 1988). Realizing these opportunities shapes the curriculum into a tool for exploring the issues of racism.

The Alberta Curriculum

In the Alberta curriculum, three important factors contribute to a language of possibility. These include the curriculum-development process itself, a lack of a prescriptive methodology, and in classrooms, the wide use of literature beyond what is recommended by Alberta Education (Program of Studies 1993). Curriculum development and implementation involves a variety of decisions that represent the values and points of view of many interest groups. As part of this process, curriculum reviews are taken periodically to specify areas for improvement and change. Teachers working both as project managers and curriculum writers provide the bulk of curriculum writing, receiving feedback from a variety of committees whose members represent a wide range of interests and backgrounds. As drafts of the programs of studies are created and rewritten, they are field-tested and/or validated by teaching in schools before final feedback and approval is sought from the Minister of Education. All this mediation takes place in a political, social, and economic atmosphere that claims varying degrees of interests in the knowledge, skills, and attitudes that students will learn in Alberta schools. This lack of a complete dominance by any one interest group is reflected in the curriculum process.

Another major influence within the curriculum development process in Alberta is the balance of power that exists between the dominant curriculum learning theories and the political, social, and economic interests. Constructivist theories of learning have recently shaped two of the programs of studies, Social Studies and Language Learning. Neither program describes an antiracist education, but they both offer opportunities for teachers and students to go beyond a mechanistic and narrow interpretation of the specified knowledge, skills, and attitudes, and connect these with issues related to racism. In each program, the introductory sections present a meaningful description about the nature of student learning within society in general. It describes students as problem-solvers who make sense of learning experiences while learning the skills (Program of Studies 1993, Language Learning 1991, Social Studies 1990). This premise of an active learner is a beginning point for teachers and students to interpret and implement these programs within a constructivist perspective.

A language of possibility also exists in the ways teachers and students interpret and implement the specified concepts within each program. Many of these specified concepts have the potential to be elaborated upon by exploring the different personal and cognitive understandings with the issues related to racism. For example, in a Grade 1 social studies topic entitled "My School," the issues related to racism can be introduced through the specified concept of respect by highlighting the ways different people in the school community show respect for each other, and by identifying alternative solutions for problems that others face within the community (Social Studies 1990). By including relevant examples of cultural and racial diversity, teachers and students begin to use these concepts to develop an awareness of racist issues within the shared and personal experiences. This experiential and conceptual knowledge is then further developed within a variety of contexts that challenge and extend the acquired understandings of both the specified concepts and racial issues (Reed 1993). For example, the specified concept of bilingualism from a Grade 4 social studies topic entitled "Alberta: A Comparative Study with Quebec," begins by developing an awareness of and respect for the prescribed cultural diversity. This understanding can be extended by including examples of conflict and/or confrontation that involve local concerns, or bilingual issues related to cultural and racial diversity. By enlarging the context of study for students, opportunities to link racial issues with the curriculum are more easily realized (Social Studies 1990). These brief descriptions illustrate how the inclusion of racist issues can invite teachers and students to work within and move beyond a multicultural curriculum and include the larger social world as a part of the meaning-making.

The constructivist perspective is further developed in the Language Learning Program of Studies. One of the principles of this program is that language learning is enhanced through interaction with others and with the learning environment, including vicarious experiences as shared through literature (Language Learning 1991). Awareness and understanding of issues associated with racism can be developed as students experience presentations of relevant literature selections. Specified concepts from the Program of Studies can direct and organize ways for students to think and use language in response to selected literature selections and racial issues. Examples of these concepts can be seen in the following.

- The ability to make associations and connections is essential to the understanding and communication of meaning.
- The ability to think analytically is necessary for critical reading, listening, and writing.
- The ability to synthesize is necessary to the understanding and retention of ideas and information.
- Learning is enhanced when learners assume responsibility for checking their growing understanding.
- Students grow as independent learners when they reflect on and evaluate their learning experiences. (Language Learning 1991)

By providing literature that supports cultural and racial diversity, issues related to racism can become part of the context of such learning. The language-learning concepts help to direct and extend this learning. These concepts are based on students' ability and willingness to use language and thought to make sense of their world while acquiring skills to better understand and shape this knowledge (Language Learning 1991). Through the language of possibility, teachers and students discuss their understandings and develop their critical and political thinking (Giroux 1988, Reed 1993). The actualization of the possibilities that arise from these opportunities provides teachers and students with more than one point of view to transform a complex issue or vicarious experience into the fabric of their own knowledge, understanding, and language.

The Approaches

Alberta Education's practice of mandating curriculum but not methodology is the second factor for developing a language of possibility for both teachers and students. Teachers are able to choose from a variety of accepted classroom approaches for implementing the Social Studies and Language Learning Programs of Studies (Program of Studies 1993). Common approaches, such as inquiry-based, interactive workshop, or literature-based, focus on teachers and students constructing meaning and knowledge as they develop understanding of the prescribed knowledge, skills, and attitudes.

In Alberta, the teacher is accountable for implementing the mandated curriculum but can choose which approach or approaches to take in organizing the curriculum learning. These two programs (Social Studies and Language Learning) provide an opportunity for teachers to choose a constructivist approach and to include issues related to racism and the role of conflict. To develop an understanding of these issues involves a growing awareness of the points of view that surround conflict. This leads to student activity that develops elements of critical thinking and learning, and to a change in the relations of power between students, and between students and teachers (Bishop 1992, Giroux 1988, Reed 1993). The teacher becomes more than a conveyor of information. Through such approaches everyone responds to experiences, collaborates as learners, dialogues together, uses reading, writing, and talking as learning tools, and participates in projects to extend and demonstrate their understanding. The language of possibility has its roots in a constructivist approach to learning that involves, shapes, and legitimizes both individual and group knowledge.

Literature Selections

A third factor shaping a language of possibility is the use of nonprescribed literature selections (Program of Studies 1993). Teachers can include a range of literature along with the recommended resources to implement the two programs and for developing an understanding of racial issues. As representations of lived experience, the use of story through selected picture books and novels helps teachers and students to explore specified concepts from the two programs and connect these to issues of racism. Through the meaningful context of a story, teachers and students can develop a more critical understanding of racial issues, and other related and equally valuable social experiences (Bishop 1992, Reed 1993).

Story can provide a universality to life themes and issues that touch and enlighten its participants, thus shaping a language of possibility. The power of story is found both in its ability to share information and in its invitation for others to make sense of experience. Through the sharing of literature, teachers and students develop awareness of the roles they and others play in life, and empathy for how humans ought to treat each other. The clarity of a story can cross many barriers, such as cultural experience, a time period, or a dialect. The strength of literature as a tool for learning is embedded in our shared cultural history. It has the transformative power to influence, shape and improve understanding (Bishop 1992, Giroux 1988, Rosenblatt 1978).

Teachers develop a language of possibility within the curriculum by selecting literature that either focuses on an appreciation of different cultures or explores an issue related to racism that is part of a common experience. For example, literature by an author like Michael Kusugak or author-illustrator Patricia Polacco is often used in Social Studies to highlight the specified concepts that deal with cultural similarities and differences. Kusugak shares personal experiences from his Inuit background by depicting a northern lifestyle. Polacco tells stories of her family as immigrants from Eastern Europe who maintain their rich heritage while becoming a part of a larger community. Literature selections such as *How Pizza Came to Our Town* by Dayal Kaur Khalsa, *The Lotus Seed* by Sherry Garland, and *Amazing Grace* by Mary Hoffman present a specific aspect of an issue related to racist and cultural diversity. These take place in imaginative and empathetic story contexts that serve as common experiences from which teachers and students can share and dialogue about different points of view (Reed 1993).

As teachers and students become more able to deal directly with issues related to racism, the selected literature presents a more explicit portrayal of related issues such as cultural differences, conflict, change, immigration, and social acceptance. Sensitivity to students' feelings and their ability to absorb and understand the issues guides the teacher's choice of a literature selection. The stories chosen most often offer a sense of resolution and a feeling of hope. These include selections like Paul Yee's *Tales from Gold Mountain: Stories of the Chinese in the New World*, Michelle Maria Surat's *Angel Child, Dragon Child*, and N. Sadiq's *Camels Can Make You Homesick.* These stories are about the experiences and feelings immigrants face in a new country (Bishop 1992, Reed 1993).

Literature that deals explicitly with racist issues is more strongly connected to the learning expectations found in the Program of Studies for students in the higher grades as they develop the knowledge, skills, and attitudes to make sense of differing points of view. Novels provide these students with a more intense opportunity to develop a deeper understanding of the complexity surrounding racism and how these differences can be acted upon. Novels such as *Maniac Magee* by Jerry Spinelli, *Number the Stars* by Lois Lowry, and *Naomi's Road* by Joy Kowaga develop these issues within three different worlds: a town divided between Blacks and whites, Denmark during the Nazi movement, and a Japanese-Canadian prison camp. Stories such as these portray a sensitive and balanced look at fear and hope, and destruction and the power of love as the forces of change shape and limit possibilities (Bishop 1992, Reed 1993).

Literature is part of the public sphere in which issues such as racism are mediated by various interest groups. The stories mentioned above and similar selections represent lived experiences that illustrate racial issues and share more than one point of view. Through story narrative, these literature selections are able to "talk" in an authentic voice about personal experiences regarding racial issues. It is this authenticity that invites the reader to engage personally in the issues, and through dialogue and reflection come away "knowing more" or "knowing differently" about our shared world (Bishop 1992, Giroux 1988, Reed 1993, Rosenblatt 1978).

Literature provides a powerful source of knowledge for teachers and students, and by purposely choosing literature selections to share in classrooms, the process for understanding racism has the opportunity to be legitimized as knowledge and to contribute towards a language of possibility.

Conclusion

An antiracist education curriculum is not the only vehicle for developing a knowledge and an understanding of the issues related to racial and cultural diversity. There are teachers who, as agents of change, implement the prescribed curriculum and move through its limitations looking for possibilities to include elements of an antiracist education. In Alberta, while antiracist education is not a mandated part of the curriculum, a language of possibility does exist. These possibilities occur because the elements of liberalism and constructivism are inherent in the Language Learning and Social Studies Programs of Studies. The choice of approaches for implementing these programs can be based in constructivism, and can include literature as a fundamental source of knowledge and experience. The use of literature is multifaceted, as it can personalize racial issues, provide a vicarious and/or safe experience, revisit a situation from several points of view, and help to mediate conflicting emotions. Literature is a form of legitimized knowledge that can link racial issues with the implementing of curriculum, and the personal experience of both teachers and students. This language of possibility exists for teachers who are both culturally sensitive and able to consciously mediate both the mandated and the hidden curriculum. These teachers view learning as the active reconstruction of personal and relevant life experiences, and use literature as a powerful vehicle to develop the life themes and issues of racism. Until the forces that shape the mandated curriculum are willing and able to formally address an antiracist education, this is one way for teachers to create a language of possibility in which teachers and students learn to appreciate and understand people that are different from themselves.

Discussion Questions

1. Authors often use literature to discuss relevant social issues. There is the message the author wishes to share with the reading audience, as well as a message each reader constructs in understanding the story. Choose a literature selection that includes an example of racial and cultural diversity. Think about the author's assumptions. Think about your response to the story. What potentials for developing awareness and understanding would there be in sharing this selection with others?
2. There is a demand in our schools to ban literature selections that appear to be racially and culturally offensive. At the same time, others feel it is a teacher's

responsibility to choose literature selections because he or she knows his or her students, the curriculum, and the school culture. Should a literature selection be banned if the racial diversity, cultural diversity, or both, are portrayed negatively? What constitutes a negative portrayal? Who will decide whether the portrayal is negative or not? Have you ever wondered about the validity of the cultural and racial content of a literature selection?

3. An antiracist education curriculum can focus on key concepts such as respect, or relevant issues like immigration, or both. What concepts or issues do you consider important enough to include in such a curriculum? Which concept or issue would you choose as a way of introducing this curriculum? Why? Look at a relevant curriculum, such as Social Studies, for key concepts, language, and activities, that give a teacher flexibility for including elements of antiracist education.
4. During your years in school, do you recall a memorable experience in which racial and cultural diversity were not respected? What were your thoughts and feelings? Who were involved? Could there have been another way of resolving this situation?

Notes

1. S. Bowles and H. Gintis. 1976. *Schooling in Capitalist America.* New York: Basic Books.
2. G. Klein. 1985. *Reading into Racism: Bias in Children's Literature and Learning Materials.* London: Routledge & Kegan Paul. pp. 75-6.
3. Ibid. p. 80.

References

Alberta Education. 1990. *Program of studies*, Social Studies. Edmonton, AB.

———. 1991. *Program of studies*, Language Learning. Edmonton, AB.

———. 1994. *Bibliography of learning and teaching resource to support cultural diversity.* Edmonton, AB.

Anyon, J. 1979. Ideology and United States history textbooks. *Harvard Educational Review* 49 (3): 361-86.

———. 1981. Social class and school knowledge. *Curriculum Inquiry* 11 (1): 3-42.

Aoki, T. 1992. "Layered voices of teaching: The uncannily correct and the elusively true." In *Understanding curriculum as phenomenological and deconstructed text*, ed. W. F. Pinar and W. M. Reynolds, 17-27. NY: Teachers College Press.

Apple, M. W. 1979. *Ideology and curriculum.* London: Routledge & Kegan Paul.

———. 1985. The culture and commerce of the textbook. *Journal of Curriculum Studies* 17 (2): 147-62.

Benedict, R. 1968. *Race: science and politics.* NY: The Viking Press.

Bishop, R. S. 1992. "Extending multicultural understanding." In *Invitation to read: More children's literature in the reading program*, ed. Bernice Cullinan, 80-91. Newark Delaware: International Reading Association.

Castenell, L. A., Jr., and Pinar, W. F., eds. 1993. *Understanding curriculum as racial text.* NY: SUNY Press.

Collins, R. L. 1993. "Responding to cultural diversity in our schools." In *Understanding curriculum as racial text*, ed. L. A. Castenell, Jr. and W. F. Pinar, 195-208. NY: SUNY Press.

Edmonton Public Schools. 1990. *Literature to support the social studies*. Edmonton, AB.

Foucault, M. 1980. *Two lectures*: Power/knowledge: Selected interviews and other writings. NY: Pantheon.

Giroux, H. A.; Penna, A. N.; and Pinar, W. F. 1981. *Curriculum and instruction.* CA: McCutchan.

Giroux, H. A. 1988. Literacy and pedagogy of voice and political empowerment. *Educational Theory* 38 (1): 61-75.

Hass, G., and Parkay, F. W. 1993. *Curriculum planning: A new approach.* Boston: Allyn & Bacon.

Klein, G. 1985. *Reading into racism: Bias in children's literature and learning materials.* London: Routledge.

Larrain, J. 1989. *Theories of development: Capitalism, colonialism and dependency.* Cambridge, UK: Polity Press.

McCarthy, C. 1988. Reconsidering liberal and radical perspectives on racial inequality in schooling: Making the case for nonsynchrony. *Harvard Educational Review* 58 (2): 265-79.

———. 1993. "Multicultural approaches to racial inequality in the United States." In *Understanding curriculum as racial text*, ed. L. A. Castenell, Jr. and W. F. Pinar, 225-46. NY: SUNY Press.

Pinar, W. F. 1975. "Currere: toward reconceptualization." In *Curriculum theorizing: The reconceptualists.*, ed. W. F. Pinar, 396-414. CA: McCutchan.

———. 1984. *Teaching the text.* Occasional paper no. 30. Department of Secondary Education, University of Alberta.

Pinar, W. F., ed. 1988. *Contemporary curriculum discourses*. AZ: Gorsuch Scarisbrick.

Pinar, W. F., and Reynolds, W. M., eds. 1992. *Understanding curriculum as phenomenological and deconstructed text.* NY: Teachers College Press.

Reed, C. A. 1994. *Children's literature, an antiracist education: A language planning project.*

Rosenblatt, L. n.d. *The Reader, the text, the poem: The transactional theory of the literacy work.* Portsmouth, NH: Heinemann.

Selden, S. 1988. "Biological determinism and the normal school curriculum: Helen Putnam and the NEA Committee on racial well-being, 1910-1922." In *Contemporary curriculum discourses*, ed. W. F. Pinar, 50-65. AZ: Gorsuch Scarisbrick.

Sharp, R., and Green, A. 1975. *Education and social control.* London: Routledge & Kegan Paul.

Swartz, E. 1988. *Multicultural curriculum development.* Rochester, NY: Rochester City School District.

Taubman, P. M. 1993. "Separate identities, separate lives: Diversity in the curriculum." In *Understanding curriculum as racial text*, ed. L. A. Castenell, Jr. and W. F. Pinar, 287-306. NY: SUNY Press.

Troyna, B., and Williams, J. 1986. *Racism, education and the state.* London: Croom Helm.

Welch, S. D. 1985. *Communities of resistance and solidarity.* Maryknoll, NY: Orbis Books.

Wexler, P. 1982. "Structure, text, and subject: A critical sociology of school knowledge." In *Cultural and economic reproduction in education*, ed. M. W. Apple, 275-303. London: Routledge & Kegan Paul.

Further Reading

There are several books that provide a good selection for children's literature. Some of these are:

Garland, S. 1993. *The lotus seed.* NY: Harcourt Brace & Company.

Hoffman, M. 1991. *Amazing grace.* NY: Scholastic.

Khalsa, D. K. 1989. *How pizza came to our town.* Toronto: Tundra.

Kogawa, J. 1986. *Naomi's road.* Toronto: Oxford Univ. Press.

Lowry, L. 1989. *Number the stars.* NY: Houghton Mifflin.

Sadiq, N. 1985. *Camels can make you homesick.* Toronto: Lorimer.

Spinelli, J. 1990. *Maniac magee.* NY: Harper Collins.

Surat, M. M. 1983. *Angel child, Dragon Child.* NY: Scholastic.

Yee, P. 1989. *Tales from gold mountain: Stories of the Chinese in the New World.* Vancouver: Douglas & McIntyre.

Author Notes

Alberta Curriculum is the general description of what students are to learn. In Alberta, this is defined in the Program of Studies.

Alberta Education is the provincial department responsible for curriculum development and evaluation.

The Program of Studies in Alberta is primarily a description of the expectations for student learning. The content focuses on what students are expected to know and be able to do across all the subject areas, and is organized according to subject areas.

The knowledge, skills, and attitudes are determined through the grade levels for each subject area. All students develop these specific learning expectations as they go through school.

Social Studies and Language Learning are two school subjects found in the Program of Studies. Social Studies assists students to acquire the basic knowledge, skills, and positive attitudes needed to be contributing members of society. Language Learning takes place within and across content areas, as students use language and the tools of language — reading, writing, and talking — to think and learn.

Specified concept is a term used in this article to generally describe the learning concepts outlined in the Program of Studies.

Inquiry-based, interactive workshop, and literature-based are examples of approaches teachers use in organizing the curriculum. For further information, refer to literature by Donald Graves, Lucy Calkins, Nancie Atwell, and Regie Routman.

6

POINT OF VIEW IN LITERARY TEXTS: A PERSPECTIVE ON UNEXAMINED RACIST IDEOLOGIES IN THE HIGH SCHOOL ENGLISH CURRICULUM

Ingrid Johnston

> *Can we not say that, when modern literature is brought into the classroom, the subject being taught is betrayed by the pedagogy of the subject? We have to ask ourselves whether in our day too much does not come within the purview of the academy. More and more, as the universities liberalize themselves, turn their beneficent imperialistic gaze upon what is called Life Itself, the feeling grows among our educated classes that little can be experienced unless it is validated by some established intellectual discipline.*[1]
>
> *L. Trilling*
>
> Race, Identity and Representation in Education

Introduction

No work of fiction can be free of ideological freight. Books express their author's personal ideologies, either consciously or unconsciously, openly or indirectly. As Hollindale (1992) reminds us, writers cannot hide their values. Even if these beliefs are passive and unexamined, the texture of language and story will reveal them and communicate them. Such values are usually taken for granted by the writers, and often by the society in which they live.

Students reading novels as part of their high school English curriculum will also take such unexamined, passive values for granted unless they are helped to notice them. I believe that the powers of reinforcement vested in such quiescent and unconscious ideology should not be underestimated. Canadian English teachers are beginning to acknowledge the changing demographics of our classrooms and the increasingly heterogeneous nature of our students; we need to consider not only *what* students read, but also *how* they read. I suggest that teachers can select texts situated within a variety of cultures, with varying points of view and diverse narrative voices, and then encourage students to begin to engage critically with the ideological assumptions of the texts they read.

The Power of Ideology...

> The power of ideology is inscribed within the words, the rule-systems, and codes which constitute the text... When a text is written, ideology works to make things more natural to write; when a text is read, it works to conceal struggles and repressions to force language into conveying only those meanings reinforced by the dominant forces of our society.[2]

What is Ideology?

John B. Thompson (1984) outlines two different senses of ideology. The first sense is a neutral conception, whereby writers assume that ideology provides members of a society with collectively shared values and norms. Such systems of belief or symbolic practices act as a sort of social cement. The second sense is linked to a process of sustaining asymmetrical relations of power and maintaining dominance. This critical conception of ideology has the more negative connotation that has been conveyed by the term through most of its history and is the one that Thompson uses. He defines ideology thus: "Ideology, broadly speaking, is *meaning in the service of power*," and he argues that to study ideology is to study the ways in which meaning serves to sustain relations of domination (1990, 7).

Ideology often assumes a narrative form; stories are told that justify the exercise of power by those who possess it. Stories contribute to the formation of the cultural imagination of the young by creating a network of patterns and templates through which we articulate our experience. Watkins (1992, 183) explains: "The stories we tell our children, the narratives we give them to make sense of cultural experience, constitute a kind of mapping, maps of meaning that enable our children to make sense of the world. They contribute to children's sense of identity that is simultaneously personal and social; narratives, we may say, shape the way children find a 'home' in the world."

What significance does such ideology have for our students? Do we care that the narratives students read equip them with forms of values and beliefs relevant to the general reproduction of the current social order? Or should we encourage students to look more skeptically upon a social force that constitutes their relations to a power structure through what Eagleton (1991) calls "affective, unconscious, mythical or symbolic dimensions of ideology?"

How Do Texts Teach?

Narrative texts are highly organized, structured discourses that may deliberately advocate particular social practices, or implicitly encode such practices. Texts may appear to promote a particular ideology while implicitly inscribing one or many others through a number of crucial discourse components, which include narrative voice, order of events and, perhaps most significantly, point of view.

We are all familiar with the overtly didactic book that purports to help children or teenagers to confront and deal with problems in their lives, or encourages them to behave in a particular exemplary manner. Most adolescent readers are able to resist such a deliberate form of ideology. However, books that are invested with invisible ideological propositions may be more powerful in their effects and more difficult to recognize. Such implicit authorial control can perhaps be best resisted by teaching students to recognize how conceptual and perceptual points of view are constructed in discourse. To understand the significance of such narrative strategies, we need to consider the books that we deem worthwhile offering to students in the classroom, and then look at how narrative strategies operate in these and other texts.

Teachers hope that reading literature will contribute towards a positive self-concept for all students, including those from minority groups, by eradicating notions of gender, racial, or class superiority. Recently, a number of teachers in Canada have attempted to offer students books that critically address tendencies to assume that the world is male, white, and middle class.

Issues of gender have been addressed with enthusiasm since the early 1980s. Priscilla Galloway's (1980, 2) study of the literature being taught in Ontario high schools concluded that women were absent both as authors and as important people in the literature being studied by high-school students. They were present either as victims or "only in relation to other people, as wives and mothers." This situation has improved in the past decade. Some of the most frequently taught literature in Canadian high schools today is written by women authors, including Alice Munro, Gabrielle Roy, Margaret Laurence, and the American writer Harper Lee. Many of the female characters in these texts, such as Hagar in Laurence's *The Stone Angel* and Morag in *The Diviners* are both strong and independent.

Efforts to consider issues of race have been less successful. Certainly, attempts are being made in elementary and junior high schools to introduce students to books that are situated within the culture of a social group that is not white. The success of such books as Eleanor Coerr's *Sadako and the Thousand Paper Cranes*, Jean Craighead George's *Julie of the Wolves*, and Barbara Smucker's *Underground to Canada* attest to this concern. Other novels on school recommended-reading lists, for example, Theodore Taylor's *The Cay* and Cam Hubert's *Dreamspeaker,* attempt to address concerns of racism, primarily through focalizing a narrative through white narrators, whose experiences shift their assumptions about another race or culture. Similar narrative strategies are evident also in fiction for older readers taught in schools; two such books, which I will consider in more detail later, are Harper Lee's novel *To Kill a Mockingbird* and Laurence's *The Diviners*.

All of these books are written by white authors. In all them, which are considered important texts both for their literary qualities and for their antiracist stance, the narrative is focalized through a white protagonist. Readers are encouraged to identify and to align themselves with the main character, through whom events in the story are seen. Readers are invited to share the narrator's view of the world and to subject themselves to the ideas of self constructed by the text. Reinforcing this textual subjection is the widely promoted pedagogical strategy of encouraging students to "lose themselves in a book" by engaging empathetically with the protagonist of the novel. Most readers hardly need this encouragement; we know that the books we enjoy the most are often the ones that engage our emotions the most convincingly. We suffer agonies of despair or soar to the heights of excitement in unison with the character with whom we have identified. It is precisely in this state, as Stephens (1992, 68) suggests, that we are most at risk of being manipulated by the text:

> In my view, the present habit of stressing reader-focussed approaches to text in combination with advocacy of identification with focalizers, inconsistent as this combination may be, is a dangerous ideological tool and pedagogically irresponsible. It fosters an illusion that readers are in control of the text whereas they are highly susceptible to the ideologies of the text, especially the unarticulated or implicit ideologies.

So what does Stephens recommend as an alternative? We know that it would be impossible to read imaginative fiction with any real sense of satisfaction without engaging our emotions and, to an extent, identifying with the protagonist, especially in a book with a first-person point of view. What Stephens suggests is a dual orientation, whereby readers become aware that their perceptions and attitudes are being conditioned as they read. Such a distancing strategy, while not guaranteeing freedom from conditioning, will help readers critically to question the narrative stance that they are being led to take.

When reading books that purport to be culturally diverse, Stephens (1993, 83) suggests that students can be encouraged to ask questions such as the following:

> Are cultures and experiences which are not those of a white middle class represented as inferior or ineffectual; do characters demonstrate subjectivity, or are they objects or even caricatures; does the book's language implicitly assume the superiority of a form of a "standard" English; and do illustrations adequately represent distinctive physical features, and avoid cultural stereotypes?

Ten Quick Ways to Analyze Children's Books for Sexism and Racism

> Young children are exposed to racist attitudes both in schools and out. These attitudes repeated over and over become accepted as reality over time. Children should be taught to detect stereotypes and myths. Here are ten guidelines that can be used to evaluate children's books for bias:

1. Check illustrations.

> ***Look for stereotypes.*** A stereotype is an oversimplified generalization about a particular group, race, or sex, which usually carries derogatory implications. For example, Native Americans are described as the naked savage or "primitive" craftsperson and his

"squaw." While you may not always find stereotypes in the blatant forms described, look for variations which in any way demean or ridicule characters because of their race or sex.

Look for tokenism. If there are minority characters in the illustrations, do they look just like whites except for being tinted or coloured in? Do all minority faces look stereotypically alike, or are they depicted as genuine individuals with distinctive features?

Who is doing what? Do the illustrations depict minorities in subservient and passive roles or in leadership and action roles? Are males the active "doers" and females the inactive observers?

2. Check the story line.

The liberation movements have led publishers to weed out many insulting passages, particularly from stories with Black themes and from books depicting female characters; however, racist and sexist attitudes still find expression in less obvious ways. These checklist suggests some of the subtle, covert forms of bias to watch for: standard for success; resolution of problems; and role of women.

3. Look at lifestyles.

Are people from the developing countries and their setting depicted in such a way that they contrast unfavourably with the unstated norm of white, middle class suburbia? If the minority group in question is depicted as "different," are negative value judgements implied? Are minorities depicted exclusively in ghettos, barrios, or migrant camps?

4. Weigh the relationships between people.

Do the whites in the story possess the power, take the leadership, and make the important decisions? Do minorities and females function in essentially supporting, subservient roles? How are family relationships depicted? In Black families, is the mother always dominant? In Latino families, are there always lots of children?

5. Note the heroes.

For many years, books showed only "safe" minority heroes — those who avoided serious conflict with the white establishment of their time. Minority groups today are insisting on the right to define their own heroes (of both sexes) based on their own concepts and struggles for justice. Ask the question: whose interests is a particular hero really serving? The interests of the hero's own people, or the interests of the white established group?

6. Consider the effects on a child's self-image.

Are norms established which limit any child's aspirations and self-concepts? What effect can it have on children from the developing countries to be continuously bombarded with images of the colour white as the ultimate in beauty, cleanliness, virtue, etc., and the colour black as evil, dirty, menacing, etc.? Does the book reinforce or counteract positive associations with the colour white and negative associations with the colour black?

7. Consider the author's/illustrator's background.

Analyze the biographical material on the jacket flap or the back of the book. If a story deals with a minority theme, what qualifies the author or illustrator to deal with the subject? If the author and illustrator are not members of the minority being written about, is there anything in their background that would specifically recommend them as the creators of this book?

8. Check the author's perspective.

No author can be entirely objective. All authors write from a cultural as well as from a personal context. Children's books in the past have traditionally come from authors who were white and who were members of the middle class. With any book in question, read carefully to determine whether the direction of the author's perspective substantially weakens or strengthens the value of the written work.

9. Watch for loaded words.

A word is loaded when it has offensive overtones. Examples of loaded adjectives (usually racist) are savage, primitive, conniving, lazy, superstitious, treacherous, wily, crafty, inscrutable, docile, and backward.

10. Look for the copyright date.

The copyright dates can be a clue as to how likely the book is to overtly racist or sexist. Some books appear as a result of certain events. Outdated books are also used to show that things have not changed a great deal.[3]

Who Sees? Who Tells: What Texts Offer?

Of course, we can never know exactly what happens when a reader reads. We assume a dialectical relationship between a reader and a text that will vary according to an enormous diversity of factors, including the context of the reading, the past experiences and reading history of the reader, and the reader's own cultural context. A work of fiction will offer a reader a number of interpretive positions made possible by particular features and narrative strategies of that text, but in literature as in life, we have to start from where the students are, in this case, with their own, often inarticulate, ideology. Hollindale (1992, 35) reminds us that, "Ideology is not something which is transferred to children as if they were empty receptacles. It is something which they already possess, having drawn it from a mass of experiences far more powerful than literature."

This is one reason why obviously didactic texts may have little effect on the students who read them. Such surface ideology speaks persuasively only to those already converted. For others, it leaves them with their own divergent ideology. Similarly, it would be naive to assume that a consciously antiracist text will effortlessly reform those readers whose racist ideologies are already well-established. In some instances, it may actually reinforce these readers' intransigent beliefs.

As teachers, if all we do in the classroom is to bring in texts that we consider promote the right message about racism and expect our students to absorb the lesson, we will be doomed to disappointment. As Britzman et al. (1993, 198) warn, "Simply presenting students with the effects of racism or sexism in imaginative fiction will not move them through stable borders of race, class and sexuality into some new 'inner truth' of an antiracist or anti-sexist knowledge already existing in the text."

Instead, prompted by an interrogation of textual strategies that influence the way we read and interpret texts, students can be helped to articulate and to challenge their own cultural values in the context of the classroom.

Such interrogation is particularly crucial in texts with reliable first-person narrators who situate readers in a subject position effectively identical with that of the narrator. Asking "Who sees?" and "Who tells?" when reading such texts, enables us to decide how much credence we, as readers, give to what the texts offer. These are the questions I wish to consider in relation to the two popular high-school literary texts mentioned earlier: Harper Lee's *To Kill a Mockingbird* and Margaret Laurence's *The Diviners.*

To Kill a Mockingbird: Enlightenment Assumptions

Harper Lee's novel has been a staple of the Grade 10 English curriculum in Canadian and American schools since the 1970s. Innumerable study guides have encouraged teachers to offer the novel to students with elaborate curriculum material and high praise for the novel's "serious themes, complex universal problems, and highly developed characters" (1983, 174). An early study guide summarizes the plot as follows (1967, 3):

> This recent Pulitzer Prize winner by Harper Lee tells the story of two children and their widower-father in a small Alabama town during the 1930s. Their father's defense of an innocent Negro makes a lasting impression upon both the children and all their neighbours.

This novel has been lauded as a profound meditation on a universal moral theme. Society, in this liberal humanist tradition, is reduced to an homogeneous grouping with the universal "we" eliminating all considerations of power, class, culture, and social order. Atticus, the altruistic white lawyer described in the 1967 guide saves the "innocent Negro" from unjust racist treatment. In this novel, Atticus is a fully described, complex human being. Tom Robinson, the unfortunate Black man, is described sympathetically but one-dimensionally. If we ask the crucial questions "Who sees?" and "Who tells?" in this novel, the answer to both is the white, middle-class, child-narrator Scout, whose perspective alternates between that of a young child and that of a mature adult reflecting on her experience. The novel is rich in imagery and language, but limited in its perspective. Black culture and experiences, although portrayed with compassion in the novel, are nevertheless represented, both deliberately and unconsciously, as ineffectual and inferior to those of the white middle-class protagonists.

The novel may indeed speak forcefully to those white students whose ideological assumptions are already attuned to the inequalities of a racist society. It will do little but confirm the beliefs of minority students that power in Western society is vested in the white middle class. Students reading the novel need to be made aware of the implicit ideological assumptions of race and hegemony contained in the text.

The Diviners: Laurence as Mediator of Race and Culture

Margaret Laurence is one of Canada's finest writers. Her major novels deal imaginatively with the complex lives and relationships of people from all classes and races. As a writer, she challenges the sex stereotyping so common in fiction by portraying women who are struggling to establish their own identities. In *The Diviners*, Morag, the central character, breaks out of a stifling relationship with her husband, Brooke, in two ways. She has a child with Jules Tonnerre, the Metis friend of her prairie youth, and she also maintains her independence as a writer. As a mature woman, Morag comes to accept the importance of her own rejected past in the small prairie town she hated, as well as the value of the "Tonnerre Tales" for Jules and for their daughter Pique. Morag, Jules, and Pique come to recognize not only the importance of a past to their pride as people, but the mixing of truth-of-fact and truth-of-imagination in creating and preserving the legends of the past.

The narrative voice of *The Diviners* is an interplay of the third person, with its implied objectivity, and the first person, with its implied subjectivity. But there is an immediacy about the third-person narrative that captures the illusion of Morag describing herself in the past as she develops into a writer. The focalizer of the novel is, at all times, the character of Morag herself.

Unlike the shadowy Black characters described by Harper Lee, Laurence's characters are all full-blown idiosyncratic people, many of whom achieve symbolic dimensions in the text: Christie, the scavenger and the first diviner of Morag's life; Royland, her counsellor and friend, who, with his gift for water divining, takes on the role of shaman; Jules, the angry and proud defender of his Metis people's past embodied in the character of Louis Riel; and Pique, the unsettled and uncertain teenager struggling to find her own place in the world between the cultures of her mother and her father. In this rich, epic novel, with its complex structure that contains many of the elements of heteroglossia Bakhtin (1981) describes, there remains the particular focus provided by the singular point of view.

In *The Diviners*, Laurence offers readers insight into the traditions and richness of the Metis culture, but the portrayal is still limited to the perspective of Morag, the white writer. As a marginalized character herself in the novel, Morag is empathetic to the experiences of the Metis people, but her viewpoint is of necessity one-directional.

To Compare and Contrast

No one, I believe, would accuse Laurence of cultural appropriation in writing a novel that affirms and illuminates the human spirit as powerfully as *The Diviners*. Students reading and discussing a book such as this in school may well begin to engage critically with issues of gender, class, and race raised in the text. However, a more profound understanding of the power of ideology embedded in point of view in literary texts, can, I suggest, be gained by looking comparatively at a number of texts written from different perspectives. As Gerald Graff (1992, 108) points out, "Contrast is fundamental to understanding, for no subject, idea, or text is an island. In order to become intelligible 'in itself,' it needs to be seen in relation to other subjects, ideas, and texts."

Acknowledging that culture is a debate, rather than a monologue, opens up possibilities for teachers to offer students a range of texts with different voices that provide a space for students to confront their own values and assumptions in a process of dialogue with each other and with their teacher. Patrick McGee (1993, 287) reinforces this idea, "English studies should no longer be the domain of a monological voice, but the field of open debate and dialogue between different voices, backgrounds and subjectivities."

What this means is not that we should stop teaching books such as *To Kill a Mockingbird* or *The Diviners* because the focalizers of these texts are white and European, but that we might consider offering them in conjunction with books written from other points of view.

An African-American Perspective

Mildred Taylor's novels of the Logan family are set in the American South of the 1930s and 1940s, and provide an admirable parallel to Harper Lee's novel *To Kill a Mockingbird*. In Taylor's novel *Roll of Thunder, Hear My Cry*, the depression era of the American South is seen through the eyes of a young, Black girl, nine-year old Cassie Logan. As the only Black land-owning family in the area, the Logans struggle to resist pressure from the white land-owner to sell their land. Taylor attempts to provide strong characterizations of both African-Americans and whites in the novel. Whereas Harlan Granger, the white land-owner and his friends are portrayed as prejudiced and cruel, Jeremy, the young white friend of the Logan family, is loyal and affectionate. Cassie and her brothers, although subjected to the injustices of living under white power, learn the value of maintaining human dignity in the face of oppression and remain loving and steadfast, but their friend T.J., embittered by his experiences, makes poor decisions that lead to tragic consequences.

In both this novel, and in Taylor's subsequent novels of the Logan Family, *Let the Circle Be Unbroken* and *The Road to Memphis*, the African-American writer offers an imaginative Black perspective on the human-rights issues of justice and respect that are focalized through a white protagonist in *To Kill a Mockingbird*. Individually, each of these novels can offer a worthwhile reading experience, but reading the two together in the classroom allows students an opportunity to engage both emphatically and critically with the varying points of view.

A Native-Canadian Perspective

Ruby Slipperjack's novel *Honour the Sun*, although lacking the complexity and narrative richness of Laurence's *The Diviners*, offers a sensitive and honest portrayal of an Ojibway girl growing up in a Northern Ontario Native community and her family. In many ways, this character's experiences complement those of Morag and Jules Tonnerre in the fictional Manawaka. Written in the form of a journal, the novel records the perceptions of the young narrator, nicknamed the Owl, from the summer of 1962, when she is ten, to the summer of 1968, when she returns to her village from residential school.

Seen through the young girl's eyes, the Native community is paradoxically nurturing and debilitating. The narrator's early happiness is ensured by the love, stability, and hard work of her widowed mother who struggles against the forces of violence and alcoholism in the community to safeguard her children's well-being. The novel emphasizes the security of family closeness and the strength of traditional Ojibway values while acknowledging the frustrations and destructive powers of poverty and lack of opportunities that played a part in leading the narrator's mother toward drink.

Reading a novel such as *Honour the Sun* in conjunction with *The Diviners* allows readers to engage more convincingly with viewpoints other than those of the white narrator with which most Western readers are familiar. Reading for comparison and contrast challenges readers to acknowledge that literary texts cannot be reduced to transparent expressions of ideology, either good or bad. Rather, they need to be seen as arenas of conflicting and often contradictory social values embedded within the varying contexts in which they are written and read.

Pedagogical Perspectives

Offering students novels with diverse narrative voices is a beginning place for acknowledging the plurality and heterogeneity of our world and the diverse nature of our students' backgrounds. For some students, simply reading these novels may lead to further reflections on racism and perhaps a sense of personal change; but for other students, with more deeply entrenched racist frames of reference, an isolated reading experience may not be enough to encourage them to ponder their own unexamined beliefs or to begin to understand racism in a social and historical context to which they themselves are inextricably connected.

What we hope to achieve as teachers is to offer students a supportive framework within which they may begin to question and challenge their own constructions of race.

As Mohan (1992, 30) suggests, we need to help students to read texts as "counter-narratives that challenge, interrupt, or undercut the regimes of knowledge" and encourage them to see the texts' potential for enabling a "critical consciousness of our implication in oppressive social arrangements." Minority voices that contest the idea of a monolithic Western voice need to be introduced in a dialogic and critical context that allows teachers and students to engage in genuine dialogue about the nature and meaning of knowledge and power and to consider how these create uneven relations of domination and subordination. Reading a variety of novels may challenge students to consider and discuss issues of race, class and power, while still allowing space for them to engage pleasurably with the texts.

Ideology, as Hollindale (1992, 37) explains, is not a political policy that can be changed, itemized, imposed, and legislated into reality. Instead, it is a climate of belief that is vague, holistic, pliant, and stable, and can only evolve. One possibility for teachers is to offer students books with varying points of view and to create the dialogical space for them to examine and clarify the ideology that is working in the texts. Reading can then become an active process in which readers try to make sense of the messages they receive, to relate to them, to share them with others, and to engage actively and critically in a process of self-formation and self-understanding.

Conclusion

Finding good books with varying points of view that will appeal to young readers can be particularly challenging for teachers who may be unfamiliar with a range of multicultural fiction. Good stories enthral and enrich readers by helping them to imagine the lives of others; such stories can break down barriers by allowing readers to know people as individuals in all their particularity. No one book can do it all or pretend to carry a whole ethnic group experience. School librarians are admirable resources for helping teachers to select good books for classroom reading. In addition, teachers can consult a variety of literary resources that recommend multicultural texts and include in their annotations considerations of literary quality, setting, characterization, themes, point of view, readability, and an examination of stereotyping and ideology. The following resources are particularly useful for school reading:

Miller-Lachman, Lyn. 1992. *Our family, our friends, our world: An annotated guide to significant multicultural books for children and teenagers*. New Province, NJ: R.R. Bourlier.

Rochman, Hazel. 1993. *Against borders: Promoting books for a multicultural world.* Chicago and London: American Library Association.

Discussion Questions

1. Select a novel with a first-person point of view that you have read in the past year. Try retelling the story from the perspective of one of the minor characters in the novel. Consider these questions: How does this different point of view change your understanding of the events of the novel? Does this different perspective offer new insights into any of the characters in the novel? Why do you think the writer chose to tell the story in the way he or she did?

2. All texts contain assumptions about race, class, and gender. Have you ever read a book with assumptions about a particular race or class, or males and females, with which you disagreed? Think about the reasons for your objections.
3. All writers are situated within a particular time and culture. Think about how these factors may influence their writing. Consider how a particular novel you have read is a "construction," rather than a "reflection," of reality.

Notes

1. L. Trilling. In *Race, Identity and Representation in Education.* Edited by C. McCarthy and W. Crichlow, 1993. London: Routledge. p. 15.
2. Gary Waller. 1986. *English Poetry of the Sixteenth Century.* London and New York: Longman. p. 10.
3. Louise Derman-Sparks and the A.B.C. Task Force. 1989. *Anti-Bias Curriculum. Tools for Empowering Young Children.* National Association for the Education of Young Children, Washington D.C., pp. 143-5. Adapted with permission from *Guideline for Selecting Bias-Free Textbooks and Storybooks.* Copyright 1980 by the Council on Interracial Books for Children.

References

Bakhtin, Mikhail, M. 1981. *The dialogic imagination: Four essays by M. M. Bakhtin,* ed. Michael Holquist, Austin: Univ. of Texas Press.

Britzman, Deborah P.; Santiago-Valles, Kelvin; Jimenez-Munoz, Gladys; and Lamash, Laura M. 1993. "Slips that show and tell: Fashioning multiculture as a problem of representation." In *Race, identity and representation in education,* ed. C. McCarthy and W. Crichlow, 188-200. New York and London: Routledge.

Coerr, Eleanor. 1977. *Sadako and the thousand paper cranes.* NY: Putnam.

Eagleton, Terry. 1991. *Ideology: An introduction.* London and New York: Verso.

George, Jean Craighead. 1972. *Julie of the wolves.* NY: Harper & Row.

Graff, Gerald. 1992. *Beyond the culture wars: How teaching the conflicts can revitalize American education.* New York and London: N.W. Norton & Co.

Hollindale, Peter. 1992. "Ideology and the children's book." In *Literature for children: Contemporary criticism*, ed. Peter Hunt, 19-40. London and New York: Routledge.

Hubert, Cam. 1989. *Dreamspeaker.* Toronto: General Paperbacks.

Laurence, Margaret. 1978. *The diviners.* Toronto: McClelland & Stewart.

———. 1961. *The stone angel.* Toronto: McClelland & Stewart.

Lee, Harper. 1960. *To kill a mockingbird.* NY: Little, Brown.

McGee, Patrick. 1993. "Decolonization and the curriculum of English." In *Race, identity and representation in education*, ed. C. McCarthy and W. Crichlow, 280-8. New York and London: Routledge.

Mohan, Rajeswari. Dodging the crossfire: Questions for postcolonial pedagogy. *College Literature: Teaching Postcolonial and Commonwealth Literatures.* Double Issue 19.3/20.1, 1992, 1993.

Slipperjack, Ruby. 1987. *Honour the sun.* Winnipeg: Pemmican Publications.

Smucker, Barbara. 1977. *Underground to Canada.* Toronto: Clarke, Irwin.

Stephens, John. 1992. *Language and ideology in children's fiction.* London and New York: Longman.

Taylor, Mildred. 1990. *The road to Memphis.* NY: Dial Books.

———. 1981. *Let the circle be unbroken.* NY: Dial Press.

———. 1976. *Roll of thunder, hear my cry.* NY: Dial Press.

Taylor, Theodore. 1969. *The cay.* NY: Doubleday.

Thompson, John B. 1990. *Ideology and modern culture: Critical and social theory in the era of mass communication.* Cambridge: Polity Press.

———. 1984. *Studies in the theory of ideology.* Cambridge: Polity Press.

To Kill a Mockingbird: Experiencing the novel. 1983. Curriculum Unit. The Center for Learning: Wm. C. Brown.

To Kill a Mockingbird Study Kit. 1967. Logan, Iowa: The Perfection Form Company.

Waller, Gary. 1986. *English poetry of the sixteenth century.* London and New York: Longman.

Watkins, Tony. 1992. "Cultural studies, new historicism and children's literature." In *Literature for children: contemporary criticism*, ed. Peter Hunt, 173-95. London and New York: Routledge.

Further Reading

Hayhoe, Michael, and Parker, Stephen. eds. 1990. *Reading and response.* Milton Keynes, Philadelphia: Open Univ. Press.

Johnson, Laura, and Smith, Sally. 1993. *Dealing with diversity through multicultural fiction: Library-Classroom Partnerships.* Chicago and London: American Library Association.

Naidoo, Beverley. 1992. *Through whose eyes? Exploring racism: Reader, text and context.* Stoke-on-Trent: Trentham Books.

Author Notes

I would like to thank Margaret Mackey and Rebecca Luce-Kapler for their helpful comments during the writing of this chapter.

7

RACISM AND REALITY IN THE INTERNATIONAL CLASSROOM

Terrance Carson

Whose school is it, anyway? (Gold and Miles)[1]

M. Fullan
The New Meaning of Educational Change

Introduction

Racism surely exists in Canadian schools, just as it does in Canadian society in general. Schools reflect the society in which they are located, and the potential for racism is no different in Canada than in any other country. These are two possible ways of responding to the reality of the internationalism that now characterizes our classrooms.

This chapter is about choosing to cultivate communities of diversity. Doing this depends upon an appreciation of how culturally diverse Canadian classrooms now are — the reality of the international classroom — and an appreciation that racism is always a possible way of responding to difference.

Racism Is Not Only About Race

Racism does not require much to get started. A person can be discriminated against for any number of reasons, skin colour, religion, ethnicity, sexual orientation, body shape, or place of origin. In fact, psychologists note that it is the minor differences that can loom largest in the imagination. What allows us to call it racism is that this discrimination is used as a justification for oppression. Thus, while we normally speak about racism as having to do with race, the dynamic of racism is really about how we use difference as a justification to oppress.

It's Their Depravity

> If you are robbing somebody, oppressing them, dictating their lives, it's a very rare person who can say: "Look, I'm a monster. I'm doing this for my own good." Even Himmler didn't say that.
>
> A standard technique of belief formation goes along with oppression, whether its throwing them in gas chambers or charging them

> too much at the corner store, or anything in between. The standard reaction is to say: "It's their depravity. That's why I'm doing it. Maybe I'm even doing them good."
>
> If it's their depravity, there's got to be something about them that makes them different from me. What's different about them will be whatever you can find.[2]
>
> **The Notion of Race and Racism**
>
> Many of us automatically think of the continued disadvantage and persecution wrought on people of colour by whites. However, the idea of race is not just about the colour of one's skin but also about ethnicity which takes into account physical features, language, religion, ideas of nation and culture. These are things people use to define themselves as a group. Often, when people refer to different races, they use now one criterion, now another. Academics are increasingly putting the word "race" in quotation marks to show that it is an ill-defined and misleading term.
>
> More clear is how the notion of race is used. Racism is about people from dominant groups exerting their power unjustly over others. The only justification they can offer for their behaviour is that they belong to a "superior" race.[3]

Thus, race is an ill-defined term, but racism is not. What makes the topic of racism vital for Canadian educators today is the changing composition of the classroom and the culture. We now confront differences every day in our schools, in our communities, and in the media. The encounter with difference is a fact of life. How these differences are encountered will determine if our newly internationalized classrooms will be the seedbeds of racism or the beginnings of communities of diversity.

Communities of Diversity: An Alternative to Racism

A community of diversity is one that draws its identity and strength from the many cultures that make up the contemporary classroom. This is an alternative to racism. It is a community that acknowledges difference in such a way that gives "the other" (the one who is different) her or his just due. This is not simply the opposite of racism. More than freedom from oppression, a community of diversity appreciates the importance of culture and difference and the contribution that these differences make in sustaining the community. The question is this: Can our internationalized classrooms become communities of diversity?

Working to develop communities of diversity does not deny the importance of combating racism. But care must be taken to not exclusively focus on antiracist education. Such a focus unavoidably positions teachers and schools as part of the problem. Rather than focusing on deficiencies, we need to recognize that teachers, students, and parents already have many of the pedagogical resources, but these can become submerged and subverted in various ways. We can develop communities of diversity by building upon these resources in such a way that respects teachers and students as the active and thoughtful participants in improving education and the quality of life in schools.

The Reality of the International Classroom

We can begin a description of the international classroom with a few generalizations. In most urban Canadian classrooms, the cultural and family backgrounds of the children can be quite different from those of their teachers. In Toronto, Vancouver, and Montreal, for example, increasing numbers of students have neither official language as their native tongue. These students and their families come from all over the world, from China and Vietnam, from Mexico and the Caribbean, from East Europe and the former Soviet Union, from the Middle East and the horn of Africa, and from India and Pakistan.

Probably the best way of describing the reality of the international classroom is with a concrete example. Alex Taylor Community School (see Chapter Nine) is a small, inner-city elementary school in Edmonton with about 160 children from kindergarten to Grade 6. Yet, these 160 children represent over twenty different ethnic groups. As one teacher put it "English as a Second Language (ESL) isn't just a program here, it's our normal practice. We expect to do it every day with every subject."

The children in the Grade 6 class at Alex Taylor show the settlement patterns of modern Canadian cities and reflect the ebb and flow of global conflict. There are Vietnamese boys and girls here who came as young children in the early 1980s. There are East Europeans who come with vivid memories of ethnic cleansing. There is a boy from El Salvador whose family arrived half-a-dozen years ago, having fled the civil war and the death squads in that troubled land. Also in this classroom are two Cree boys whose families moved into Edmonton from Northern Alberta hoping to find a better life in the city.

In Edmonton, more than one school child in eight is classified as an English-as-Second-Language student. But these statistics downplay the reality of the international classroom. Many children are first-generation Canadians whose parents do not speak English in the home and find the dominant culture strange. At home, there can be real tension between mainstream Canadian youth culture and the values and traditions held by the parents in the home.

The Failure of Educational Experts

The internationalization of Canadian classrooms has happened behind the backs of educational planners and teacher educators. Thus, teachers have been left to deal with this new reality with little assistance from organized programs or traditional sources of professional development. Nowhere is this more true than in university faculties of education. In teacher education, we have had a long standing habit of looking upward for theories to explain teaching, all the while ignoring the shifting ground we stand upon. So our usual practice has been to teach new teachers as if there were a seedbed of "normal students," while the culturally different child is regarded as an anomaly.

In a sense, much of traditional educational theory has been caught in a kind of "nowhere land," trying to use quantitative research to shape an image of the universal child and a universal teacher. This universal child and universal teacher come to inhabit the pages of our textbooks on learning theory, child development, and instructional methods. It is a model of "theory into practice." And in this model the theory always runs late, coming behind the actual conditions in schools. Student teachers remind us of this when they return to the university after their field experiences with tales of the incredible cultural diversity and learning differences they have encountered.

An even more damaging legacy of our teaching and research in faculties of education has been to propagate an habitual over-reliance on the authoritative voice of theory. In the process, classroom experience is devalued and teachers are discouraged from interpreting and acting in accordance with the realities that they live with daily. Had we been more attentive to the teachers, we would be more ready to see that cultural differences are not anomalies in most urban classrooms.

A Multi-Layered Understanding of Curriculum

Curriculum policies, too, have often been careless of the stubborn particulars of classroom life. Ted Aoki, a Canadian pioneer in rethinking curriculum studies, directs our attention to the problem of thinking of the curriculum as simply a document to direct teaching. He draws a distinction between the generalized curriculum-as-plan and the curriculum it is lived in the classroom.

> The province-wide voice of the curriculum-as-plan is necessarily abstract, but its rightful place is not in its primacy. It needs to be opened to allow a place for the curriculum-as-lived, because it is only when the teacher, having lived through the joys and struggles with the students, receives the curriculum-as-plan and interprets it so it makes sense in the classroom situation that it can shed its inertness and come alive.[4]

Aoki's distinction cautions us against mounting aggressive curriculum development projects as a way to bring about educational reforms. Teachers today are feeling the effects of a seemingly endless cycle of new programs that respond to problems. Particularly for secondary-school teachers and students, the curriculum-as-plan is increasingly directed towards standards and standardization that are reinforced and maintained by testing and rising post-secondary entrance requirements. Because it sets its sights firmly on educational outcomes, the curriculum-as-plan forgets that teaching is a pedagogical relationship. The plan is unconcerned with the hopes, joys, and frustrations that teachers and students experience inside classrooms.

It is important to consider that giving primacy to the curriculum-as-plan has, in large part, been responsible for the neglect of the ethnic and cultural diversity that exists within classrooms. Increased attention to regulation and standardization encourages us to regard differences as problems to be solved or aberrations to be ignored. The more powerful the plan, the greater the risk of dividing teachers' loyalties between the children as they are and idealized representations of teaching.

Signs of New Thinking in Curriculum and Teacher Education

Curriculum policies and teacher-education programs have been changing. The work of Jean Clandinin, Michael Connelly, and others on teachers' narratives have given a new prominence to stories of teaching. School-based action research is another promising direction. Action research is founded on the principle that teachers can create new understandings and new practices by their own efforts. Both teacher narrative and action research have proven to be fruitful places for collaboration between teachers and university-based educators.

Stories from the International Classroom

Stories provide insight into the possibilities that classrooms have for becoming communities of diversity. Many stories can be told from Alex Taylor Community School, which observes celebrations of the various cultures in its school community. From there we can hear stories about the Chinese New Year festival, or about how First-Nations students perform the Sweetgrass Ceremony on a regular basis. The person who witnesses the noise and the colour of the dragon dance, or who inhales the aroma of the sweetgrass cannot help but be drawn into the diverse cultures of that school.

Culture in the international classroom cannot be a museum piece, or a mere object of curiosity that is brought out periodically for purposes of display. Cultural traditions are understood as existing in the world as it is, responding to change while the traditions themselves are altered in this engagement. The story of the *Kinderwereld Atelier*, in Belgium is an example of such an engagement.

The Kinderwereld Atelier

> In an old warehouse in an industrial section of the busy European port city of Antwerp there is a "Children's World Workshop" that has been built and staffed by a group of teachers. It operates on a shoestring budget, inviting children from the local schools to share and experience some aspect of Belgium's relationship with the world.
>
> Entering from the street, the visitor is met by Bert de Wolf. Bert occupies a small, rather cramped office cum resource library. Bert explains that the *Atelier* has been established to help engage Belgian school children in questions of culture and economic development. He explains that there are three "worlds" in the Children's World Workshop. The worlds are Turkey, Peru, and Zaire. Each has both contemporary and historical links with Belgium: Turkey supplied many guest workers to Belgian industry in the 1960s, Belgian priests work as missionaries in the *barrios* of Lima, and Zaire is the former colony of the Belgian Congo.
>
> Bert then leads the visitor into the world of the Turkish experience. A group of twelve year old Antwerp school children have

> already travelled back in their imaginations to the coal fields of 1962. In a simulation they have "experienced" the overcrowded housing and the jeers of the Belgian paymaster at the mine site. But the money is good and now they have saved enough to go back to their Turkish homeland for a holiday.
>
> The students have now come to another room in the Centre which has been made into a simulated Turkish village. In the room there are corners representing a coffee house, a tobacco farm and a mosque. The students begin to tell of their mixed "experiences" in Belgium: the good pay, the racism, and their living conditions in a strange city that has customs different from theirs. During the course of this role play the visitor watches fascinated as to how these Flemish speaking children can become Turks. Suddenly one of these children goes to the "Mosque" and begins to pray. The others suddenly look at her with a newfound admiration. They had not realized before that their classmate was a Moslem of Turkish descent.

In the story of the *Kinderwereld Atelier*, the children's discovery of the cultural other in their midst is made by chance. It has come about in context of the pedagogical work of teachers who have decided to deal with a real question of culture and immigration in their community.

Making linkages between the global and the local at the classroom level is difficult. The "cultural other" often appears as a problem to be solved, rather than a person who embodies another possible history and a unique cultural experience. The cultural other as a problem is the underlying stance of traditional ESL programs. Both teacher and student come to see the educational problem as a question of deficit — the student is here because he or she lacks English. Both student and teacher realize that English is a necessity for success in jobs and further education, so they willingly co-operate to focus exclusively on correcting this language deficit. The second story from the international classroom is how an ESL teacher moves beyond a stance of the "cultural other as a problem."

The Story of Maria

> Maria has two faces, one for when she knows she is being seen and another for when she thinks she is anonymous. The second face prevails. Etched for eternity across her face are untold stories of horror in El Salvador. Her eyes look, not out the window, but through it, not at what lies across the street but what lies across time and space, beyond hope. Her body is tensed with that particular anger which has no listening target and thus never quite springs loose but rather hovers within her, intensifying the lines of anguish in the skin around the eyes, nose and mouth. When I speak to her, this mask of pain instantly gives way to a former face complete with wide smile, intelligent eyes and hopeful keenness. She listens, speaks and laughs and when you see this, here is a lovely person you want to know. But then, her

> eyes back on her writing, the mask of her past returns and I am locked out again, wondering if I really could handle knowing her. As long as I do not know, I cannot be responsible. As long as the words and pictures of the newspaper remain just that, words and pictures of far-away places, then I can remain comfortable a voyeur, clucking my tongue at man's stupidity and clinging gratefully and somewhat smugly to my own comfort and security. If, however, I were to choose to listen to Maria and she were to choose to tell me her story, could I remain distant from those events? Could I turn my face from her pain come evening, knowing that that which caused the pain is still happening and still affecting countless others like her who may, it they live, come to Canada, perhaps next year, or ten years from now? I am not sure I want to build that bridge. It feels like an uncomfortable place to go.[5]

Possibilities of deep and sustained linkages between the global and the local are hinted in this experience recounted by Virginia Sauvé. In this paper, carrying the provocative title of "Journeys and Bridges," she speaks of her work in a program for immigrant women. Sauve's own journey, after 23 years experience of teaching ESL, has brought her to the realization of the importance of understanding what it is like for the other to be an immigrant woman. Encountering the other person authentically as "the other" is a process of "bridge building." She implies that this begins when we start to see our students as they are in the moment and not as we would like them to be. For her, as a teacher, this is not a comfortable place. But should comfort be our primary goal? Listening to Maria's story hits upon a profound and yet simple truth that the other person is "us." This produces a kind of global consciousness that is no longer abstract, one that really does see the global in the local. It results in an identity that transcends both standardization and difference. It is a deepened sense of identity with others that can only come about after we first genuinely encounter our difference.

From the International Classroom to Communities of Diversity

Many and varied possibilities exist for cultivating communities of diversity in the internationalized classrooms of Canada. Much depends upon support for teachers at the classroom level. The reality of the international classroom is essentially a local affair. A classroom in an Edmonton elementary school like Alex Taylor (see Chapter Nine) will have a different cultural mix than a classroom elsewhere; each will be international in particular ways at particular times. We need to ask what allow each of these classrooms, in their variety and particularities, to develop and flourish as communities of diversity.

Here are possibilities for building communities of diversity.

- Move from bureaucratic management to local control.

Over the past half century, urban school districts have grown and developed as large, bureaucratic organizations. This movement has had many benefits, but also a few problems. On the positive side, bureaucracy provides expertise, fairness, and certain centralized efficiencies to school systems. On the negative side, it weakens local initiative and creativity. Over the long term, bureaucratic management becomes unresponsive and less efficient. Now there are strong movements toward transferring control of education from large school boards to local parent councils. This can be a positive development for communities of diversity, because it opens the possibility for parents, teachers, and students to work together more closely. It can also be negative, however, in that these local councils can be captured by the elite or by special-interest groups.

- Recognize that there is more to people than their cultures.

In respecting culture, we should not fix people in their cultural identities. Identities are multiple.

- Build capacity for development.

Supporting classroom narratives and collaborative action research as the means for building capacities for ongoing change.

Conclusion

We should recognize that racism exists in schools, just as it does in Canadian society. Unless we recognize this fact, we will be unable to deal with it. Our classrooms have changed and most schools have a culturally diverse school population. For immigrant and minority children, racism is a living experience. They are an oppressed group. The current school system has failed to deal effectively with racism in schools. To address the racial issue, one should go beyond the concept of race. Race does not tell us how groups are marginalized, but racism does.

Discussion Questions

1. The classroom is becoming truly international. Examine current teaching practices and indicate whether teachers are taking into account the cultural diversity that exists in the classroom.
2. Does ethnicity matter?
3. What problems do immigrant and minority children encounter in the school? How to they try to cope with their daily experiences?

Notes

1. M. Fullan. 1991. *The New Meaning of Educational Change*. Columbia University: Teachers College. p. 227.
2. Noam Chomsky. 1993. *The Prosperous Few and the Restless Many*. Berkeley: Odonian Press. p. 65.
3. Dinyar Godrej. 1994. *Unlocking Prejudice. New Internationalist*. October. p. 5.

4. Ted Aoki. 1992. "Beyond the Half-Life of Curriculum and Pedagogy." In *Talks to Teachers: Inspiriting Curriculum and Pedagogy.* Edited by T. Aoki. University of Alberta, Department of Secondary Education, Curriculum Praxis Series.

5. Virginia Sauvé. 1990. "Journeys and Bridges," Plenary Address to the National Conference of Teachers of English as Another Language. Vancouver. March.

References

Aoki, T. ed. n.d. *Talks to teachers: Inspiriting curriculum and pedagogy*, University of Alberta, Department of Secondary Education. Curriculum Praxis Series.

Chomsky, Noam. 1993. *The prosperous few and the restless many.* Berkeley: Odonian Press.

Fullan, Michael. 1991. *The new meaning of educational change.* Teachers College: Columbia University.

Godrej, Dinyar. 1994. Unlocking prejudice. *New Internationalist.* October.

Sauvé, Virginia. 1990. Journeys and bridges. Plenary Address to the National Conference of Teachers of English as Another Language, March, Vancouver.

Further Reading

Cogan, Karen, and Ramsankar, Steve. 1994. *Alex Taylor Community School: A quarter century of programs and promises.* Alex Taylor: Edmonton.

Elsthain, Jean Bethke. 1993. *Democracy on trial.* Concord, ON: Anansi.

Freire, P., and Macedo, Donald. 1987. *Literacy. Reading the word and the world.* MA: Bergin & Gravey.

PART III

Strategies for Overcoming Racism

INTRODUCTION

How do we deal with racism? What is antiracist education? How can teachers meet the challenges of teaching in a culturally diverse classroom? These are some questions examined in this section. The authors present case studies of schools and programs that are attempting to create positive race relations in the school and in the community. It is argued that antiracist education offers the possibility of eradicating racism through awareness, challenge, and confrontation. It is necessary that schools adopt antiracist policies to remove discriminatory barriers, both personal or systemic.

Schools have witnessed conflicts of different nature, from violence to conflict arising out of political interest. In Chapter Eight Myrna Berlin and Ibrahim Alladin examine Kipling Collegiate Institute, a school in Etobicoke, Ontario. This school, which was until recently marked by violence and racial problems, has developed a unique model to bring students and teachers to address racism and racial issues. Kipling is a multicultural school serving a diverse population. It has taken several initiatives to bring multicultural understanding and awareness in the school community. At Kipling multiculturalism is practised every day.

Chapter Nine is another example of an inner-city school that has developed special programs to address the needs of the community. Alex Taylor Community School in Edmonton, Alberta, is one of the oldest schools in the city. It was once considered one of the most violent and difficult schools in the province. But the commitment of a dedicated team of teachers and volunteers has made Alex Taylor a truly community school. It has successfully responded to concerns of parents and students, particularly those who were victims of racism. At Alex Taylor, the curriculum is more than a government-mandated program of studies. In addition to the regular curriculum, the teaching staff has developed a co-creative effort to address the concerns of the whole community.

In Chapter Ten John Rymer and Ibrahim Alladin suggest ways to effectively deal with racism. The authors argue that antiracist practices are needed to challenge the power relations in society. The school system has not been successful at eliminating social and racial barriers that exist in school. Antiracist education offers the possibility to alter the role relationship and power structure between teacher-student. Racism is a social construction, and both the teacher and the student have to be involved in the deconstruction and reconstruction process.

The chapters in this section are:

Chapter Eight: The Kipling Collegiate Institute Story: Towards Positive Race Relations in the School (Myrna Berlin and Ibrahim Alladin)

Chapter Nine: Dealing with Racism in the Community: Response from the Alex Taylor Community School (Ibrahim Alladin and Steve Ramsankar)

Chapter Ten: Strategies for an Antiracist Education (John Ewan Rymer and Ibrahim Alladin)

8

THE KIPLING COLLEGIATE INSTITUTE STORY: TOWARDS POSITIVE RACE RELATIONS IN THE SCHOOL

Myrna L. Berlin and Ibrahim Alladin

Freedom is never voluntarily given by the oppressor; it must be demanded by the oppressed.[1]

Martin Luther King Jr.

Introduction

Canadian society is becoming culturally more diverse. This diversity is often reflected in the school. The classroom is becoming international. Recent changes in immigration policy, and our manpower needs, will likely alter the demographic profile of Canada. To contend with cultural diversity, Canada officially adopted a policy on multiculturalism two decades ago. While politicians and academics debate the future of multiculturalism in Canada (Alladin 1993, Bullivant 1981, Kallen 1982), some schools are living with the challenges of having a culturally diverse student population. To meet the needs of the students, the school has to respond favourably. This chapter studies Kipling Collegiate Institute and its attempt to bring different cultures together. Kipling, once considered to be a violent school marked with racial incidents, has become the epitome of multiculturalism.

Kipling Collegiate Institute: Early Days and Enrollment Patterns

When Kipling opened in 1960, with 423 students in Grades 9 to 11, and 23 teachers, most students came from white, middle-class homes in the neighbourhood. From time to time a few Asian students enrolled, but there were no Black or East-Indian students. Students of Italian origin made up the largest single cultural group. The school population grew during the 1960s and 1970s, but culturally remained essentially the same.

As declining enrollments hit Etobicoke secondary schools in the 1980s, it was feared that Kipling might have to close. With a declining student population, it became difficult to provide a viable academic program. New initiatives were investigated and introduced to stop the loss of students and to attract others to the school. An adult re-entry program (adults returning to school to get their diploma or up-grade their skills and/or knowledge for college or university admission) was introduced and, as more and more students registered to take advantage of this opportunity, the program gradually expanded. A quadmestered timetable was introduced in 1987, providing four entry points in the school year and flexibility in subject offerings and student choices. This also helped to boost enrollment. At the same time, the character and mix of the student body became increasingly multicultural. In 1989, an informal survey revealed that the student body of Kipling represented 57 different countries of origin. This was in large part due to the closeness of Lester B. Pearson International Airport, which had become a major gateway for a large influx of landed immigrants and refugee claimants. These people often settle in central and northern Etobicoke in general, and in the Kipling community in particular, owing to the available housing in the area. Adults were attracted by the re-entry program, adolescents were served by the quadmester timetable and, as more immigrant and refugee students arrived, it became necessary to expand the ESL program, which in turn attracted more adult and adolescent students.

On Assimilation

> "The process of becoming Canadian in outlook has gone far in the Canadian-born children of immigrants. It will go on to completion in their children, or at least their children's children... At the same time community conflicts and institutional disturbances tend to retard it (assimilation) and render doubtful the seeming advantages of a sudden precipitation of new peoples into a great variety of contacts with those who differ so widely from themselves. It is for this reason that assimilation...is such a disturbing matter for all concerned." (Carl A. Dawson)[2]

The dynamics of the changing student demographics can be seen by looking at the Secondary School September Report, which is a summary of school enrollment submitted to the Ontario Ministry of Education. It is a snapshot of enrollment at the school on one day, September 30. It also reports on the changes in enrollment during the previous school year, such as new admissions to the school, transfers, and retirements. Newly admitted students from outside of Ontario were asked where they came from. This information provides a clear picture of the growing diversity and multicultural nature of the KCI student body.

Changes in Enrollment

As can be seen from Figure 8.1, enrollment grew steadily from 1987 to 1992. Although many students left the school for one reason or another, there was a steady net gain in enrollment for the school during these years. Many of these students came to Kipling

FIGURE 8.1

Changes in Enrollment for Kipling Collegiate, 1987-1993
September 30 Report

	1987	1988	1989	1990	1991	1992	1993
New Admissions	475	923	1166	1515	1567	1699	1363
Retirements/Transfers	485	839	1005	1403	1468	1627	1367
Total Enrollment	669	753	914	1026	1125	1197	1193

from other schools in Etobicoke, but in each year a significant proportion of the new admissions came from outside the province. In the years 1990, 1991, and 1992, these students accounted for 45 percent, 51 percent, and 43 percent, respectively, of all new admissions. Although many students moved on to other schools and communities, many stayed and contributed significantly to the steadily growing multicultural mix of the school.

Figure 8.2 shows the origins of the students who came from outside Ontario. Unfortunately, the categories that the Ministry of Education provides for reporting this information create limitations. The countries or areas used for reporting the origin of new students did not adequately reflect the students' nationality or cultural origin. The vast majority of the students listed under West Indies came from Jamaica and Trinidad. The majority, if not all, of the students listed under Ethiopia and Kenya in 1989 and 1990 were probably Somalis who came to Canada as refugee claimants through these two countries. The large numbers listed for Other African (countries) in 1991 to 1993 would, again, reflect mostly Somali immigrant or refugee students. Also, under Other Asian (countries) would be counted all the students from Sri Lanka, Pakistan, Afghanistan, and the countries of the Middle East, such as Iran, Syria, Iraq, Lebanon, and Saudi Arabia. Adding to this multicultural mix are the students who transfer in from other schools and represent other races, religions, and cultures. Each year, there is an influx of younger students from Grade 8 who also complement and add to the wide variety of diverse backgrounds and cultures.

As a result of the changes in student enrollment over the last six or seven years, the classrooms, halls, cafeteria, auditorium, library, and gyms of Kipling have assumed a unique, multicultural, and cosmopolitan character. Faces of many colours, a variety of hair styles, and a vast array of different, colourful, and interesting clothing, all characterize the halls and classrooms. A multitude of languages can be heard as students from similar backgrounds gather to talk to one another. Young Sikhs in their *partikas*, older Sikhs in their turbans, Muslims in their *khamis* (robes), young Somali girls in their traditional *shash* (headdress) and flowing robes, yet other young Somali girls in jeans and Doc Marten boots, and sometimes Indian and Pakistani girls in their traditional *saris* can be seen in classrooms. Figure 8.3 illustrates this multicultural mix. It is an interesting but challenging time at Kipling.

FIGURE 8.2

Breakdown of Area of Origin of New Admissions from Outside Ontario, 1987-1993

	1987	1988	1989	1990	1991	1992	1993
Other Provinces	24	25	29	39	22	28	16
United States	3	5	11	16	11	10	7
West Indies	10	14	28	45	46	30	26
Central America			2	3	24	17	11
Other N. A. (Countries)			3	1	10	29	29
Guyana				1	5	12	4
Peru						2	
Other S. A. (Countries)	7	12	20	14	15	27	13
France	1	1	3	1			2
Poland	16	15	1	7	28	73	67
Portugal	1		3			3	
United Kingdom	8	18	13	14	15	10	10
Other Euro. (Countries)	5	14	36	57	41	33	28
Ethiopia			109	180	11	10	7
Kenya			55	63	7	1	3
Other Afr. (Countries)	16	64		89	339	332	176
Hong Kong	8	8	5	28	18	11	4
India	31	72		4			
Indochina	4		2	1	5	1	2
Philippines				9	3		
Other Asian (Countries)			95	107	200	122	106
Oceania		5	3	3	3	1	5
Total	**134**	**253**	**418**	**682**	**803**	**742**	**516**

FIGURE 8.3

Students' First Language by Grade, 1993-1994

	Grade 9*	Grade 10 *	Grade 11	Grade 12*	OAC*
English	73	101	91	84	31
Somali	85	22	0	0	0
Punjabi	22	0	0	0	0
Polish	19	0	0	0	0
Other	28	40	39	38	31
Total	**227**	**163**	**130**	**122**	**62**

* Based on high-school credits earned

Kipling Today: The Challenges of Learning in a Culturally Diverse Environment

In the 1980s, Kipling Collegiate's ESL program served immigrant students from Europe and Asia. African students from Somalia started arriving in 1989. This first group of students had strong academic backgrounds, but required additional language classes. In 1990, Kipling experienced an influx of Somali students fleeing the civil war. These refugee students had suffered extensively and had little or no English, with limited educational backgrounds.

Students' special needs in Math and English led to the creation of new courses. But, more initiatives were required as we began to receive high-school-age students from Somalia and Guyana who had no formal schooling. The Board of Education for Etobicoke responded to our need by funding a Literacy Program, the first of its kind in Etobicoke. In this full-time program, students are taught the fundamentals of school. Students spend from six to eighteen months in this nurturing, structured environment.

In the past, the ESL program could not offer a full timetable to students and so, of necessity, ESL students were placed in regular classes. Many of these students lacked sufficient English skills and the background knowledge to cope with the regular curriculum. Although ESL teachers provided support in these classrooms, the students lacked the skills to fully participate and succeed. In an attempt to assist ESL learners with the transition into mainstream classes, Kipling now offers Grade 9 courses specifically designed for our ESL learners. These classes are scheduled to correspond to the mainstream programs, so that students can make the transition from the former to the latter as soon as they have a reasonable chance of success.

The ESL Department's initiatives have not been limited to programming. In-services about the Somali community have been held for educators. A special all-day workshop by Somali health educators was hosted for our female Somali students around the issues associated with Female Genital Mutilation (FGM), a procedure most of the girls have undergone and that has lifelong health ramifications. We continue to respond to needs as they are identified — one of the most recent being gender equality.

In the fall of 1993, Kipling Collegiate experienced problems it had never had before. Racial incidents escalated to point where large groups of students began to face off against one another. The origin of these occurrences was racial tension, which had existed in the community over the summer, and an incident, which developed outside of the school, involving a few of the students. In the initial stages, the racial conflict was between Blacks and Somalis. Later, it was between East Indians and Somalis. Large, menacing crowds would gather at lunch time and after school, and we were never sure what would happen next.

The school and the community were in shock. The violence had erupted so suddenly it took everyone by surprise. After all, many students and staff had worked hard to bring about understanding among the various groups in the school, an acceptance of the multicultural nature of the school and the view that racism would not be tolerated. The work of Kipling's Anti-Racism Committee had culminated in a successful antiracism assembly presented by students for the rest of the school in the spring of 1993. A highlight of the program was the showing of a video called "Join Together," produced by the students of the Communications Technology department, which celebrated the diversity of the Kipling student body. So, how could racism and violence have become an issue at Kipling? Let us examine the Kipling experience.

From Violence to Mediation

A frightening incident occurred on the Friday before the Thanksgiving week-end in 1993. Two groups of youths gathered on a nearby playing field. One group was Somali, the other East Indian. There were weapons. Crowbars and baseball bats were seen. About a dozen staff members positioned themselves between the two groups. Fortunately, the police arrived before anyone was hurt.

The response to an affront against one person of an ethnic group literally led to ganging up on the alleged offender. This ganging up escalated to large groups confronting one another. The concept of solving a problem one-on-one did not exist. The solution to any confrontation was to get more "soldiers" to fight. Many participants in these activities were not KCI students, but members of the community at large.

In response, the Etobicoke Board supplied additional security in the form of walkie-talkies, resource personnel, and conflict-resolution training for staff. The board's Antiracist Department made personnel available. Experts came to the site to work with staff and students. The issues were discussed openly. Both staff and students wanted to resolve the racial conflicts in a positive way.

Policy and Guidelines for Race and Ethnic Relations

The Board of Education for the City of Etobicoke realizes:

- that it has a major responsibility for the development of positive attitudes in all people under its influence;
- that the people influenced by its mandate and operations come from many cultures and have many different racial and ethnic backgrounds;
- that the educational process must begin with and be supported by a belief in the inherent dignity of people.

Because of these realizations, the Board of Education for the City of Etobicoke commits itself to continue:

(a) develop, promote and support positive race and ethnic relations for staff, students and community;

(b) take steps to communicate the commitment to this principle to staff, students and community;

(c) take appropriate action when this principle is challenged or undermined in any way.

The Board of Education for the City of Etobicoke condemns and refuses to tolerate any expression of racial or ethnic bias in any form by its students, staff or trustees.[3]

The school is the focal point or meeting place for the different cultures in the immediate community. This "town-square" effect often causes students to be uncertain about their individual identities and they feel the need to exert themselves to prove who they are and what position they hold in the school and in the community as a whole. Often, high-school students are jockeying for positions of leadership and respect within the school setting.

But, as well as the normal teenage emotions, racial identity has become a concern of several of the immigrant groups within the school and the community. Since over 50 countries are represented at Kipling, this need for identity is understandable. To add yet another concern, students from the same background do not want to be associated with others of their own culture because of the "class" or "clan" designation they held in their homelands.

Sometimes, nonracial issues must also be dealt with in the school. Some students have emotional problems and have traumatic experiences from living in a refugee camp. As well, new immigrant communities in the Toronto area sometimes feel the need to protect their members from "Canadian" ideas that are divisive to their heritage and culture. To do this, some community leaders insure a stronger ethnic identity by encouraging new arrivals to become very conservative and fundamental in their beliefs and behaviour. This causes the students and their families additional stress, because there can be a great difference between what the school offers and what the home and community expect. This can be anything from gym classes and suitable sports uniforms to class discussions of issues that may be seen as unsuitable to discuss in the home culture, for example, the mandated sex or drug education programs that are part of the core curriculum at Kipling.

The problems between the various racial groups in the community had not gone unnoticed by the media. Reporters from the CBC had been working on a story for *Prime Time Magazine* on the conflict. Camera crews visited the school and caught on tape the tension at the school and the concerns of the staff. In the late fall of 1993, "A Place Called Dixon" was aired by the CBC. Although Kipling was shown to be dealing positively with the racial conflicts, both students and members of the community were very displeased with the way in which the program depicted the community and race relations in the area.

Exercise

The Meaning of Ethnicity

The show was over. It had been a rather spectacular demonstration of Hungarian folk dance. The costuming and the choreography, and the vibrant faces of the young performers was really impressive.

I watched them sing the words of those folk songs in their native tongue. I could see their parents in the wings beaming with pride. They were first generation immigrants from Hungary who still had fond memories of their homeland. Now they were passing those traditions on to their children.

"Great show!" I said to several of the youth after the performance. "You've got a great heritage and you represent it well. By the way, do you all speak Hungarian at home?"

"Once in a while" or "occasionally," several suggested.

"Not me," exclaimed a tall male. "I'm not even Hungarian. I'm the only one in the group who isn't Hungarian."

Somewhat surprised, I countered, "But why did you join the group?"

"It's neat to be part of some tradition," he retorted.

Questions to consider

What do you think being Hungarian means to the young people?

Why might being part of an ethnic tradition be considered "neat" — even if it is not your own? In what sense might emphasizing an ethnic tradition be at risk? (Hiller 1986, 165)

Soon cameras from the CBC were back on the Kipling campus. A producer from its "Man Alive" program had become interested in the issue of violence in high schools and thought that Kipling, as a result of its troubles in the fall, might provide the focus and material for this theme. But, what they found was that as a result of a mediation process and focus groups, Kipling had settled down and had become a shining example of a school where multiculturalism works. The school had actually dealt with racial violence and was promoting positive race relations. The program, entitled "School Colours," aired in March, 1994, had the second-highest audience (720 000) of any "Man Alive" segment in the 1993-1994 season.

The staff and administration have seen, as one of our needs, the necessity to increase awareness of the background of the learners and the issues that they see as pressing. Staff development sessions and workshops are seen as essential to provide the staff with an understanding of the community and its needs.

It is beyond our scope to fully understand what our immigrant and refugee students have lived through. Many have no immediate family members with them in Canada. Some have seen parents and siblings killed in politically torn countries. Others have spent their whole lives in refugee camps. Many have lived in half a dozen countries while they have tried to get to Canada and the freedom that we offer. The tragedies and atrocities that many of the students have suffered are beyond our understanding. Taking this into consideration, the Kipling staff work diligently to assist the students and to try to understand their emotional conflicts. The teachers have taken an interest in working co-operatively with the students.

Meeting The Challenges of Multiculturalism: The Kipling Way

The racial incidents at Kipling created a deep concern. The school could not ignore a serious community problem. Etobicoke had become an immigrant ghetto and with it all the social problems were becoming visible. At the community level, multiculturalism had failed to bring the people together. The federal initiatives on multiculturalism had little impact on the social life of the community. An apparent lack of understanding divided the people of Etobicoke and racial discrimination became evident. While Canada can take pride in its policy on multiculturalism, it has ghettoized many immigrants. Etobicoke is an example. The policy has not prevented racial discrimination in Canadian society. Racism in schools is increasing. Kipling therefore, responded positively to deal with this issue.

To diffuse tension and promote closer interaction, the Etobicoke Board has hired a part-time Somali School-Community Liaison Assistant to work at Kipling Collegiate and several local elementary schools. Important aspects of this person's mandate are communication, translation, and cultural issues between students, family, community, school, and staff.

As well, the Etobicoke Board has hired an Outreach Worker/Counsellor for Kipling Collegiate to help with specific concerns that have arisen. The job description includes:

- liaising with parents regarding academic issues, especially in regards to punctuality and school attendance;
- meeting with attendance counsellors to monitor problematic attendance;
- arranging special tutoring where necessary;
- reinforcing behavioural expectations with members of our various communities;
- holding seminars for specific groups of students, parents, and guardians;
- facilitating professional resources from the community to be presented in a warm and welcoming atmosphere into the school.

The Outreach Worker also deals with specific cultural concerns and assists the newcomer to make a smooth transition into Canadian society. Issues of culture, understanding of Canadian legal procedures, equity, health and access to medical care, and religion are also addressed. This type of citizenship education is crucial to empower new Canadians.

There is also an opportunity to deliver workshops and seminars to staff so that they become more aware of the changing needs and concerns of the community. It is important that the expectations of the various cultures, backgrounds, and religions are familiar to the school personnel. Staff development and increased awareness of the multi-cultural community is an important initiative that Kipling has launched. Through this initiative, staff will receive additional awareness training. The school is also seeking to educate parents on how to become more involved in the education of their children. This sense of school/community partnership has given Kipling the opportunity to help parents become more interested in the school. Kipling encourages parents to attend the Parent/Teacher Association (PTA) meetings, where childcare is offered for their convenience.

Focus Groups and Peer Support

One positive response to the violence in the fall was the establishment of focus groups involving every student in the school. Thirty staff members volunteered to help and were assigned a group to chair. The groups were formed completely at random and contained approximately twenty students each. Students of both sexes and from every ethnic background and grade were in each group. The students were encouraged to be open and frank. The Etobicoke Board provided supply teachers to take over classes for teachers who were holding focus groups.

Discussions were loosely structured around the following questions:

- What is going well at Kipling?
- What is your opinion of the present climate in the school?
- What areas are to be improved?
- How can you make things better?
- How can we prevent further conflict in the future?

The following are the compiled highlights of what the students said:

1. The students had high regard for the staff and felt that the school was good academically. The people in school were warm and accepting on the whole. They like the multicultural aspect of the school.
2. Students spoke about the lack of school spirit. They felt that students from all ethnic backgrounds should contribute and that perhaps there was a tendency for some groups not to get involved. Students tended to socialize only with others in their own group. They spoke their own language in these groups.
3. Different cultural groups need to accept others and not cling to their own culture so much. They need to become more mainstream "Canadian."
4. Suspensions need to be handled differently. They should be served "in" school as opposed to at home. Parents, even of students of legal age, should be informed of suspensions.
5. Some students feel that adult students (Re-entry program) should not be in the same building.
6. Anyone with a weapon should be expelled.
7. Students should be friendly and help everyone, no matter what his or her ethnic background. More students need to contribute to the school program and extra curricular activities. We need to learn more about all cultural groups in the school.
8. The groups involved in the fighting need to understand how problems are solved (for example, not by fighting and escalation, but by mediation). Students need to solve problems on a one-to-one basis. Programs should be developed in anger control, conflict management and problem solving. Keep the media and trouble-makers out of the school.

The focus groups seemed to have a calming affect on the school. Everyone was able to express his or her own views. Two of the counsellors work with a focus group composed of class representatives to continually gain student input about what is going on in the school. One of Kipling's graduates, a former student council president and now a university student, has volunteered to work with the student council on leadership initiatives.

Another group of students is trained in peer mediation. This group mediates disputes on an ongoing basis when called upon to do so. Peer mediation through the Kipling Peer Facilitator (KPF) group is a vital part of the school. Students are helping students — that is the focal point of this group. Students who have an issue that must be resolved can approach the mediation team at anytime. It is very positive when students can resolve their own issues. Anyone has the right to ask for assistance over any issue of concern. The sessions are always confidential and two highly trained student facilitators operate each group.

Although the administration is not involved with the operation of this group, it can refer students to the KPF in order that they work out their concerns. Often, issues that are not disciplinary in nature may end up in the school's office for resolution. In these cases, students have been asked to work through their concerns at the mediation level. Most often this works well. It is gratifying to know that in most cases, students can resolve issues and solve problems themselves. Consensus is often reached by all the parties concerned. Where an issue is clearly disciplinary in nature, it is handled by the staff and/or administration. Kipling's KPF is the envy of other high schools in the area. It has developed a mediation model that seems to work well with the students. Conflict resolution by students seems to be more effective.

Staff and students dealt with the problems in a number of different ways. Teachers took advantage of class time to deal with antiracist education. Staff and students of the school's Anti-Racism Committee planned and put on another assembly to underscore the view that intolerance would not be an accepted part of life at Kipling. The Communications Technology students produced a video, "Together We Are," to reinforce the multicultural and antiracist nature of the school.

One of the school's drama teachers found a unique way to take a proactive approach to concerns regarding potentially racist situations. After the fall incident, the students began discussing their concerns openly in class. The teacher saw this as an opportunity and encouraged the students to talk out their feelings and express their innermost thoughts through media and drama. The result appeared in the annual school drama presentation. The drama focuses upon the development of appropriate behaviour and correct responses to issues dealing with equality, and in particular racist incidents that the students might have encountered in their lives.

School's Peer Mediation: Program Helps Teens Sort Out Problems

> Now that he's an adult, Don Melnychuk can laugh about some of the punch-ups he had growing up in a tough inner city neighbourhood. Melnychuk is a school counsellor at Ross Sheppard High School, where he helped teens sort out conflicts peacefully.
>
> That's not to say he was an angel growing up in Boyle Street in the 1960s. Fights among kids were common, and Melnychuk was in

> his fair share. If someone made an ethnic slur about his Ukrainian heritage, Melnychuk decked him. Or tried.
>
> Melnychuk is part of a growing movement across Canada to resolve school conflicts before they get serious. The need for peaceful solutions has never been more urgent.
>
> Prompted by an increasing number of school-yard assaults, Edmonton's public school board last year passed a tough new code in student conduct. Nineteen students have been expelled so far this school year, the same as for all of last year.
>
> At the beginning of the school year, Melnychuk trained several students at Ross Sheppard in the art of peer mediation. The principles are simple. Two students involved in a conflict are encouraged to express their feelings without blaming others. They must listen to the other person's side of the story and look at solutions. Conflicts can range from teasing to serious violence.
>
> "It's the way of the future," said Ben Berger, 17, one of the six members of the program.
>
> "The goal of the program is to defuse any type of problem before it gets to the point where authorities have to be brought in."
>
> Berger said the process could defuse potential racial conflicts among groups of students. However, he said it can only work if both sides really want to resolve a problem.[4]

The students wrote the dialogue for the play. Under close supervision by the teacher, the play developed along, with many friendships and bonds. The thirteen members of the cast and the five-piece rock band became "We Are" (poems written by students provided the central theme for this play; see the Appendix on p. 146). This special production embodies the multicultural nature of the school, the joys and sorrows of such a diverse school, and the process of attempting to transcend the difficulties that all students face. It is a unique piece of drama that tells the story of the dilemmas and accomplishments of multiculturalism in Canada. Aside from a successful run at the school, the play was invited to tour in local elementary and secondary schools in Etobicoke.

The teacher's concerns over inappropriate behaviour of his students, plus his ability to listen to their needs led to the development of his caring, proactive vision for the school. This vision has increased awareness of:

- what a racial incident is;
- why such behaviour should not be tolerated; and
- how best to stop being a victim or a perpetuator of racial attitudes, behaviour, or comments.

The responsibilities placed on today's high-school students have changed over the years. In addition to the multicultural concerns already mentioned, the school is expected to provide more than an academic education. The students themselves have expressed concern about the fact that for many of them, home is a place where they only drop in between school, their job, and their social life. They live in single-parent homes, where they cannot spend much time with their caregiver because that parent must work at more than one job. In one focus group, a young man made the point that his parents do not know how to "parent." He wished they had better training so that they could help him with his concerns as he matures and grows into adulthood.

Some students at Kipling have to spend a great deal of time caring for younger siblings. Their responsibilities do not allow them much time to have the fun to which they feel they are entitled. These extra burdens continue to put pressure on young people. Attending school to acquire an education is no longer their only concern, but just one of many they must carry. Some teenagers are on their own and must be totally responsible for themselves physically, financially, and emotionally.

The students have serious concerns about their future, including the following.

- Will there be space at the colleges or universities that they wish to attend?
- When they graduate in their chosen fields, will jobs be available?
- How can one deal with growing racism in Canada? Will the ethnocultural background of the students be a liability when they wish to enter the work force?

For immigrant youths going to school, these are some challenges they have to face.

How to Deal with Racial/Ethnic Incidents

1. Create a positive and open atmosphere for communication.
2. Clarify what constitutes a racial/ethnic incident.
3. Discuss the cause of the incident. Do not avoid, deny, or trivialize the issue. Emphasize that regardless of the circumstances, the use of racial/ethnic slurs is never appropriate or acceptable.
4. Discuss how racial/ethnic harassment affects people.

   (a) For the victim:

   i. The feeling of anger, frustrating, and powerlessness.

   ii. The sense that his/her racial/ethnic identity and self-worth are being devalued.

   iii. The inability to function effectively.

   (b) For the aggressor:

   i. The misuse of power relations (finding oneself in a privileged position).

   ii. The false sense of racial and ethnic superiority.

5. Discuss alternative responses to disagreements (if it resulted from a disagreement).
6. Discuss strategies for future positive interaction and seek commitment.

7. Discuss the Board's policy regarding racial and ethnic incidents.
8. Provide the parents/guardians with a copy of the Board's policy.[5]

It should not be assumed that every incident at Kipling is racial or involves ethnic conflicts. As would be the case in any school where large numbers of people come together, disputes are likely to occur and young people do not always resort to the most appropriate solutions for conflict resolution. For example, a fight between a Black student and a white student may not be racially motivated. It can be simply a case of two youths fighting. It is important to understand youth culture so as not to interpret every clash involving different ethnic groups as racial.

Conclusion

Kipling Collegiate Institute is truly a multicultural school. The racial incidents that occurred in the fall of 1993 were caused by factors external to the school. The failure of government agencies to meet the changing needs of an immigrant community triggered a series of events that culminated into racial violence in the school. Multiculturalism, as a policy, has not been able to deal with the concerns that newcomers to Canada face. Some programs are ineffective and they often lack the commitment to implement change. As Canadian society becomes culturally more diverse, racism is on the increase. Schools such as Kipling are left to deal with a social problem that requires more than changes at the school level. Multiculturalism, as it is practised, has done little to combat or reduce racism in Canada.

The racial incidents at Kipling shook both the school and the community. However, Kipling put together a number of initiatives to promote positive race relations. It became actively involved, developed antiracist education campaigns, and has had success in bringing the parents together. This partnership between the school and the community has given Kipling the new image of "peace-maker." With support from the staff, the Etobicoke Board, and the community, Kipling has been able to "get a handle" on the concerns within the school. However, outside the school, major concerns still remain. As long as broader social problems, such as racism, unemployment, and various forms of discrimination, are not addressed, schools like Kipling will continue to have a fragile existence.

Discussion Questions

1. Racism is a complex problem. Racial incidents in schools can be triggered for various reasons. If a school is experiencing racial violence, what course of action can be taken to resolve the problem?
2. Are teachers sensitive enough to deal with problems such as racism in schools? What type of support do teachers require to deal effectively with racism in schools?
3. School boards throughout Canada are instituting an antiracist education policy. What attempts are being made in your school jurisdiction to implement an antiracist policy?

Notes

1. Martin Luther King Jr.
2. Excerpt from Harry H. Hiller. 1986. *Canadian Society. A Macro Analysis.* Scarborough: Prentice Hall Canada. p. 165. Reprinted with the permission Prentice Hall Canada Inc.
3. The Board of Education for the City of Etobicoke.
4. *The Edmonton Journal*, February 28, 1994. p. B1. Reprinted with permission of *The Edmonton Journal.*
5. The Board of Education for the City of Etobicoke.

References

Alladin, Ibrahim. 1993. *Multiculturalism in the 1990s. Policies, practices and implications.* Edmonton: EISA Publishers.

Bullivant, B. M. 1981. Multiculturalism — Pluralist orthodoxy or ethnic hegemony? *Canadian Ethnic Studies* 13 (2): 1-22.

Hiller, Harry H. 1986. *Canadian society. A macro analysis.* Scarborough: Prentice Hall Canada.

Kallen, Evelyn. 1982. Multiculturalism: Ideology, policy and reality. *Journal of Canadian Studies* 17 (1): 93-102.

Further Reading

A series of reports on antiracist education has been developed in Ontario. The Etobicoke Board of Education for example, has several studies that are useful. See *Changing Perspectives* (1992); Goldgrab, Sheila. (no date). "How Communities and Organizations Can Overcome Racial Inequalities? Anti-Racism Project of the Etobicoke Social Development Council; Atkins, R. (no date). *From Policy to Practice. A Guide For Developing School Based antiracist Action Plans.* Etobicoke Board of Education; Ontario Ministry of Education and Training. (1993). *Antiracism and Ethnocultural Equity in School Boards. Guidelines for Policy Development and Implementations*; Hope, H. F. *Local School Antiracist Policy.* Etobicoke.

Author Notes

The authors are grateful to the following, all of Kipling Collegiate Institute, for their help: Karl Sprogis, former Vice-Principal; Donna Gorbold, Head of Student Services; Lesley Macdonald, Head of English as a Second Language; Anthony D'Andrea, Communications Technology; Raymond Gallant, Computer Coordinator; Jane Robbie, Library Resource Secretary; and the students who participated in the research.

APPENDIX: WE ARE...

Appendix 1

WE ARE...
ONE PEOPLE, ONE NATION, ONE WORLD.
AND SINCE TIMES ARE CHANGING
THE TIME HAS COME FOR REARRANGING
WE HAVE TO LIVE OUR LIVES
TOGETHER AS ONE
IN ORDER TO SURVIVE, LIVE AND LOVE,
WE'VE GOT TO STOP OUR CRUEL JOKES AND LIES.
AND IF WE DON'T OUR SPIRIT DIES.
WE'VE GOT TO LIVE OUR LIVES TOGETHER AS ONE.
WE ALL HAVE DREAMS AND HOPES
BUT OUR FEARS TEND TO GET IN THE WAY
THE FEAR OF WHAT PEOPLE MAY THINK OR SAY

THE RACISM
THE PREJUDICE
THE SEXISM
THE HURT
THE PAIN
THE SUFFERING

ALL IN THE NAME OF WHAT
IF SOMEONE IS DIFFERENT FROM ANOTHER
DOES THAT MAKE HIM ANY LESS OF A BROTHER?
AND EVEN IF WE'RE BLACK, WHITE OR GREEN
IT'S NOT OUR COLOURS THAT SHOULD BE SEEN
WE'VE GOT TO LOVE EACH OTHER FOR WHAT'S INSIDE
OUR HERITAGE WE SHOULD NOT HIDE
BE PROUD OF WHAT YOU ARE
AND THAT YOU'VE COME THIS FAR
WE'VE GOT TO LEARN TO ACCEPT AND ACKNOWLEDGE
WHAT EVERYONE HAS DONE
AND THAT'S HOW WE'LL LIVE OUR LIVES AS ONE.

-KIM MITCHELL

We seem to spend our lives
Planning for the future...
tomorrow is always in our thoughts,
While today slips away,
And yesterday sometimes returns
to remind us of our mistakes.
We try to hold the special moments
forgetting that the best is yet to come;
that tomorrow is another day,
another chance to take,
another chance to fulfill
the dreams for the future.
-Lisa Ransom

Unknown

Unfamiliar Faces and Culture
Two totally different worlds
There is my world
Then there is yours.
My world seems strange to you
But it is normal to me.
And your world seems strange to me
But it's your home.
We learn to accept our differences
And as we do, we gain knowledge
Knowledge of different beings
Knowledge of the Unknown.

-Nasra Adan-

9

DEALING WITH RACISM IN THE COMMUNITY: RESPONSE FROM ALEX TAYLOR COMMUNITY SCHOOL

Ibrahim Alladin and Steve Ramsankar

"Teach in an inner-city school! You're crazy," a friend warned me. "You'll ruin your career!"[1]

Peter McClaren
Life in Schools

Introduction

Racism is the social attitudes, social structures, and actions that oppress, exclude, limit, and discriminate against nondominant ethno-racial groups. As an ideology, it treats one group as superior to other groups and some groups are deliberately excluded because of certain physical attributes. Since this form of racism exists, the systemic breaking down of barriers requires effort from all institutions in the society. The school, as this chapter shows, can become an important catalyst in bringing the community together and challenging racist behaviour. Indeed, it is argued that the school has a responsibility to first, recognize that racism exists in Canadian society and second, to take positive steps to reduce it. Alex Taylor Community School, in Edmonton, Alberta, provides an example of a school's commitment to the pursuit of race equity and community-wide change.

This is the story of a school in Edmonton's inner city — a school where every student is hugged every day. For almost a quarter of a century, Principal Steve Ramsankar and a devoted team of teachers, support staff, and volunteers have worked together to meet the educational, social, physical, and spiritual needs of children at Alex Taylor Community School.

Alex Taylor Community School: The Red-Brick House

The red-brick building known today as Alex Community School opened in 1908, in the heart of what was then the small city of Edmonton. It is situated in a commercial area known as Boyle Street, and was the centre of the town's most respectable and affluent middle class. Many Alex Taylor graduates from those early days are today prominent members of the business and professional communities. Over the years, urban expansion, redevelopment, and economic depression has radically altered the Boyle Street neighbourhood. Increasing immigration and migration from the rural areas to the developing city resulted in dense population, competition, and the need for affordable housing. This changed the face of the Boyle Street area from a small-town city centre to a neighbourhood with an inner-city profile. According to Cogan and Ramsankar (1994, 10): "Prostitution, alcoholism and drug dealing were the biggest problems in the neighbourhood." Alex Taylor became part of this tough neighbourhood. The school was in no better condition than the neighbourhood itself. Janis Blakey, a professor at the University of Alberta describes the school as follows:

> It was a scary place. There were bolted safety screens on all of the windows; there were signs of vandalism and the police were constantly having to patrol the area. It was not a pleasant place to be and teachers did not want to work there (Cogan and Ramsankar 1994, 10).

According to the 1990 Neighbourhood Crime Statistics from the Edmonton Police Media Relations, the Boyle Street area is characterized by high levels of homicide, sexual assaults, robbery, break and enter, thefts, assaults, child abuse, morality crimes (prostitution), drugs, and liquor violations. The area is so neglected and run down that it is unlikely to attract the affluent middle class it once did. In 1989, the average individual income in the area was $12 200. This figure often represents a family's entire income. Because of the cultural challenges and financial pressures, over 40 percent of the students have special needs, such as nutritional deficiencies, lack of warm clothing for the winter months, language difficulties, academic, emotional, psychological, and social problems. Many of the students have more than one of these challenges.

The city police have played an active role in the school since 1972 with the preventative police liaison program. Despite the efforts by the police, the inner city has continued to decline economically. The population is transient and families move as their financial circumstances permit. This is reflected in the high rate of transience at Alex Taylor. For example, from September, 1992, to June, 1993, the initial enrollment of 167 students increased to 183. Sixty-six students had transferred into the school and 50 had transferred out of it. But in spite of the high rate of transience, absenteeism is extremely low. Unlike many schools today, which face rising absenteeism, the students at Alex Taylor Community School attend classes regularly. In the 1992-1993 academic year, for example, the average room-attendance rates ranged from 90.1 to 94.2 percent throughout the year. Many children have received perfect-attendance certificate awards.

Alex Taylor is not simply an elementary school. It is a community school, and it provides programs and services to the community. It welcomes everyone and there is an openness about the school. Each person is perceived as an individual with unique, basic needs, and the school attempts to understand and meet those individual needs. The guiding principle for such an approach is expressed through the metaphor school is a family. The principal reminds the children that, "We are a family. All of us help each other. The school is a home away from home."

A Multicultural School

The inexpensive housing in the area has attracted many immigrant families. The school enrollment ranges from 130 to 200 students in the kindergarten classes through to grade 6. The classrooms have become truly international — over the years the students have represented 30 different language groups and a glance at the children in the school's bustling hallways confirms the image of the diverse Canadian population. In the 1992-1993 academic year, the September enrollment of 167 students included Chinese (about 40 percent), Vietnamese, Salvadoran, Metis, Irish, German, Cambodian, Guatemalan, Jamaican, Cree Native, Italian, Dutch, African, Romanian, Turkish, and Chilean backgrounds. Alex Taylor is indeed a reflection of the Canadian mosaic.

When Steve Ramsankar arrived at Alex Taylor in 1970, the school was reputedly one of the toughest in Edmonton. In this inner-city community there was low-cost housing, single-parent families, and many families who lived below the poverty level. Owing to restricted financial resources, new immigrants gravitated to the city core. By 1993, the school had an enrollment of 167 students from different ethnic and racial backgrounds (Cogan and Ramsankar 1994, 11). Despite the drastic changes that have occurred for the better at Alex Taylor Community School, the surrounding neighbourhood has mostly remained unchanged. The neighbourhood has:

> All of the characteristics of a run-down, rough inner city core... Scattered with abandoned, boarded-up buildings, bath houses, low income housing, prostitution, alcoholism, drug dealing and homeless people, the area is not really conducive to the raising of young children. According to 1990 Neighbourhood Crime Statistics from the Edmonton Police Media Relations, the Boyle Street area is still characterized by high levels of homicide, sexual assaults, robbery, break and enters, thefts, assaults, child abuse, morality crimes (prostitution), drugs and liquor violations (Cogan and Ramsankar 1994, 11-12).

It is in this situation that school serves as a haven to children and parents from the disillusionment of living in a neighbourhood of inner city problems. As Robert Whitt states in *A Handbook for the Community School Director*:

> Whatever crises the kids in the inner city area are struggling with in their family lives, they know that there is a special place that they can turn to and depend on that very day.
>
> The school cannot go into the home and change the home patterns that have developed over the years, but the school can change its own patterns. The time has come when the school must focus on those elements over which it has control... There is one place in the cultural milieu that pupils may find a constant — the classroom. The inner-city, with all of its turmoil and grinding poverty, can provide a haven to which the slum pupil may withdraw from the pointings of society (Cogan and Ramsankar 1993, 13).

With an attempt to integrate the school and the community, Dr. Ramsankar has developed a philosophy at the school that is translated into the various programs at the school.

The highlight of the year at Alex Taylor is the celebration of the Chinese New Year, usually in February. For twenty years, the school has brought parents, teachers, politicians, community leaders, businesses, and churches to celebrate the festival. A large city is transformed into an integrated community that participates in what Sergiovanni (1984) has described as "culture building" and the "practicing of purposing." Through this cultural celebration everyone learns to understand and respect one another.

Racism in the Inner City

A survey conducted by the Edmonton Social Planning Council in September, 1992, revealed that racism in Edmonton, particularly in the northeast of the city, is widespread. Eighty-seven percent of the respondents indicated that racial incidents in their neighbourhood were high, especially among teenagers. People experienced racism in schools, at the workplace, and were discriminated against when looking for employment and housing.

According to the Federal Census of 1986, Edmonton is, after Winnipeg, the second-most ethnically diverse Canadian city. One fifth of its population is made up persons born outside Canada. In the 1960s, this population was predominantly from European countries. Since then, immigrants have come mainly from South East Asia, and Central and South America. In 1986, about one in ten Edmonton area residents (9.3 percent) belonged to a visible minority. Visible minorities are here defined as belonging to one of the following groups, whether born in or outside of Canada: Blacks, Chinese, Filipinos, Indo-Pakistanis, Japanese, Koreans, Latin Americans, other Pacific Islanders, South East Asians, West Asians, and Arabs (Edmonton Social Planning Council 1991, 4-5).

Are We Racists?

Canadian Society Not Immune to Racism

> Canada is not immune to racism and we must learn how to deal with it. First, we must accept that racism exists. Its forms are not as brutal as the policy of "ethnic cleansing" in the former Yugoslavia or the stone-throwing at the homes of foreigners in Berlin, but racial confrontations in Montreal and Toronto, the activities of Keegstra, Zundel and the skinheads speak loudly about the extent of prejudice and intolerance in Canadian life.
>
> According to the latest poll (February, 1994) about 16 percent of Canadians are hard core xenophobes (people who hate or fear foreigners). Such attitudes can result in action ranging from name-calling to rewriting hate propaganda directed at a specific group, property damage or physical violence. More widespread and more difficult

> to deal with is the existence of systemic discrimination, or "polite prejudice," in our institutions and daily life.[2]

It is important to note that while conflicts exist among different ethnic groups, it does not mean that there is perpetual war of all against all, or of class against class, in Edmonton. Rather, the situation in the inner-city has to be understood in terms of the adjustments people have to make. In studying a zone of the city, one must find out who lives there, what primary community ties they have, and what their housing situation, economic position, and status aspirations are, what associations they form, how these associations interact and how far the various groups are incorporated into urban society as citizens (Rex and Moore 1967, 11).

We Are Not Racists But...

> Alberta continues to witness cases of discrimination and ill-treatment against nonwhites and some religious groups. Jewish synagogues and cemeteries have been defaced; Aryan Nations have burned crosses in southern Alberta. Natives, Sikhs and Moslems face public ridicule about their dress; turbans have been banned by local legions and there was a long and loud provincial furor against turbans in the RCMP. Workers express fear that immigrants take away their jobs and somehow cheapen the labor force. Vietnamese are made responsible for the existence of ethnic gangs. "Paki" taxi drivers are refused by customers. Even Alberta politicians have joined in denouncing multiculturalism legislation.[3]

As the Boyle Street neighbourhood declined from being a prosperous community into an inner-city ghetto, immigrants moving into the area were subjected to discrimination. Immigrants from Central America and Asia moved in and bought property. Established, white Canadians felt threatened. Race relations deteriorated as the new immigrants developed ties with fellow immigrants to build a primary community. In this case, they attempted to reproduce some of the social institutions of their homeland and provide themselves with norm-governed homes into which they can retreat from the world of work. As this primary community became more extensive, the new immigrants started "living in the colony," which according to Rex and Moore (1967) kept them from falling into a state of complete demoralization and anomie. Established, white Canadians simply see the new immigrants as resisting any attempt to integrate into the society. Therefore, they become the targets of racism.

Alex Taylor: A Partnership Between the School and the Community

A hundred years ago, the school was the focal point of the community. The school served a number of social and educational functions. Political gatherings, social events, and literary activities were held in the school. But as towns and cities became more urbanized and industrialized, the school lost some of these functions. The role of the school within the community was lessened to that of an educational institution, no longer linked to the other aspects of community life.

Exercise

How Antiracist Is Our School?

This exercise can assist in determining whether a school is effectively combating racism. Examine the following nine questions.

1. Is there a policy on antiracist education in your school jurisdiction?
2. Are parents and students informed about this policy?
3. Are languages, other than English used in the school to display notices, announcements and news items?
4. Are opportunities provided to ensure that ESL students are welcomed to the school and that they work co-operatively with students who are fluent in English?
5. Are racists incidents such as name-calling dealt with seriously by the staff and student-support groups?
6. Do learning materials reflect the diversity of cultures in Canada?
7. How does the school or teachers deal with bias in learning materials?
8. Does the school regularly review its policies and practices as they relate to curriculum, assessment, evaluation, interviews, and parental involvement?
9. Does the school encourage extracurricular activities where students can explore their cultural heritage and backgrounds?

The community plays a central role at Alex Taylor. The school has created a sense of belonging. It has revived interest in the school and extended some activities that involve the local people and parents. Alex Taylor is truly a community school. This spirit of community has helped Alex Taylor deal with issues such as racism and the school has developed ways to reduce racism in the community.

One of the most powerful strategies used at Alex Taylor to minimize social conflict is that of the family approach in education. The idea that we are a family regardless of one's race, creed, or ethnicity, is emphasized continuously. The students, staff, and community members provide public education to promote the goals of a multicultural society.

Through a series of exercises, the concept of the family is discussed. For example, students are asked questions such as, "What does the family mean?" They answer, "It means love for each other. It means caring for each other, sharing with each other, and respect for one another." Students participate in activities that foster positive relationships and avoid situations that will hurt people. In this way, they develop an understanding that Canada is a multicultural society.

The Thursday morning assembly at Alex Taylor serves to promote a sense of citizenship. New Canadians are given a "buddy" who becomes a friend. This buddy system provides students and parents with the chance to get together and interact more often. Cultural barriers are overcome faster. People get accustomed to another language and do not feel intimidated by the presence of someone who looks different.

The school has reached out to the community to help it ease racism. It encourages parents to recognize and understand cultural differences. For example, Native students have the opportunity to perform the Sweetgrass Ceremony. Other cultural groups are invited to celebrate different events and festivals important to their culture. The concept of one and oneness within the family is reinforced in all these activities.

The Co-Creative Curriculum

At Alex Taylor, the curriculum is more than a government-mandated program of studies. In addition to the regular, prescribed curriculum, the school staff, in a co-creative effort, has developed programs and services that relate to the needs of the community — parents, students, seniors, and preschoolers. The curriculum is redefined to meet the changing needs of the community.

Alex Taylor has developed a variety of educational and cultural programs in addition to the instructional programs for kindergarten through Grade 6. Some programs are the following.

- a baby-sitting service, for children aged 6 months to 5 years, that enables parents to attend adult-education classes at the school
- a nutrition program to supplement children's diet
- a self-esteem program
- Cub Scouts, Big Brothers, Brownies, and Girl Guide programs both during and after school
- cultural exchange and travel programs
- social, and physical and mental health programs for children and adults
- voluntary summer program for inner-city children
- food and clothing banks for needy families
- ESL classes for new Canadians
- citizenship programs to introduce children and their parents to the ideas of multiculturalism
- special events to celebrate cultures and festivals

The variety of programs at Alex Taylor indicates how the school tries to reach out to the community and educate all the people the school serves. The co-creative curriculum seeks to involve the community; it strives to educate everyone.

Easing Racism

Besides addressing the cultural and spiritual needs of the community, the school has a clearly defined position on antidiscriminatory education. The school has embraced a multicultural approach to eliminate prejudice and discrimination. It has initiated several measures to promote antiracism both at the school and in the community.

> We cannot legislate against discrimination because no one can legislate that I should love you or you should love me...you have to live it, you have to practise it daily...you have to be an example of what it is to be accepting...It saddens me to see the conflict and racial disharmony in our society. If we don't take these unhealthy trends seriously and educate all our people to love and accept one another, no matter how much we advance in technology, we will end up in chaos (Cogan and Ramsankar 1994, 37).

As Cogan and Ramsankar (1994, 38) aptly put it, "By studying and recognizing different cultures and cultural events, the school celebrates the Canadian mosaic and teaches the children respect and acceptance of differences." Through the celebration of Native traditions such as the Sacred-Circle Program and through a variety of other activities, including foreign-language classes, dances, songs, and culture-awareness sessions describing and exploring traditions and customs of other countries, Alex Taylor Community School has found unique strategies to deal with the diversity of its student population. This has enriched its approach to harmonious race relationships among the members of the faculty and the children. Problems of xenophobic nature, which are usually attributed to unawareness of foreign traditions, are proactively dealt with through pre-emptive actions of bridging the gap between individuals and groups. Overseas educational tours have been conducted to enable students and teachers to obtain first-hand experience of traditions, customs, and cultures of other countries. Ramsankar (1994, 39) explains the usefulness of such exercises:

> The experience of travelling in another country gives the students a worldliness and an understanding and acceptance of other cultures and traditions. Teachers also integrate these themes of multiculturalism into their curriculum and classrooms, so that a bond is formed between the students regardless of their color, religion, culture, or ethnic background. Understanding each other's uniqueness often serves to join the children together and make them forget their differences...Through understanding and knowledge, racial prejudice is all but eliminated and cultural differences becomes a uniting rather than divisive force.

Responsibilities are delegated to each staff member, giving ownership to the individual. Every person is an important team member who makes a significant contribution according to his or her expertise. The staff members ignore the weaknesses of each student, and instead capitalize on their strengths.

In most cases, racism and racial prejudice are due to ignorance of other cultures. One of the most successful strategies that Alex Taylor has used to ease racism is the family model in education. Everyone recognizes that he or she belongs to the Alex Taylor family, regardless of race, creed, or colour. At this school love for fellow human beings is taught. Here, love means respect, reaching out, caring for and sharing with each other, and touching the spirit in another human being. We must learn to understand, appreciate, accept, and love each other to minimize racial discrimination.

To ease racism in our society, the school and the community have to work together. Without the full participation of all citizens, racism will remain a serious issue. The school alone cannot eliminate racism, but it can raise awareness and can empower students and teachers to develop a more positive attitude. Furthermore, by fostering a closer relationship with parents, the school can become a focal point for debate and discussion. Alex Taylor has successfully developed programs both for students and parents to address important social issues. For example, the morning-snack program has important messages: poverty in the inner city, the need for a nutritious diet, feeding children and families, and sharing food. Similarly, the adult ESL classes recognize that new Canadians cannot fully participate in the society without an adequate knowledge of English. True citizenship requires participation and new Canadians should not excluded or treated separately.

One of the strengths of the approach used at Alex Taylor is the emphasis on self-esteem. Self-esteem involves reciprocal encouragement of the self and others. The attempt to demonstrate that the school must teach everyone to feel good and proud has instilled values such as sharing and respect. The family environment at the school also fosters self-esteem. By creating understanding and respect for other cultures, Alex Taylor has eased racism in the school and in the community.

Conclusion

A key question is whether the school can play a significant role in dealing with issues such as racism. The Alex Taylor story clearly indicates that the school can play three important roles towards the elimination of racism. First, it has to create an atmosphere for open discussion and recognize the fact that racism exists both in the school and in society at large. Second, the school should develop antiracist education programs. Third, the school should bring students, teachers, and parents together to address racism and to work towards positive race relations. Without redefining the curriculum, the case study shows that there are limitations. Educators have to become cognizant of the fact that social transformation cannot take place if we maintain rigid structures. By taking the needs of the people it serves into consideration, Alex Taylor has tried to provide a common understanding among all citizens based on the concept of love and sharing. By bringing people together, it has become a truly community school.

Discussion Questions

1. The classroom is becoming truly international. Visit a school in the city and examine whether the school environment reflects cultural diversity. Does the curriculum encourage or promote the goals of multiculturalism?
2. What actions can students and teachers take to deal with racism in the school?
3. Education cannot build a better life for Native people and minorities in Canada if other Canadians continue to exclude them. What kinds of changes should be introduced into the schooling of children to ensure a more egalitarian society?

Notes

1. Peter McClaren. 1989. *Life in Schools*. New York: Longman. p. 26.
2. *The Edmonton Southsider*, August 1994, p. 4.
3. Edmonton Social Planning Council. 1992. *Alberta Facts*. Edmonton, Alberta. Number 10, March.

References

Cogan, Karen, and Ramsankar, Steve. 1994. *Alex Taylor Community School: A quarter century of programs and promises*. Alex Taylor: Edmonton.

Edmonton Social Planning Council. 1992. *Because of the color: A study of racial tension in Northeast Edmonton*. Edmonton, ESPC. September.

———. 1991. *Tracking the trends*. Edmonton, ESPC. September.

Edmonton Southsider. 1994. Edmonton, AB. August.

Rex, John, and Moore, Robert. 1967. *Race, community and conflict: A study of Sparkbrook*. London: Oxford Univ. Press.

Sergiovanni, Thomas J. 1984. Leadership and excellence in schooling. *Educational Leadership* 41. February.

Further Reading

There are several sources on Alex Taylor Community School. Some programs started at Alex Taylor may be useful to others and those interested should look at Steve Ramsankar and Charles Hart's "Creative Curriculum for an Inner City: A Case Study of Alex Taylor Community School," *Journal of Curriculum and Supervision* (1992); CBC "Man Alive" documentary (January 15, 1985); and the video "Alex Taylor Community School: Learning With Love," Mark Boiko in association with Lone Buffalo Productions in co-operation with the National Film Board of Canada (NFB). The NFB has produced a number of antiracism video resources. See, for example, "A Kid's View of Canada"; "Your Country, My Country"; and "For Angela".

10

STRATEGIES FOR AN ANTIRACIST EDUCATION

John Ewan Rymer and Ibrahim Alladin

> *The pedagogy of the oppressed, as a humanist and libertarian pedagogy, has two distinct stages. In the first, the oppressed unveil the world of oppression and through the praxis commit themselves to its transformation. In the second stage, in which the reality of the oppression has already been transformed, this pedagogy ceases to belong to the oppressed and becomes a pedagogy of all people in the process of permanent liberation.*[1]
>
> *Paulo Freire*
> Pedagogy of the Oppressed

Introduction

Race relations in Canada are undergoing profound changes. The shift from assimilation to multiculturalism as formal policy is a reflection of the changes. Political responses to racial and ethnic relations are conditioned by this policy shift. In spite of the pluralization of Canadian society, the treatment of racial differences is marked by contradictions. Racial criteria are still used to justify the exclusion of certain minorities from full institutional involvement (Elliott and Fleras 1992, 320). Special measures are being promoted as devices to eliminate barriers that preclude equality of opportunity for many visible groups. Antiracist practices are emerging to challenge the spate of negative events that seek to divide Canada along racial and ethnic lines. This chapter examines how racism is manifested and dealt with in the classroom. It questions current classroom practices and offers alternative strategies for an education that is inclusive and antiracist.

Racial Encounters in the School

Persistence of Racism in Schools

> My first classroom, 20 years ago, seemed like any other, 24 white students with European names, three were aboriginal, bigger, stronger and older than the others students in the room, and Miko, a girl of Japanese descent. Each of the Native boys was repeating the grade, officially due to poor achievement, unofficially they had "bad

> attitudes." All three had learned to cope with school the best they could, but would not complete the year.
>
> To the class Miko was different. She was barraged daily in all of her classes with derogatory remarks, driving her to tears. She was chided about her appearance and failures in mathematics. Japanese children are good at math, right? The Native boys were never teased or tormented like she was, probably because they would have dealt with such aggression with quick justice. Miko felt powerless, the only Oriental and female. Not every student participated in the teasing, yet the "silent majority" never stood up for her or befriended her. So began my learning in antiracist education, the challenge being how best to raise the students' awareness of racism and deal with racism in a constructive manner.
>
> Just a few months ago, an East-Indian student complained to the school's administration that they did not deal with the racial problems he perceived in the school. The initial response of some staff members was disbelief and their comments indicated that they believed there was not a problem with racism in the school because there were too few students from visible minorities for there to be a problem. This illustrates a common misconception found in schools and other social institutions that racial problems only exist when a certain number of students of varying ethnicity are in contact with each other. It is almost as if they believe that a specific critical mass must first be reached for racism to become problematic. It raises the question as to how individuals define a racial problem. Is the verbal abuse of a solitary student a racial problem? Or does a racial problem involve gangs and bloodshed? Once again, how best can we create awareness of racism, this time among colleagues.

The examples given in the "Persistence of Racism in Schools" illustrate the realization that racism exists in the classroom and in schools as both an individual problem and an institutional one. It poses, for the educator, the challenge of how best to deal adequately with this social issue. One must first of all recognize it as a complex problem. Imagine being posed with this situation, which Epstein (1993, 1) describes:

> In the playground of a middle school, two white girls in Year 7 shout at some boys "F*** off, Pakis." The teacher on playground duty overhears them and, horrified, is about to tell them off. Just before the teacher reaches the group, the boys turn on the girls, with the taunt "Lezzies, lezzies!"

Praxis

Faced with this scenario, how should the teacher best handle abuse and counter-abuse? Rarely do we find a single incident of discriminatory action to be a clear and simple situation. For each of the three examples given, as for any discriminatory situation, ready-made answers do not exist. One must be more aware of the whole situation. In some situations, such as the one described above, an instant response may be required; in others, more time can be taken to facilitate antiracist education. In all cases, the teacher needs to have developed praxis, a dialectic harmony of theory and action. Praxis exists when theory and action are entwined in a process that causes action to inform theory and theory to explain action. Rather than separate action and theory by reductionism, one realizes that both can occur simultaneously while in the act of teaching. The concept of praxis is difficult to envisage using the English language, but a reasonably close explanation is provided by Schon's view of the reflective practitioner.

Schon (1987) describes a situation that he termed knowing-in-action. This describes action in which it appears that thought is not engaged. Obviously, the action has occurred so many times that it is essentially spontaneous and is assumptional in nature. It is the kind of action that one can engage in yet at the completion of the act be unable to describe what actually happened. Schon describes the reflective practitioner as one who can engage reflection-in-action while in the act. For Schon, a unique situation is needed; for our purposes this situation is a discriminatory act. This allows the practitioner to question the assumptional nature of knowing-in-action. The practitioner reframes problematic situations such that a repertoire of past experiences and understandings may be brought to play (Pearson 1989). In so doing, the problem may be viewed in a new light. The reflection-in-action provides insights into the action, possibly different perspectives, that modify the action. In a simple manner, this provides a small insight into the nature of praxis.

Praxis is developed over time through reflection upon the experiences we encounter. The first level of reflection should be directed at one's self. Before one embarks on the processes involved in the antiracist education of others, it is essential to investigate the roots of our own misconceptions, suppositions, biases, and stereotypic beliefs. After years of working in multicultural settings and with a variety of ethnic groups one can pride one's self in being free of erroneous assumptions. Only through being aware of the anomalies that may be present in our daily experience can we investigate the roots of racism that exist in all of us.

The reflection necessary for the development of praxis is informed by the nature of the context in which the teacher experiences classroom dynamics. The context is comprised of the pedagogical, social, psychological, and emotional aspects of classrooms, as well as the political and structural components of the school. Troyna and Hatcher (1992) have provided a theoretical framework, their levels of analysis (Figure 10.1), upon which one can hang the information gained by experience. Racist situations are inevitably complex and accordingly no two situations encountered in schools will be exactly the same. The understanding one may gain from each situation requires analysis on both the "micro-level as well as the more general level" (Epstein 1993, 5). A critical examination of the nature of racism in schools requires that we identify and judge individual acts of racism and then place those acts within the context of broader society and the inequities inherent to it (Simon et al. 1988).

Figure 10.1 illustrates a hierarchical structure that may be useful in gaining an understanding of discriminatory acts and linking them to broader society.

FIGURE 10.1[2]

Levels of Analysis

Structural: What are the differential relations of power? What is the structurally induced conflict between groups?

Political/ideological: What were the prevailing systems in play at the time of the situation?

Cultural: What is the lived experience and common-sense understanding found within the community?

Institutional: What are the procedures and practises which are sanctioned by the school?

Subcultural: What are the children's subcultural worlds?

Biographical: What are the factors, characteristics, and personal histories specific to the individuals involved?

Contextual: What was the immediate history of the racist incident?

Interactional: What actually happened in the incident?

Some Serious Considerations

It should be realized that there are four factors that must be considered upon entering into antiracist education (Simon et al. 1988, 9):

- the *controversial nature* of serious examinations of discrimination
- the *roles of teacher and student* in such examinations
- the *critical posture* required when evaluating discrimination
- the importance of entertaining a *discourse of possibility.*

A serious study of racism in schools and society will inevitably create controversy. It has been argued that racist practices have been so integral to our history that they have gained acceptance (Simon et al. 1988, Brandt 1986, Larocque 1991, Shadd 1991, Buchignani 1991). Certainly, racism will be "close to home" for many students, and may be a very real component of their lives. The nature of antiracist education is oppositional, therefore controversy is inevitable. Certainly it will challenge the concepts of the status quo, particularly the nature and distribution of power in society. "Discrimination contradicts the very foundations of a democratic society" (Simon et al. 1988, 10) therefore the challenge is to reconstruct a nondiscriminatory society. Many teachers prefer to avoid controversy because it unsettles both themselves and their students. It is often necessary, however, for students to be puzzled to stimulate the development of critical thinking skills (Passmore 1980). Bewilderment is not the desired outcome, but is the vehicle to the discussion of the puzzling questions they face. It also allows the students to understand the type of evidence that is relevant to the questions that trouble them.

The teacher-student role relationship and power structure are altered in antiracist education. The traditional didactic pedagogy is unsuitable for the process and aims of such an education. The teacher cannot act like an executive, managing the learning of the students. Rather, in antiracism education, the teacher may be better described as a liberationist (Fenstermacher and Soltis 1986). The student's ideas and opinions are valued, and seen as functional and accurate, given their life experiences. The teacher constructs a classroom climate that encourages the sharing of ideas, even those that may be unpopular or offensive to the teacher. A climate of mutual respect is beneficial for it not only frees the students to speak, challenge ideas, and evaluate perspectives, but it provides the especially needed emotional and physical safety that supports appropriate disclosure and introspection. The key to this approach is the teacher's manner and ability to model the values that are fundamental to the liberationist approach including: honesty, integrity, fair mindedness, justice, open mindedness, regard for evidence, curiosity, a reflective habit, and judicious skepticism (Fenstermacher and Soltis 1986, 40). The students and teacher will be investigating racism beyond the limited perspective of ignorance or malice and questioning the socially sanctioned practices that maintain discrimination.

Racism has developed through human thought, therefore it is a social construction. For the students to deconstruct and ultimately reconstruct their own knowledge, the use of constructivist epistemology will be required. The idea of critical posture is inherent to constructivist pedagogy. Traditional education expects, and to a degree, values passive learning. Many teachers still consider the noisy classroom to indicate a lack of control. Critical posture is related to action as the students are required to be involved for learning to occur. Learning of this nature tends to be highly experientially based. As active participants, the students must view the information presented as a construction based on a specific point of view. The point of view held is historical, therefore the students must inquire into its nature, its history, the benefits it seeks to derive, and the social implications of its acceptance or rejection.

The final consideration is the discourse of possibility. This refers to the dialogue that reconstructs the nature of democratic social life. It allows the student to question the taken-for-granted world they live in and to engage in the search for plausible alternatives to current discriminatory practices and structures. It affords the students the opportunity to evaluate the struggle and implications for transformative social action in the broader social milieu.

Aims of Antiracist Education

It is important that as educators seeking to address both individual and institutional acts of discrimination that we begin a serious level of reflection. On one hand, we endeavour to investigate and define our own values, beliefs, assumptions, and knowledge. On the other hand, we need to reflect and analyze each situation to gain a clearer understanding of the nature of racism.

Upon reflection, we may identify values that may stand us in good stead for the creation of an antiracist curriculum. Some of these values may be used as the aims of an antiracist education. Three such aims are derived in this manner: equality, justice, and emancipation. These aims may be seen as being in opposition to the intentions of the school system, depending on the perspective used. For example, when Brandt (1986) coined these aims he did so from the premise that the state was racist and therefore the education system was not designed "necessarily in the interest of the racially defined 'dominated groups'" (Brandt 1986, 125). Clearly, antiracist education can be debated as oppositional to the reproductive nature of schooling. The antiracist educator does not intend for the education system to continue to reproduce the social structure that it operates within. The purpose of this education is to influence social change.

These aims also cause antiracist education to be viewed differently from multicultural education. Where multiculturalism is aimed at the tolerance and appreciation of differing cultures, the development of esteem, and the reduction of ignorance, then antiracist education is directed at exposing, defining, and transforming power relationships, through equality, justice, and emancipation. It challenges current practices and seeks to eradicate racism through awareness, challenge, and confrontation. Augie Fleras, in Chapter Four, compares and contrasts multicultural education and antiracist education.

Antiracist education seeks to alter the structures that may be seen to maintain or sanction discriminatory practices. Education is known to maintain the inequalities that exist in society. The students attending schools in poorer or marginal areas of the country generally do not have access to the same resources that those in affluent urban communities may have. For example, urban schools are able, through higher salaries and greater opportunities, to attract teachers who will stay longer. However, as many northern Native communities have found, teachers in remote rural schools usually stay only long enough to obtain a permanent teaching certificate, usually two or three years, and then leave. Students in such communities are less likely to receive the benefits of prolonged teaching experience. The antiracist educator strives to ensure not only equal treatment and the provision of equal opportunities to all students, but to identify, question, and attempt to alter the structures and practices that restrict equal opportunity in educational institutions and the broader society.

Justice is both a moral and legal imperative. Democracy is founded upon the belief that all citizens are valued equally. As a result, each has the same rights necessary to operate within society and benefit from membership in the society. The democratic society is itself seen to benefit from the justice inherent in equalized opportunity. This is not, as some fear, the provision of a "free ticket" at the expense of the taxpayer. It is the maintenance of just treatment between individuals, before the law and within social institutions for the betterment of all. Civilization is always at risk; it is far too easy for humans to regress to simpler historic power relationships that wrested even greater proportions of power in the hands of the elite. The contemporary growth of large organizational structures in a scientific society can lead to the consolidation of power in the hands of an elite few, resulting in a loss of freedom for the common man (Russell 1952). A society may be better judged by the measure of justice provided to its most marginal members than by the grandeur of its material achievements.

Liberation or emancipation seeks to free both the oppressor and the oppressed.

Racism is not a benefit to any individual or state. By limiting the opportunities or freedom of a racial or ethnic group the entire nation suffers politically, socially, and economically. The potential contribution of the oppressed to the betterment of the total society is diminished. If we were to look at the social benefits of slavery, we would find that only a small number of people benefited from it and maintained that slavery was essential to the quality of life for all in the community. On more critical inspection, we would find that slavery diminished the value of the working-class person in the society. Advocacy of slavery had then, limited the economic benefit for a broader spectrum of society. Owing to the limited economic opportunity, both slaves and the poor, common folk were unable to participate in the political and broader social facets of the society. Liberating the oppressed is only one aspect of emancipation. Emancipation of the oppressor "liberates the conscious or unconscious racist from the bondage of ignorance or worse, ideological miseducation" (Brandt 1986, 126).

The interest of this orientation is to improve the human condition. This is done by causing tacit assumptions to be exposed as the initial step toward a transformative process. Transformation itself implies action or work, but is conducted as praxis.

Are There Positive Outcomes to Discrimination?

> When we investigate discrimination we tend to focus on the examples that have clearly negative results. But consider the situation where a boy or girl is seen as more attractive because they are the only person of a particular race in a school. Alternatively, consider yourself as a member of a visible minority in a foreign country and store keepers or bankers ignore others in their premises because of your presence. They may physically move you to the head of the queue, ahead of others who have waited for hours. These may be seen as positive outcomes, greater attention, greater opportunity. But is this desirable? What about affirmative action, selecting individuals from visible minorities to fill positions that have traditionally not included minority groups? Does this practice lead to positive or negative outcomes? Critically examine the possibilities.

How may one develop equality, justice, and emancipation in the classroom and society? The process of reconstructing knowledge will require an emphasis upon dialogue, experiences, and the appropriate modelling by the antiracist educator. Education of this sort is aimed initially at creating personal awareness or greater understanding of racism and commitment to resisting it. The second phase is to take action in society to foster social change. The ideas presented are appropriate to any level of antiracist education, from the elementary to post-secondary levels. We propose Figure 10.2 as a model for antiracist experiential learning that may provide a focus for dialogue and reflection.

Creating an Appropriate Climate

School is not a voluntary, ad hoc gathering of strangers, but a selected collection of individuals grouped by age and required by an unequal power structure to act as if

FIGURE 10.2

Phase 1 Personal Awareness and Understanding

Posing the Challenge

Exploration
Focusing
Grounding
Structuring

Activity or Experience

Defining a Method
Investigation

Formalization of New Knowledge

Experiential Criticism
(a) Description
(b) Interpretation
(c) Evaluation

Phase 2 Action in Society

Communication
Application

alone while in the presence of others, for the purposes of evaluation (Jackson 1968). The classroom, from the perspective of the antiracist educator, needs to reflect the learner's needs. Being learner centred, the setting for the educational experience must be realistic, uncontrived, and include trust and respect.

A climate of mutual trust and respect evolves out of negotiation and testing involving the teacher's acceptance and respect for individual differences. This is aided by the recognition that each person's starting point is different and he or she will evolve dynamically through the process he or she experiences. This climate grows out of a concern for social responsibility. The classroom will provide the environment to exercise the rights and responsibilities of citizenship. This environment will foster individual responsibility as well as respect for the rights of others and a responsibility for the maintenance of those rights. Mutual trust and respect are critical elements for the attainment of equality, justice, and emancipation.

A logical outcome of such a climate is voluntary participation. Forced participation ignores respect for the right of another to exercise his or her own decisions. Coercive antiracist education would merely model a negative aspect of institutionalized authority, unequal power. Voluntary participation may seem threatening to a traditionally minded teacher concerned with controlling the classroom; however, it is believed that curiosity is a primary characteristic of people. Given a climate of trust and respect, emphasizing personal safety, both emotional and physical, students will be drawn to participate out of curiosity.

A Child's View of the Language of Differences

> "Dad I don't understand why they call Africans black and us white. And why do they call those people coloured? They're not green or blue. Africans aren't black, they're brown and we're not white, we're just a lighter brown. This is stupid!"[3]

The Challenge

As educators, it is important to determine what it is that the students currently believe or know. Children are often confused by the racist remarks that adults make. Fortunately, their openness provides an opportunity for dialogue and critical reflection. Children can provide adults with the opportunity to question critically, to reflect upon the taken-for-granted words and concepts that we encounter daily. It is through a process of exploration that one investigates the level of knowledge present and at the same time develops in the students the essential sense of ownership of the experience they will engage in. Exploration is facilitated through a series of questions that become increasingly focussed on the knowledge the students have. After varying periods of time, the exploration will become grounded upon a concept or train of thought that will provide the foundation for the structure of the question that will be posed as a challenge. Simon et al. (1988) propose the following questions.

Sample Exploratory Questions

1. When are forms of inequality unjust and unacceptable? Do you think there are any forms of inequality that are accepted? Why?
2. When can we say that an act of discrimination has occurred?
3. Discuss examples of discrimination that you have either heard or read about or experienced first hand. How were they based on a person's membership in a racial group, cultural group, or age group?
4. Discuss the differences between individual and social acts of discrimination. Can you classify the examples of discrimination that you gave as either individual or social (institutional)?
5. What do you think is meant by the phrase "but our experience is not just ours"? What problems do you think might limit the

effectiveness of anti-prejudice advertising campaigns or school programmes in reducing discrimination in Canada?

Richards (1992) proposed a number of principles for creating problems which, although oriented to outdoor experiential situations, are appropriate for this discussion. The key element in structuring a challenge is to develop the sense of ownership on the part of the students for the actions they will be involved in. The students' knowledge, made public through the exploratory and focusing questions, is used to create the challenge or problem they seek to solve. This contributes in large part to the development of ownership. The challenge or activity used in antiracist education needs to be concrete, recognizable, manageable, and solvable. The teacher's role is to ensure that these criteria can be met. The best challenges involve a worthwhile consequence.

Students often talk about the real world as being separate from school. This is usually because they sit passively in class and listen to a teacher mediate their interaction with the real world. The idea behind these challenges is to take the students into the real world by making them active through a critical posture and holding them responsible for ownership of their own learning. By making the challenge in the real world, it may involve the students holistically. This will allow them to engage their "internal processors" — will, memory, reasoning, feelings, sensing, intuiting, and imagining (Mulligan 1992). A team approach often best facilitates attainment of holistic involvement. If one plans to continue this process with a group of students, it is important for the students' academic and personal development to have the ensuing challenges become progressively and incrementally more complex.

Ultimately, a challenge or activity must be posed. Depending upon the situation and context of the teaching occurring, the teacher may have to pose the question, although, as students acquire experience and sophistication, it is preferable that they do so. By setting their own challenge or task, the students achieve a greater sense of empowerment. The level of inquiry that students attain can be surprising and often unexpected. Elementary students, often assumed to be unsophisticated in their thought, can provide extremely insightful ideas. Not every situation, however, lends itself to student-directed inquiry. Frequently teachers will develop and plan the activities. Even so, it is vital to get the students to "buy in" to the activity. The success of the project requires the students to take on the teacher's plan as their own. This is accomplished in the same manner, using exploratory and focusing questions. Innovative ideas have been created by teachers at all levels of education to stimulate students' investigations into racism and discrimination.

The Experience

The next phase of the model proposed involves the actual activities to be used. Once again, after the challenge is posed it may be useful to further explore the question to ensure that the students understand the task. The means by which the challenge will be handled needs to be determined. If the students are to seek their own solution, an appropriate method must be defined. This will normally require considerable discussion and negotiation. More frequently, the teacher may have a specific approach that he or she feels is most appropriate for the context in which they work. Any number of techniques are useful and it is valuable to investigate a variety for use with classes.

A few examples to note would include the ideas of Beverly Naidoo (1992), Roger Simon et al. (1988), Louise Derman-Sparks and the Anti-Bias Curriculum Task Force (1989), and Jane Elliot. Naidoo explores racism through the use of literature in a British context. Her premise is that students' social and political consciousness is influenced by the literature they read. She investigates with students racism in local, European, American, and South African contexts using books like *Roll of Thunder, Hear My Cry,* and *Waiting for the Rain.* Naidoo also found that dramatic interpretation allowed students to connect with the feelings and concepts of racism.

Simon et al. (1988) provide an insightful approach to dealing with racism in Canada through the use of film. This curriculum, based on Canadian film, is well designed and presented in a useful format. For a teacher seeking a new way of approaching discrimination with his or her students, or for the novice just approaching this curriculum, this is an excellent resource.

Derman-Sparks, working in concert with the Anti-Bias Curriculum Task Force, presents a comprehensive curriculum seeking to reduce bias in society by educating young children. This curriculum addresses the American concerns about bias as it is related to race, handicap, gender, and culture. This is a well-written curriculum that will meet the needs of elementary and kindergarten teachers.

A Class Divided

> "Blue eyed people are smarter than brown eyed people. They are cleaner than brown eyed people. They are more civilized than brown eyed people." So starts the television program outlining the daring experiential learning process Jane Elliot developed for her third grade class in 1968. This learning experience was developed for her students after the assassination of Dr. Martin Luther King confused and upset her class. The class had just recently named Dr. King their Hero of the Month and could not understand why anyone would want to murder him. The program views the process from the eyes of the students fourteen years later in 1984. The program shows how as Jane Elliot explores the concept of discrimination she draws from the student's experience the knowledge they have about racial discrimination. The challenge she poses is "Do you think you know how it would feel to be judged by the colour of your skin?" She then adapts this to her context, rural Iowa, by asking if the students would be interested in finding out what it is like to be judged by the colour of their eyes. The blue eyed people are made the better people for the first day and the learning began. The ensuing experience profoundly affected the students, as can be seen by their responses fourteen years later. This program is a definite "must see" for observing how an experiential process can be developed. Jane Elliot's use of this technique with prison staff is also shown.

A word of caution: Any role play has the potential to be emotionally or psychologically damaging if the teacher is not familiar with the potential hazards. It is imperative to take abundant time to "debrief" or critically examine an activity such as this.[4]

Formalizing New Knowledge

Through the course of any experience, each student will be assessing the congruence of the activities, insights, and feelings he or she has had with his or her experiences. To maximize learning, it is essential for the students to deconstruct and reconstruct their ideas. One may refer to it as "unpacking" the experience. For this process Eisner's ideas of criticism and connoiseurship (1978, 1985) are particularly useful. Eisner presents the idea of criticism as a public act for the purposes of "illumination of something's qualities so that an appraisal of its value may be made" (1985, 218). The purpose of this is two-fold; it allows the students and teacher the opportunity to draw the essential observations and perceptions of the experience into a public forum for critical examination; and it allows the students to construct their own ideas about the value of discriminatory action. This public presentation of the experience and the ideas associated with it, coupled with peer comment and assessment plays a critical role in shaping knowledge.

As knowledge is a social construction, dialogue is critical. Having shared a common experience the students may, through dialogue, collectively shape their knowledge. This allows for the critique and testing that ideas require. Obviously, since the students have taken an active role in the creation of the knowledge, it may have greater meaning to them than knowledge that has been presented didactically. The teacher must also be aware of great importance the affective dimension has for cognition. Eisner (1978) believes emotion plays a critical role in human understanding. He maintains that the failure to understand a situation emotionally may cause a failure to understand the powerful features of the situation.

Experiential criticism is composed of three phases. The first phase is descriptive. Experience is identified, characterized, portrayed, and rendered in language such that the relevant qualities of the experience are constructed. This focuses the entire group on the important aspects of the activity and provides a common focus. The second phase is interpretive in that the students attempt to provide an understanding of the ideas and concepts they have encountered. The students and teacher construct a framework upon which to understand discrimination and racism. The final phase involves evaluation, an attempt to place a value upon the knowledge that they have gained. This final step attempts to link the individual's experience with the larger world. In this phase the importance of the experience is determined and awareness of it is expanded to link to the broader world view of the individual. The public dialogue throughout the criticism process provides for multiple perspectives to be witnessed, thereby each individual may gain a broader appreciation for the concept of racism.

Action in Society

Two aspects may be pursued at this phase of antiracist education, communication and application. It is important that individuals have the opportunity to act on the basis of their newly constructed knowledge. As we all know, we love to share new ideas that give us a fresh perspective on life. Regardless of age, people who have become aware of the nature of racism may seek to make changes for the purpose of increasing justice, equality, and liberty in the community. The actions will vary in scope from the classroom, school, community, or nation.

The communication and application of this knowledge may occur in any number of ways. The beauty of antiracist education is that it provides a teacher with a focus for any number of communicative ventures. Students may write essays, poetry, speeches, dramatic productions, television scripts, news reports, or music. The teacher may encourage students to produce and present dramatic productions. They may initiate public forums or debates. The artistic may entertain the idea of an art display, possibly including sketches, paintings, sculptures, fabric, glass, or multimedia. It may be the teacher who initiates these projects, depending upon the context and the time available. However, it is more likely that the students will initiate the projects, and certainly it is more empowering if they do. Through this action the students learn other valuable skills, including organizational skills, time management, and team work. Communication allows the students to apply their knowledge to life in the broader community.

Curriculum Reconstruction and Transformation

One of the criticisms of multicultural education is that it generally targets white students and teachers. It is expected that racist attitudes towards minorities will change if these prejudiced individuals are exposed to sensitivity training in human relations and ethnic studies programs (McCarthy and Crichlow 1993, 292). Studies have shown that exposing white teachers and students to sensitivity training has not reduced or eliminated prejudice (Hall 1984). Reform in race relations based on this approach is not likely to transform attitudes.

A new approach towards eliminating discrimination in schools must go further than a critique of current definitions of racial identity. A critical approach to the fostering of multiculturalism must also seek to promote democratic initiatives in curriculum and pedagogical practices, and in social relations in schools. School programs must not be based on attitudinal models of reform. These models tend to place minority children in low or non-academic core curriculum.

The curriculum must be reconstructed that emphasizes antiracist and antisexist change and social reorganization. McCarthy (1993, 301-302) notes:

> Changes in the curriculum to address the present and the future race relations in the United States must be founded in the recognition that knowledge is socially produced and is systematically relational and heterogeneous...Efforts to redefine the curriculum in the name of multiculturalism must go beyond the narrow prescription of content addition and replacement. A critical approach to curriculum reforms must make salient the connections between knowledge and power and must build on the deconstructive and relational analysis already on the way in third world and indigenous scholarship and cultural production. Such an approach would bring the entire range of tradi-

tional and contemporary material and symbolic arrangements in the school curriculum into focus for examination with a view toward transformation.

Conclusion

For schools to eliminate discrimination, antiracist strategies must be developed. It is argued that multicultural education does not go far enough to question the social organization of knowledge. Antiracist education offers a more systematic challenge to the structure of the existing school knowledge and the curriculum. All students should have access to the same curriculum. As long as existing school practices are in place, the school population will be divided along ethnic and racial lines. Many minority children will be excluded and alienated from the school system. The dominant curriculum must be reconstructed so that it represents the interests of all children. This would constitute a fundamental step in preparing children for democratic participation in a complex society.

Discussion Questions

1. Immigrants have been accused recently of being responsible for increased social problems in our cities. These accusations have been made by politicians and covered extensively in the media. They include such claims as defrauding social welfare, violent crimes, and taking jobs away from Canadians. Critically examine the basis for these accusations and the political ideology that supports them.
2. Aboriginal self government has been raised as a political issue in recent years. Investigate the arguments that have been made for and against self-rule. Is there reason to believe that opposition to such plans is founded upon racism and unequal access to power? Explain your opinions.

Notes

1. Paulo Freire. 1970. *Pedagogy of the Oppressed.* New York: Continuum. p. 36.
2. B. Troyna and R. Hatcher. 1992. *Racism in Children's Lives: A Study of Mainly-White Primary Schools.* London: Routledge. Reprinted with permission.
3. Megan Rymer, age 9, while living in Southern Africa
4. *Frontline,* PBS program (WGBH Educational Foundation,1986) presented by KCTS Seattle, WTVS Detroit, WGBH Boston. For information on this program contact: FRONTLINE, "A Class Divided," Box 322, Boston, MA, 02134; or PBS Video, P.O. Box 8092, Washington, D.C., 20024.

References

Alladin, Ibrahim. 1993. *Multiculturalism in the 1990s. Policies, practices and implications.* Edmonton: EISA Publishers.

Brandt, G. L. 1986. *The realization of antiracist education.* London: Falmer Press.

Buchignani, N. 1991, "Some comments on the elimination of racism in Canada." In *Racism in Canada* , ed. O. McKague, 199-205. Saskatoon: Fifth House.

Derman-Sparks, L., and the A.B.C. Task Force. 1989. *Anti-bias curriculum: Tools for empowering young children.* Washington: National Association for the Education of Young Children.

Eisner, E. 1985. *The educational imagination: On design and evaluation of school programs.* 2d ed. NY: MacMillan.

———. 1978. Educational connoiseurship. Paper read at Association for Supervision and Curriculum Development (ASCD) Distinguished Lecturer Series at the 33rd Annual Conference, 4-8 March, San Francisco.

Elliott, J. L., and Fleras, A. 1992. *Unequal relations. An introduction to race and ethnic dynamics in Canada.* Scarborough: Prentice Hall Canada.

Epstein, D. 1993. *Changing classroom cultures: Anti-racism, politics, and schools.* Stoke-on-Trent: Trentham Books.

Fenstermacher, G. D., and Soltis, J. F. 1986. *Approaches to teaching.* NY: Teachers College Press.

Hall, Stuart. 1984. "Encoding/decoding." In *Culture, media, language: Working papers in cultural studies 1972-79*, ed. S. Hall, D. Hobson, A. Lowe, and P. Willis, 128-38. London: Hutchinson.

Jackson, P. W. 1968. *Life in classrooms.* NY: Holt, Rinehart, & Winston.

Larocque, E. 1991. "Racism runs through Canadian society." In *Racism in Canada*, ed. O. McKague, 73-6. Saskatoon: Fifth House.

McCarthy, C., and Crichlow, W., eds. 1993. *Race, identity and representation in education.* London: Routledge.

Mulligan, J. 1992. "Internal processors in experiential learning." In *Empowerment through experiential learning*, ed. J. Mulligan. and C. Griffin, 178-86. London: Kegan Paul.

Naidoo, B. 1992. *Through whose eyes? Exploring racism: reader, text and context.* Stoke-on-Trent: Trentham Books.

Passmore, J. 1980. *The philosophy of teaching.* London: G. Duckworth & Co.

Pearson, A. 1989. *The teacher: Theory and practice in teacher education.* NY: Routledge.

Richards, A. 1992. "Adventure-based experiential learning." In *Empowerment through experiential learning*, ed. J. Mulligan. and C. Griffin, 155-62. London: Kegan Paul.

Russell, B. 1952. *The impact of science on society.* London: Unwin Paperbacks.

Schon, D. A. 1987. *Educating the reflective practitioner.* San Francisco: Josey-Bass.

Shadd, A. 1991. "Institutionalized racism and Canadian history: Notes of a Black Canadian." In *Racism in Cañada*, ed. O. McKague, 1-5. Saskatoon: Fifth House.

Simon, R. I.; Brown, J.; Lee, E.; and Young, J. 1988. *Decoding discrimination: A student-based approach to antiracist education using film.* London, ON: Althouse Press.

Troyna, B., and Hatcher, R. 1992. *Racism in children's lives: A study of mainly-white primary schools*. London: Routledge.

Further Reading

Canadian Teachers' Federation. 1992. *Racism and education: Different perspectives and experiences* Ottawa: Canadian Teachers' Federation.

Dei, G. J. S. 1993. The challenges of antiracist education in Canada. *Canadian Ethnic Studies* 25 (2): 36-51.

Evans, W. D., ed. 1992. *Reading against racism* Buckingham: Open Univ. Press.

Lyons, C., and Farrell, M. 1994. Teaching tolerance: Multicultural and antiracist education. *McGill Journal of Education* 29 (1): 5-14.

Walkling, P. H., and Brannigan, C. 1986. Anti-sexist/antiracist education: A possible dilemma. Special Issue: Race, Culture and Moral Education. *Journal of Moral Education* 15 (1): 16-25.

The following provide excellent teaching resources:

Anderson, E.; Lebans, R.; and Evans, S. *The role of the reader in the curriculum: The fourth report, a curricular approach to antiracist education*. North York: North York Board of Education, Curriculum and Instructional Services.

Ontario Ministry of Education and Training. 1992. *Changing perspectives: A resource guide for antiracist and ethnocultural equity education*. Toronto: Ontario Ministry of Education and Training.

Scarr, M., and Paul, D. 1992. Art against racism (A teaching unit). *BCATA Journal for Art Teachers* 32 (1): 32-7.

York Region Board of Education. 1991. *Race relations: Pathways to equity*. Aurora, ON: York Region Board of Education.

EPILOGUE

RACISM IN CANADA: CHALLENGES AND PROSPECTS

Ibrahim Alladin

It would be folly to assume that in a multicultural society like Canada that policy structures are addressing the problems of racism. The issues are complex and the challenges facing central authorities are formidable. Canadian society is going through a phase of political and economic turmoil that has created conflicts among groups. Each group has a vested interest to maintain political and economic dominance. Those groups that cannot access power are simply marginalized. This marginalization of visible minorities has divided Canadian society along racial and ethnic lines. The potential for balkanization is present. Systemic racism is putting pressure on Canada's image for racial tolerance. Prejudice and discrimination is evident in employment, education, and public service. There are many forces that have created a crisis in Canadian race relations, which are examined in this book. This chapter will bring together the themes that run through the three sections.

Incidents involving racial and ethnic groups across Canada have created outcry about what is acceptable in a multicultural society. According to the recent Decima Report (1993), racism has increased and more Canadians are expressing their concern about the future of Canadian society. Younger Canadians going to school feel that a great deal of racism exists in Canada (Decima Report 1993). Although red-neck racism is in decline, it has not disappeared and recently shows signs of increased vigour (Elliott and Fleras 1992, 325).

Canadians seem to be divided when it comes to defining what is acceptable. A dichotomy is reflected in public reaction to the presence of an increasingly diverse immigrant population. Recent changes in immigrant policies have attracted more immigrants from outside Western Europe, thus creating an unnecessary fear that Canada is taking too many non-Europeans. The new Canadians, mainly from Asia, have become victims of prejudice and discrimination because they are "not like most Canadians." Some of these immigrants feel that to become like most Canadians, they have to abandon their customs, language, and dress code. Yet, there is strong public support for the principles of multiculturalism. One survey showed that 68 percent of Canadians believe that multiculturalism has made Canada a better place (Elliott and Fleras 1992, 325). There appears to be ambiguity; in the domain of race relations some key questions have yet to be addressed.

How much flexibility and accommodation is needed to avoid racial conflict? Are current policies able to manage the challenges of a multiracial society? How much willingness is there to restructure Canadian society to address diversity in a manner consistent to the principles of multiculturalism? Are institutions like schools reflecting the multicultural reality of Canadian society? These are complex questions; nevertheless, they have to be answered. The future direction of race relations and the challenges of the new pluralism in Canada will depend upon how these questions are approached and what solutions are proposed.

The elimination of racial discrimination should be an important government and public priority. There at least two practical reasons why racial discrimination should be eliminated. First, discrimination reduces the life chances of people, and there is no philosophical reason why this should be allowed. Discrimination brings psychological degradation and lowers the standard of living of those many Canadians who experience it. Second, racism is a moral issue that reflects on Canadian society at large. Like sexism, it ties us morally and intellectually to centuries-old legitimations and patterns of subordination that simply have no economic and moral justification in contemporary Canada. The persistence of racism diminishes us all (Buchignani 1991, 199).

To drive towards racial equality, we must begin by debating racism publicly and understand its nature and status in Canada. If one does not fully understand the political economy of racism, it would be difficult to discuss solutions. The lack of an open public debate on racism has left a big gap between policy and practice. It is one thing to have a multicultural society and another to manage a multiracial society.

While racism should be the concern of all, schools have to play an effective part in eliminating racism. Multiculturalism is said to give identity to Canada and distinction to Canadian society (Lawson and Ghosh 1986). The multicultural reality is significant for schools because they are responsible for preparing all students to participate fully in the multicultural social, political, and economic order.

For schools to make a difference, they must first know the aspirations of aboriginal people, women, and the visible minorities, and to reflect this knowledge in the delivery of their programs. It has been argued again and again that educational systems should build pride and identity in people. Educational systems can reflect this through curriculum content, through objective selection of instructional materials, through teachers who are sensitive, and through conscious practice. Essentially, this means an education that is inclusive, one that sees history and events as a reflection of experiences upon which to build knowledge and societies. The present status of some minorities in Canada, particularly the aboriginal people, necessitates a re-evaluation of legislation, policy, programs, and services. Without a change in support structures outside the school, there will be limited opportunity for success (Bouvier 1991, 295-96).

What direction will race relations in Canada follow in the next century? As a nation Canada has a tremendous challenge in its immediate future to solve its racial and ethnic problems. There are several reactions. Multiculturalism is still acclaimed as a major

Canadian accomplishment. For example, the Australian Advisory Council on Languages and Multicultural Education states (Cummins and Danesi 1990, 99):

> Canada, having been a multicultural society since its earliest days, has the advantage of long experience in what seems bound to become a mandatory 21st century skill: constructive co-existence among culturally and racially diverse communities. Indeed, the term multiculturalism is a Canadian creation. Canadians are to enter the 21st century as the world's best prepared country, enjoying an important advantage over her friends and competitors.

Since 1971, multiculturalism has altered the government's agenda on race and ethnic relations. As a doctrine, multiculturalism provides a political framework for the official promotion of cultural differences and social equality as an integral component of the social order. Defined in this way, multiculturalism deals with the management of ethnic and racial diversity in a positive manner (Elliott and Fleras 1992, 272).

Spurred by pressure from various ethnic groups for fundamental reforms in race relations in education and society, and to provide practical solutions to the problem of racial inequality, multicultural education emerged in the 1970s as a challenge to the established curriculum. For a brief period, gains were made — Black Studies, Asian and African History, and World Religions were added to the curriculum. Within the last decade, however, conservative educators and politicians, have launched a virulent assault on multicultural education. Debates on educational reform and the curriculum have shifted more towards the right, with the conservatives leading the way.

For visible minorities and new Canadians from Asia, Africa, and South America, multiculturalism has provided little hope. They need employment, to attain economic prosperity, to eliminate racial discrimination, equal access to education and housing, and to be treated fairly by the criminal justice system (*Equality Now* 1984). In the light of growing discrimination, visible minorities feel that the formal policy has not provided them the protection they desired. The debate has now shifted on the issue of power and resource-sharing within the context of a restructured government-ethnic agenda. Visible minorities are less concerned with festivals that seek to display dances, ethnic food, and colourful costumes.

The need for Canada to address race and ethnic relations seems more pressing now than it has ever been. The demographic changes and the cultural diversity that have emerged have made it necessary for our institutions to adjust. For institutions and agencies with an extensive visible minority population, the challenge is apparent: the environment in which they have to operate is complex, rapidly changing, and fundamentally different from a decade ago (Elliott and Fleras 1992, 287). The school and the workplace are examples of environments in which adjustments must be made.

To adapt to the new cultural pluralism, a shift from policies that routinely endorsed dominant values with little consideration for minority lifestyles is urgently needed. The assimilationist agenda has to be revised. What we now have is a "new colour-conscious philosophy that singles out racial affiliation as a basis for entitlement. Instead of the handicap they once were, racial markers now constitute a resource that entitles certain individuals to compete more equally in society. Canada's innovative employment equity measures are largely based on this set of premises" (Elliott and Fleras 1992, 320). An antiracist approach to race relations should recognize all cultures, not a selected few, and it must attempt to remove barriers that interfere with the attainment of equality.

References

Bouvier, Rita. 1991. "Education and change for aboriginal people in Canada." In *Social Change and Education in Canada.* 2d ed. Ratna Gosh and Douglas Ray Toronto: Harcourt Brace & Company, Canada.

Buchignani, Norman. 1991. "Some comments on the elimination of racism in Canada." In *Racism in Canada.* ed. O. McKague. Saskatoon, Fifth House.

Cummins, Jim and Danesi, Marcel. 1990. *Heritage Languages. The Development and Denial of Canada's Linguistic Resources.* Toronto: Garamond/Our Schools, Ourselves Educational Foundation.

Decima Report. 1993. *A report to the Canadian Council of Christians and Jews. Canadians' attitudes toward race and ethnic relations in Canada.* November.

Elliott, J. L., and Fleras, A. 1992. *Unequal relations. An introduction to race and ethnic dynamics in Canada.* Scarborough: Prentice Hall Canada.

Equality Now. 1984. *Report of the special committee on visible minorities in Canadian society.* Ottawa: Queen's Printer.

Lawson, R. F., and Ghosh, R. 1986. *Canada: Education and urban society.* Special issue on policy issues in the education of minorities, 18: 449-61. August 4.

Notes on Contributors

Ibrahim Alladin is an adjunct professor in the Department of Educational Policy Studies at the University of Alberta. He is also the Director of Cambrian International at Cambrian College. His areas of interest are mainly in the fields of race and minority relations; socio-cultural integration of minorities; education and development; and global education. Dr. Alladin's books include *Education and Neocolonialism.* CIED: University of Alberta, 1990; *Education, Politics and State in Multicultural Societies. An International Perspective* (with M. K. Bacchus). Ginn Press, Needham Heights, 1991; *Beyond the Gulf War* (with Baha Abu-Laban). MRF Publications, Edmonton, 1992; *Teaching in Global Society.* Ginn Press, Needham Heights, 1992; *Multiculturalism in the 1990s: Policies, Practices and Implications.* EISA Publishers, Edmonton, 1993; and *Economic Miracle in the Indian Ocean.* Editions de l'Ocean Indien, Rose-Hill, 1993.

John P. Anchan has taught in India, the United Arab Emirates, and Canada. He has degrees in Biological Sciences, Animal Physiology, Education, and International/Intercultural Education. He is a doctoral candidate in the Department of Educational Policy Studies, University of Alberta, where he also teaches courses in Canadian History, and on Schooling and Society.

Myrna L. Berlin, is the principal of Kipling Collegiate Institute in Etobicoke, Ontario. She has spent the last 23 years with the Board of Education for the City of Etobicoke. Her teaching and administrative experiences have taken her to seven different secondary schools in Etobicoke. Her teaching background is in Business Education and she continues to take an active interest in the business programs being offered in secondary schools. She has been a member of the Director's Safe Schools Committee, the Religions and ESL/ESD Committees, and the Metro Principals' Council. She is also taking a leading role in developing local antiracist policies for the school. Her involvement in the Improved Professional Practice Committee allows her to focus on teacher-staff development and excellence in the classroom. Myrna Berlin has a Diploma in Secretarial Science from Ryerson Polytechnical Institute, a B.A. in English from York University, and a M.Ed. in Educational Administration from Brock University.

George J. Sefa Dei is an associate professor in the Department of Sociology at the Ontario Institute for Studies in Education, Toronto, Canada. His teaching and research interest are in the areas of antiracist education, development education, and international development. Dr. Dei is currently engaged in a three-year study examining the experiences of African-Canadian students' in the Ontario Public School system. The focus is on the issue of student disengagement and dropping out of school. The study is funded by the Social Science Research Council of Canada (SSHRC) and the Ontario Ministry of Education and Training (MET). Some of Dr. Dei's publications include *The Challenges of Antiracist Education in Canadian Schools*, *Afrocentricity: A Cornerstone of Pedagogy*, and *The Social Reality of International Students in Canadian Post-secondary Institutions.*

Terrance Carson is a former high-school social-studies teacher and school district consultant. Currently, he is a professor in the Department of Secondary Education at the University of Alberta and is co-director of the University of Alberta Institute for Peace and Global Education. Dr. Carson's curriculum and teaching interests include teacher education, action research, and peace and global education. His publications include *Towards a Renaissance of Humanity: Rethinking Curriculum and Instruction* and *Exploring Collaborative Action Research.*

Augie Fleras is an associate professor in the Department of Sociology at the University of Waterloo. Dr. Fleras's areas of expertise are concentrated in the field of race, aboriginal, and ethnic relations. More specifically, topics of interest include (a) government-minority relations at the level of policy and administration, (b) the concept of institutional accommodation, with special interest on police-minority relations as well as media-minority relations, and (c) the concept of multiculturalism as society-building in Canada. Professor Fleras has published extensively and recent works include *Unequal Relations: An Introduction to Race and Ethnic Dynamics in Canada* (with Jean Leonard Elliott). Scarborough: Prentice Hall Canada, 1991; *Race, Ethnicity, and the Police. A Guide For Law Enforcement Officers* (with Chris O'Toole and Brian Cryderman). 2d. ed. Toronto: Butterworths, 1992; and *Social Problems in Canada: Issues and Challenges* (with Adie Nelson). Prentice Hall Canada, 1994.

Lenore Holychuk works for the Edmonton Public School Board as a teacher-consultant. She provides in-service on language learning, social studies, and literature, and contributes to the development of various curriculum resources. She has a M.Ed. in Political Economy of Education.

Ingrid Johnston is currently a doctoral candidate and sessional instructor in the Department of Secondary Education at the University of Alberta, Edmonton. She has an M.Ed. from the University of Alberta and a B.A. and teaching diploma from the University of Natal in Durban, South Africa. She has taught high-school English and drama in South Africa and in Alberta. She is currently co-editor of *Alberta English*, the journal of the Alberta English Language Arts Council. She has published articles in *Alberta English* and in the *Ohio Journal of the English Language Arts.*

Syd Pauls has been involved in Native education for the past 22 years. He has worked for and with Native peoples in Saskatchewan to develop and implement an educational program that respects the beliefs and traditions of Natives while, at the same time, recognizing their inherent right to manage their own affairs. He is the superintendent of education for the Onion Lake First Nation. He is also completing a Ph.D., researching the relationship between First-Nation schools and provincial departments of education. One of the areas he is interested in is the jurisdictional issues that will arise as a result of the resurgence of the inherent right to self-government.

Steve Ramsankar is the principal of Alex Taylor Community School in Edmonton. He has worked in three inner-city schools in the past 32 years and has initiated a variety of programs for inner-city schools. He has received several awards in recognition of his work on education. In 1983, he received the Order of Canada and in 1987 the Premier's Award for Excellence in Education. Dr. Ramsankar has published several papers, including a monograph, *Alex Taylor Community School: A Quarter Century of Programs and Promises* (with Karen Cogan) that appeared in 1994.

John Ewan Rymer has taught secondary school in Alberta for the past twenty years. He has also taught and been an administrator at Nyanga Secondary School in Zimbabwe. In 1993, he was the team leader for a CIDA Youth Initiatives Project studying literacy and rural development in Zimbabwe. Currently, he is completing his doctoral studies in the Department of Secondary Education at the University of Alberta. Mr. Rymer has published articles on science education in *Teaching in a Global Society*. Ginn Press: Needham Heights, 1992, and the *Alberta Science Education Journal.*

Reader Reply Card

We are interested in your reaction to *Racism in Canadian Schools* by Ibrahim Alladin. You can help us to improve this book in future editions by completing this questionnaire.

1. What was your reason for using this book?

- ☐ university course
- ☐ continuing-education course
- ☐ personal development
- ☐ college course
- ☐ professional
- ☐ other interests ______________________________

2. If you are a student, please identify your school and the course in which you used this book.

3. Which chapters or parts of this book did you use? Which did you omit?

4. What did you like best about this book? What did you like least?

5. Please identify any topics you think should be added to future editions.

6. Please add any comments or suggestions.

7. May we contact you for further information?

Name: ______________________________

Address: ______________________________

____

Phone: ______________________________

(fold here and tape shut)

MAIL POSTE
Canada Post Corporation / Société canadienne des postes
Postage paid
If mailed in Canada
Port payé
si posté au Canada
Business Reply
Réponse d'affaires
0116870399 01

0116870399-M8Z4X6-BR01

Heather McWhinney
Publisher, College Division
HARCOURT BRACE & COMPANY, CANADA
55 HORNER AVENUE
TORONTO, ONTARIO
M8Z 9Z9